NOAH DIETRICH

The co-author of this fascinating book was chief
executive officer of the Howard Hughes empire for
thirty-two years. His father was John Dietrich, who
migrated to Wisconsin from Germany and served as
a Protestant minister in a number of midwestern
cities. One of seven children, Noah acquired a high
school education and tutored himself in accounting
and qualified as a certified public accountant.

Mr Dietrich was director and vice-president of
Hughes Tool Company, director and chairman of the
executive committee of Trans World Airlines,
chairman of the board of RKO Pictures Corporation,
and director of Hughes Aircraft. He was one of the
original members of the board of regents of Houston
University and a member of the Notre Dame
University Advisory Council. For many years he served
as director and regional vice-president of the
National Association of Manufacturers, a director of
the National Bank of Commerce in Houston, Texas,
and a delegate to President Truman's post-war
labor-management conference. Currently he is a
corporate consultant with offices in Los Angeles,
California.

BOB THOMAS

Bob Thomas, co-author of this remarkable book, is
well known in journalistic circles as an Associated
Press correspondent, magazine writer, book reviewer,
and radio and TV columnist. He is also the author of a
number of books on famous personalities, including
King Cohn and *Thalberg*.

Howard
The Amazing
Mr Hughes

Noah Dietrich
and Bob Thomas

CORONET BOOKS
Hodder Fawcett Ltd., London

Copyright © 1972 by Noah Dietrich and Bob Thomas
First published 1972 by
Fawcett Publications Ltd., New York
Coronet edition 1972

Printed and bound in Great Britain for
Coronet Books,
Hodder Fawcett Ltd,
St. Paul's House, Warwick Lane,
London, EC4P 4AH
by Hazell Watson & Viney Ltd,
Aylesbury, Bucks

ISBN 0 340 16493 X

CONTENTS

HOWARD

The Amazing Mr. Hughes

Author's Preface

In 1966 John Keats, in his book *Howard Hughes,* wrote:

> Hughes was nineteen when he selected Dietrich to run the Hughes Tool Company, and the association remained mutually satisfactory for more than three decades. . . .
>
> In all that was to follow, it was said that the work was 'eighty percent Noah Dietrich's genius and twenty percent Howard Hughes' gambling blood,' but however this may be, it is also true that the whole is the sum of its parts. Both the eighty per cent and the twenty per cent, if this is the way that it was, were absolutely essential to each other. In Dietrich, young Howard found precisely the man to entrust with the day-to-day operation of his affairs.

I promise the reader I'll try to do no bragging in this book. I will recount the events as I remember them and let the reader judge for himself.

However, certain impressions are bound to appear. Howard Hughes has become such a mysterious figure that it is difficult to determine what kind of man he was and is. I use the past and present tenses, because I honestly believe that the Howard Hughes of the past is different from the recluse of the Bahamas today.

No one had a closer association with Howard Hughes over a longer period of time than did I. I knew him first as an engaging but rather eccentric young man. In our last years together, I saw those same eccentricities become debilitating, so that he was virtually unable to function on a social or business level.

Hundreds of books, magazines, and newspaper articles have proclaimed the Hughes achievement of running a $600,000 legacy into a billion-dollar empire. But not much has been written about the millions he blew along the way. I know about those millions, because on many occasions I had to take remedial measures to rescue Howard from the messes he got himself into. In some of the ventures, particularly the Flying Boat, he would not allow himself to be rescued.

Here is a box score of his major losses:

PROJECT	LOSS	LOSER
Flying Boat	$50,000,000	Hughes Tool Co.
	$22,000,000	U.S. Government
RKO	$24,000,000	stockholders
Movie production	$10,000,000	Howard Hughes
Stock market	$10,000,000	Howard Hughes
Multicolor	$ 2,000,000	Howard Hughes
Hughes–Franklin Theaters	$ 2,000,000	Howard Hughes
Hughes Steam Automobile	$ 500,000	Howard Hughes

Put it all together and you get more than $100,000,000 of his, tax-payers', and stockholders' money wasted. And there was more: $2,000,000 on his around-the-world trip; millions more spent on noncommercial airplanes; not to mention the upkeep on starlets whose careers never materialized.

During decades of high earnings the Hughes Tool Company never declared a dividend.

Throughout his business career Howard Hughes never attended a board meeting.

He never had an office at any of his enterprises, except at film studios.

He was never an officer or director of TWA or RKO although he controlled their destinies.

He manipulated politicians, but he never voted.

He was never even in my office, although I was "managing director of all of Hughes's properties" (Keats).

Why am I writing about the Hughes saga at this late date? Part of the reason is personal: I want to leave, for my children and grandchildren, a record of the role I played in a colorful subchapter of American history. Another reason: I think the American public should be informed on the uses and misuses of great wealth.

Not the least motive is that it has been fun recalling my thirty-two years with Howard Hughes. I hold no rancor toward Howard. Those years with him were wild, hectic, maddening, unpredictable, never dull. Except for him, I might have served out my years as a certified public accountant or perhaps executive of a sedate mortgage company. I much preferred the more exciting life.

In telling this story, I have collaborated with Bob Thomas. Preliminary research was contributed by James Phelan. I am grateful to both of them for their assistance.

CHAPTER ONE

The Fateful Safari

I can't tell you exactly when I decided that my life with Howard Hughes had to end.

It had been a remarkable life: three decades as the closest associate of the richest American, a man who spawned a wealth of legend. A figure of rare fascination. But, in the end, an exasperating man.

I had performed thousands of services for him, satisfying his most outlandish whims.

"Noah can do it," he often said. Noah did.

In the beginning, it was such a simple matter as installing a stock ticker at his bedside.

Toward the end, the missions were more complex, involving a half billion dollars in a single transaction.

For such duties I was well paid. I became one of the highest paid executives in the United States. Private airplanes, with pilot and co-pilot, were available at all times to take me wherever I wanted to go. I had offices in Houston, Kansas City, New York, Washington, and Los Angeles. An unlimited expense account.

That wasn't enough. Living like a shah wasn't sufficient compensation for having to be on twenty-four-hour call to a man who had become increasingly eccentric, whose impetuous decisions—or indecision—had made it all but impossible to extricate him from colossal blunders.

I kept trying. Time and again I had proved that there was nothing that Howard Hughes wanted that I couldn't provide. But at last he was seeking the impossible.

The beginning of the end might be dated from January of 1956.

Contracts began coming across my desk. Big contracts. All were signed "Hughes Tool Co. by Howard R. Hughes, President," and all were orders for jet airplanes and related equipment. They came from Boeing, Lockheed, Convair, Pratt and Whitney, and General Electric. I had no previous knowledge of the contracts. Nor did anyone else in the entire Hughes organization.

This was at a perilous period in the history of the American airline industry. Jets were soon to make propeller planes obsolete, and all the airlines had been scrambling to find financing and assure delivery of the new aircraft so that they would be able to compete in the jet age. All except TWA, controlled by Howard Hughes.

Howard had held back. While American, United, Eastern, Pan American and all the other airlines were placing orders for this jet model and that, Howard agonized like a woman trying to pick out a new hat. He simply could not make up his mind.

Now he made up for his indecision—with a vengeance! Alarmed by the maneuvers of TWA's competitors, he hastened to catch up. He made deals with aircraft companies all over the country. As always, he negotiated in secrecy, telling no one in his organization about his purchases. Not even me.

I totaled the orders and placed a call to Howard.

"You know, Howard, I've been getting a lot of contracts which you have signed," I said.

"Yeah, what about them?" he asked.

"They're big contracts. For jet airplanes. These contracts will require approval by the Toolco board of directors."

"That's no problem. Just tell those stooges to give their approval."

"But Howard—these contracts total five hundred million dollars."

There was a moment of silence at the other end of the telephone.

"You're a goddam liar," he said.

"Watch your language, Howard. I totaled the orders and they come to four hundred and ninety-seven million dollars."

"I don't believe you!"

"But I have all the figures right here in my office—quantities, specifications, delivery dates, everything. I'll send them over to you, and you can see for yourself."

"You can send me over whatever you want. But I still won't believe you."

Four days elapsed. During that time I pondered the enormity of his act. Here was a man who was neither an officer nor a director of TWA. He had committed the tool company to purchase a half-billion dollars' worth of jet planes and engines—for the benefit of TWA—while making no provision whatsoever for paying the bills.

Finally he called me. His response was typically Hughesian. He made no reference to our previous conversation. All he said was: "Noah, how are we going to pay the four hundred and ninety-seven million we owe for the jets?"

As usual, Noah had a plan.

I had already made some inquiries of New York investment bankers. They had expressed willingness to go along with my plan. Fortunately the Hughes Tool Company had available an astounding extra hundred million dollars in cash—profits not immediately required for expansion. I proposed that we use the cash to satisfy down payments and initial installments for the jets. Then we would have the New York bankers float a $300,000,000 bond issue, which would be used as insurance in case profits did not continue.

"TWA can't swing such a big bond issue on its own," I told Howard. "It will need to be guaranteed by Hughes Tool. And it won't sell unless it has a stock-conversion feature." This meant bonds could be converted into TWA stocks.

Howard responded immediately. "Absolutely not! I will allow no dilution of my ownership."

Howard was adamant. He prided himself in being sole owner of his empire. He was answerable to no one.

I remained just as firm. "You asked me for a solution,

Howard, and I have provided it. This is the only way we are going to solve this problem."

Finally he acquiesced.

I began to put the plan into motion. I arranged with Dillon, Read and Company in New York to handle the issue. The details were worked out, and the prospectus was printed. Then one day I received a telephone call from a Fred Brandi, president of Dillon, Read.

"Noah, do you know what Hughes has done?" he asked.

"What now?" I asked.

"He called me and said to stop the bond issue."

"He did that?" My exasperation was growing.

"Yes. What do we do now?"

"Sit tight, and I'll try to find out something."

I quickly telephoned Howard. He admitted that he had put a stop to the bond issue.

"I had to, Noah," he said. "For one thing, I couldn't face any possibility of the dilution of my ownership. The second reason is this: supposing the bond issue didn't sell. That would give me a black eye on Wall Street."

"What kind of a black eye do you think you'll get if you can't make the payments on those jets?" I asked.

He had no reply.

And, for the first time in our thirty-one-year association, neither did I. He waited for me to bring forth a counterproposal. I had none to give him.

"Howard, I'm tired," I told him.

"I know you are, Noah," he said. "Just stick around until we solve this problem."

"*You* solve it," I said. "From now on, you're calling the shots. You remember that I'm going on safari July first." I had notified him in January that I was taking my two sons to Africa. Now it was spring, and I was more than ever determined that nothing would interfere with the trip. It was to be my second vacation in thirty-one years with Howard Hughes.

"Oh, yeah—the safari," Howard said. "How long will you be gone?"

"Two to three months," I said.

"Okay. Just let me know before you leave."

I did. Every week since January I had sent Howard a memo reminding him of my July 1 departure. Every time I talked to his secretary, Nadine Henley, I told her to mention my safari to him. I was determined to go. All my life I had dreamed about hunting in Africa, and I had spent months planning the safari. I had laid out $15,000 to hire three white hunters, three Landrovers, a five-ton truck, and thirty natives. In addition to my sons John and Tony, I had invited two close friends to accompany me—Pat Di-Cicco and Gary Cooper.

I guess I should have realized that Howard would be up to his old tricks. But I was disarmed when he allowed me to leave California with my two boys, on the first leg of our journey.

Howard's first move came after I had checked into the Waldorf in New York. He had left several messages for me to call him. I did.

"Jesus Christ, you can't go now, Noah!" he pleaded. "Not when we're in the middle of this jet crisis."

"With you, there is always some kind of crisis, Howard," I replied. "I'm going to Africa."

"I understand you're going with Gary Cooper," Howard said, trying a new tack. "I don't understand you, Noah."

"What do you mean?"

"Well, don't you know Cooper is a pinko? I don't understand why you would associate with him."

"Coop a pinko? That Montana cowboy is no pinko. But if it will make you feel any better—Coop isn't going."

Howard continued his plea for me to remain. Finally I said, "All right, Howard, tell me what has happened since I left California that would be reason for me to stay."

He couldn't think of anything. So I reiterated my intention to go, and I hung up.

I learned of Howard's next move when I received an anguished telephone call from Pat DiCicco my hunting-companion-to-be. Pat was an amiable man-about-Hollywood who had functioned as a talent scout for Howard. But Pat had higher ambitions. He asked Howard if he could have the industrial feeding contract for Hughes Aircraft, and Howard told me to work it out. I did. That made Pat an instant Food King, since Hughes Aircraft employed 38,000 people.

"I can't go," Pat wailed over the telephone from California. "Howard says if I go with you to Africa, I'll lose the feeding contract. He said if I dropped out, you probably wouldn't go, since I'm an experienced hunter and you're not."

That made me realize how little Howard Hughes knew about me after thirty-one years. I had been hunting all my life.

"It's okay, Pat," I said. "I can understand your position. But I'm still going to Africa."

The next call came from Greg Bautzer, the famous Beverly Hills lawyer and one of the few people Howard trusted.

"Noah, Howard called me over to his house a while ago," Greg told me. "He wants me to convince you not to take your vacation. I asked him how many vacations you had taken. Howard said, 'Come to think of it, I can't remember any—except when he got married.' I think I helped your cause, Noah. I told him that something was goddam funny if a guy running his empire couldn't call the shots on his own vacation."

I thanked him and returned to preparations for our departure the following afternoon.

In the morning the telephone rang. It was Howard. This time he was conciliatory and entirely sympathetic with my position.

"I agree that you're entitled to a vacation, Noah," he said. "In fact, I'll give you six months—you've certainly earned it. But I want you to take it some other time."

"I'm not going to take any six months, Howard," I said. "I'm going to Africa now."

He pursued me all the way to the international terminal at Idlewild Airport. I answered the page-call, and Howard was on the telephone with some "last-minute problems" before my departure for Rome. The problems were strung out on an extended monologue, and I perceived his strategy.

"Just a minute, Howard," I said.

I hurried over to the TWA desk and asked for the plane's captain. He recognized me as a TWA director and chief deputy of Howard Hughes.

"I'm held up on the phone," I told the pilot. "Please don't take off without me."

I returned to Howard's rambling monologue. Finally after twenty minutes, I interrupted: "Howard, you're obviously trying to make me miss that flight to Rome. It won't do any good, because I've ordered the plane to stay on the ground until I get on it. Now I'm *going on vacation.*"

He released me, and I departed on my first real holiday from the concerns of Howard Hughes in thirty-one years.

It was heavenly. Riding through the plains of Tanganyika in search of antelope, lions, and rhinos, I felt a universe removed from Howard Hughes, his unpaid-for jets, his unflyable flying boat. There were no telephones to wake me up in the middle of the night with a request for me to go flying off on some bizarre mission. There were no impossible problems to be solved on twenty-four-hour deadlines.

Sitting around the campfire with my two sons and the white hunters, I felt a rare sense of contentment. It had been a long time since I had felt that way. I didn't want that feeling to end.

I returned to Rome to begin the second phase of my long-awaited vacation. Tony and John were returning home, and I was going to join my wife Mary, her mother, and my daughters, Susan and Ruth, for a motor tour of the British Isles. But first I had to telephone Howard from Rome, as I had promised. His response was expectable.

"Noah, you've got to come back right away," Howard implored. "I need you."

"What for?" I asked. "Is there any change in the jet financing?"

"No," he admitted.

"Then what is the number-one thing that is worrying you?"

"The flying boat."

The flying boat! That monstrosity had been a headache from the very beginning of its misconception. It had been consuming millions of Howard's money, as well as $20,000,000 from the taxpayers, and his pride would not let him abandon it. The latest development came when the Long Beach harbor cofferdam had burst, seriously damaging the boat's wooden hull. Howard had sued the city of Long Beach for $12,000,000 in damages.

"I settled the suit for five hundred thousand," Howard reported to me.

"What happened?" I asked. "I thought you wanted twelve million."

"I didn't know I could repair the boat for nine hundred thousand," Howard said.

"Then the claim is settled?"

"Yes."

"So there's no reason for me to come home. I'll call you from London."

When I telephoned him from London, his plea was even more urgent: "Noah, you must come home immediately. Something has come up that only you can handle for me."

I sighed and answered, "All right." With heavy heart, I sent the rest of the family off on the three-week tour of Britain in the car I had shipped over from America. I booked the first TWA plane and made the lonesome flight back to New York.

As soon as I arrived at the Waldorf, I checked in with Nadine and waited. And waited.

For four whole days not a word from Howard Hughes. Finally he telephoned.

"What is so urgent that I had to come home immediately?" I asked.

He told me of a typical Hughes quandary. He had hired one topnotch Los Angeles lawyer to handle his flying boat suit for a fee of $30,000. Then he had engaged another important lawyer for the same suit, promising him ten percent of any recovery. That meant the second lawyer would receive $50,000. Howard was worried that the first lawyer would hear about it and demand $50,000, too. Howard wanted me to induce lawyer number two to shave his fee to $25,000.

I was steaming. I had been summoned home from my family tour, allowed to wait four days in the Waldorf Towers, then instructed to help Howard renege on a lawyer's fee. Howard was worrying about $25,000 at a time when he faced bills for jet airplanes totaling $497,000,000!

All I could say was: "All right, Howard, I'll see what I can do."

I telephoned lawyer number two and worked my wiles on him.

"You know, Howard was very impressed by the work you did on this case," I told the man. "He's going to have an awful lot of legal work to be done in the months and years ahead. I think you could get a large share of it—if you played your cards right."

"Really?" said the attorney. "Could you give me any suggestions?"

"Well, I think your fee of fifty thousand dollars might scare Howard off."

"Maybe you're right. Supposing I cut it down to twelve thousand, five hundred."

"Let's make it fifteen thousand," I said.

Howard was as delighted as a boy with a new pony. But this time his praise had a hollow ring. It had been a nasty little job—building up the lawyer's hopes of representing the Hughes Empire, just so Howard could shave a legal fee. I shook my head over the fact that Howard's entire enterprise balanced on the edge of financial disaster while he devoted himself to hoodwinking a lawyer out of $35,000.

The plains of Tanganyika now seemed as distant as the moon. Once more I was enmeshed in the frenetic world of Howard Hughes. I was more than ever determined to get out.

CHAPTER TWO

Background and Early Association

During those hectic days of 1956 I knew that my life with Howard Hughes would soon be coming to an end. I still went through the motions of running his empire, doing his errands, satisfying his whims, and straightening up the messes he got himself into. But my heart wasn't in it. Howard's paradoxical and contradictory behavior, his eccentricities, his irrationality seemed more pronounced than ever. I was sixty-seven, and I thought that after thirty-one years of day-to-day, night-after-night contact with a monumentally unreasonable man I deserved to be put out to pasture.

Yet I couldn't quit.

For one thing, Howard wouldn't let me. He used all his cunning, all his deviousness to circumvent my plans to retire. But he wouldn't grant me the one thing that could make me remain: the chance to earn some money on a capital gains basis, so that I wouldn't be donating most of my compensation to the government.

There was another reason why I stayed. Call it blind loyalty. Perhaps it was a remaining glimmer of fascination with the quicksilver personality of Howard Hughes. Or maybe it was a nagging pride, a belief that I could still perform the impossible for him.

Whatever the reasons, I stayed.

As I lingered through the final months, my mind wandered back to the beginning of the Hughes-Dietrich association. It was in November of 1925. Los Angeles. I was

thirty-six years old, working as a certified public accountant for the firm of Haskins and Sells.

A fellow accountant gave me a tip: a wealthy young
Texan was in town looking for an executive assistant.
"He's staying at the Ambassador Hotel," my friend said.
"Why don't you set up an appointment?"

I followed his suggestion. The next afternoon I arrived
at the Ambassador, the newest and fanciest hotel in Los
Angeles. I knocked on the door of one of the luxury suites.
The door opened and I gazed upward at the handsome
face of a nineteen-year-old boy.

"You're Noah Dietrich?" he asked. "I'm Howard
Hughes."

I followed him into the suite wondering if I hadn't wasted my time in coming to talk about a job with a fellow
who looked barely out of high school. He was six feet,
three and a half inches tall, and slender as a rail, and cut a
sporty figure in his golf knickers. He had just come in
from the course and was checking over his score card.

We chatted. He told me that he owned the Hughes Tool
Company in Houston, his father having died the year before. He had bought out the other heirs and now had total
control of the firm, which manufactured drilling bits for oil
companies. He had no desire to oversee the Houston
plant. His real interest was in making motion pictures, and
he intended to spend most of his time in California. Yet he
wanted to maintain control of the tool company.

"They send me production and financial reports from
the plant, but I don't understand them," he said. "That's
why I need someone with business experience to explain
the reports to me."

I gave him an outline of my background and qualifica-
tions. He listened very soberly and asked me questions in
a calm, quiet voice. At the time I thought he was trying to
make himself seem older than his years. But later I discovered that was his manner at all times. In all the years I
knew him, I never heard him raise his voice.

"I'm looking for someone with wide general knowledge," the young man continued. "Someone who is re-

sourceful and can solve problems. You see, I intend to engage in a variety of projects. Could you tell me how a battleship finds the range on its target?"

His question took me aback. But I dug into my knowledge of mathematics and came up with the answer:

"It's simply a matter of triangulation. There are two stations on the battleship, at a known distance apart. That's the base of the triangle. A sighting from each station provides the base angles. The distance to the target is derived from the formula for the height of an isosceles triangle, given the base and the two base angles."

My answer seemed to satisfy him. Next question: "Explain the principles of the internal combustion engine."

I had recently been involved in an automobile dealership, so the internal combustion engine held no mysteries for me. I explained it to him and soon we were engaged in a lively debate over the virtues of the offset crankshaft.

Class was dismissed, and I returned to my job, speculating whether I would ever hear from the young man again. I did. Two days later I had a call to report to the Ambassador suite. Again the interrogation by the unsmiling young man.

Our second session ended with no commitment on his part, and I lost interest in the obviously indecisive young man. Another opportunity had appeared for me. I was able to purchase the Ford dealership in Phoenix, provided I could finance a loan. That seemed like an easy matter, and I began making plans to move my wife and two daughters to Phoenix.

Then Howard Hughes entered my life again.

He sent an emissary to my house. "Mr. Hughes would like to ask you one more question," the man said.

"Tell Mr. Hughes I'm not interested," I replied. "I've made other plans."

"Please—just one question," the man pleaded.

"All right. What is it?"

"Mr. Hughes would like to know how you placed in your examinations for certified public accountant."

The question seemed idiotic to me, and I didn't hide my

feelings. "Tell Mr. Hughes there is no such thing as a standing in a CPA exam. You either pass or you fail. Why on earth is he interested?"

"Well, it seems that his plant manager finished second in his class at West Point. That seemed to impress Mr. Hughes."

I sent the man away. In half an hour he returned with the message: "Mr. Hughes wants to see you." I made my third journey to the Ambassador Hotel, and this time he hired me. Salary: $10,000 a year.

"What do I do?" he asked. "Pay you a year's salary in advance?"

I was astonished at his lack of knowledge of elementary business practice. "Most of your workers are paid every week—executives probably semi-monthly," I said. "Tell the boys at the plant to put me on the executive payroll."

That was the start. It was Thanksgiving Day, 1925.

As I looked back at the incident from the vantage point of thirty-one years of service to Howard Hughes, I could recognize revelations of those characteristics which I would find fascinating. Also those which proved exasperating.

He had a searching mind, a proficiency with things mechanical, an out-of-the-ordinary manner of dealing with people. He was ambitious, willing to explore new fields, full of vision, however clouded.

But he had a developing sense of secrecy that seemed unreasonable. He had scant regard for other people; the fact that he hauled me away from my family on Thanksgiving Day showed that. He paid uncommon attention to obvious trivia. Like a spoiled boy, he insisted on having something that was denied him.

Most of all, *he could not make up his mind*.

As I look back on the first thirty-six years of my life, all my youth and background, all my education and business experience seemed preparation for the career I was to pursue for Howard Hughes.

What I needed to handle the job were resourcefulness,

perseverance, the ability to work with people, a wide knowledge of business practice—and the constitution of an ox.

My father's people came from the city of Darmstadt in Schleswig-Holstein. They were deeply religious, and they objected to the government edict that all young men had to enter the army for three years when they turned twenty-one. As my father approached that age, the Dietrichs sought to leave the country so he could avoid conscription. Like many Europeans of the mid-nineteenth century, they cast their eyes toward America. But the United States was embroiled in the Civil War, and that thwarted their hopes. But then the war ended, and in 1865 the Dietrich family sailed from Hamburg for the new world.

It was a punishing voyage. Their sailing vessel was without power, and it was becalmed for days. Food and water were exhausted, and one member of the family suffered an injury and died from lack of medical care. Finally, after six weeks, the ship sighted land and limped into New York harbor.

I don't know why my parents decided on such a biblical name for me. My two older brothers had been called Otto and Will, after the crown princes of Germany. But I was stuck with Noah, and I was taunted about it all the way through school.

The life of a preacher's family in those times was frugal. My father rose to the important pulpit of Madison; his top salary was $65 a month. He was given a rent-free parsonage, but it had to be furnished and food was needed for a family of nine. Once in a while the congregation would give us a food shower, including all kinds of home-canned foods and even a dressed pig. But in between those showers our cupboards were pretty bare.

We learned to make-do. Sixty-five dollars or less a month provided no frills, and we used our resources to create our own amusements. I loved to play ball, but my parents couldn't afford to buy me a baseball. So I had them save all the string that came on packages at the house. I didn't have a piece of rubber for a core, so I wrapped the string around a rock until I had a sphere the size of a baseball. Then I had one of my sisters sew a cover out of an old piece of leather.

I learned to be a pretty good fighter, too. You had to be, if you were the preacher's son. You were always on the outside, having to prove yourself. Every two years I was thrust into a new community as my father's assignment changed—from Batavia to Jefferson to Prairie du Sac to Fond du Lac to Madison to Chicago to Zion, Illinois. Each time I had to face a whole new crowd. Each time I had to make my way with my fists.

Understandably, ours was a religious family. Very religious. The Sunday newspaper wasn't allowed in the house on Sunday. Playing cards were forbidden. Bible readings and table prayers were part of our daily routine.

The cheerless life was not for me. I preferred to be out in the fresh air playing games or walking through the woods which were close to the Wisconsin towns where we lived. Lakes were everywhere, and it was paradise for hunting and fishing. My brother and I would go off with sticks and strings and angleworms on bent pins and come home with twenty perch for the dinner table. Nothing was tastier than that fresh-caught fish.

I was a whiz at school. Especially at mathematics. I taught myself all the shortcuts, and no one could solve problems faster than I could. One teacher had a regular routine of reciting ten long numbers at the end of each class. Who ever got the total first stood up. It was always Noah Dietrich. While she was giving out the numbers, I was adding the last digits, one by one. So by the time she had finished I was already one column ahead of the other students.

My grades were straight A's with one exception: music.

I couldn't sing worth a damn. One day the music teacher noticed I wasn't joining in the chorus. She stopped the class and said, "All right, Noah, you'll sing it alone."

I was so nervous I couldn't utter a note, and she expelled me from school. It was the only black mark I received during my educational career.

When I graduated from Janesville High School in 1906, I had hoped to go on to the University of Wisconsin. Alas, it was not to be. My father had retired from the pulpit, and my two older brothers had left home. It was up to me to get a job and help support the family.

In 1910 I married a petite miss from Greenville, Mississippi. I moved my bride out to Maxwell, New Mexico, where I had been offered the position of cashier of a bank. It was a frontier town with unpaved roads and a population of sixty Americans and one hundred and twenty-five Mexicans. My salary was $100 a month. Room and board cost $50, so that left us with $50 to spend. I splurged on a horse and saddle, and my wife and I took turns riding it.

After six months in New Mexico, I continued westward to the booming town of Los Angeles. I became auditor for the Los Angeles Suburban Land Company, a syndicate that included Gen. Harrison Gray Otis, owner of the Los Angeles *Times,* and his son-in-law, Harry Chandler. They had purchased two big ranches in the San Fernando Valley—50,000 acres at $50 per acre—that spread from Lankershim (now North Hollywood) to Calabasas. The floor of the valley was sold to sugar beet and bean farmers for $350 an acre. The syndicate was unable to sell the slopes on the south side of the valley, so members were compelled to take five-hundred-acre parcels at $50 per acre. This is now one of the most valuable districts of Los Angeles.

When the syndicate shut down, I took a position as auditor for the Janass Investment Company which was selling home sites in the San Gabriel Valley for $350 per acre and were beginning to develop Westwood.

In 1917 I joined the E. L. Doheny Oil companies and became assistant comptroller with offices in the Equitable Building in New York City. It was a responsible position for a man of twenty-eight; I had seventy people under me. But my wife didn't like the East, and she took our two daughters back to California. I followed her.

My next job was with Haskins and Sells, certified public accountants, I realized that I couldn't go far in the profession unless I became a CPA. So in 1923 I gave up all pleasures for three months to study for the three-day examination by the State Board of Accountancy. I got copies of previous tests and studied them, and passed with no difficulty.

For five years I was comptroller for an automobile distributorship for three western states, and that experience led to the opportunity for a Ford dealership in Phoenix. That plan was interrupted by a skinny young man from Texas.

It was a lucky happenstance for both of us. The following year was a disaster for Ford dealers. The engineering department made a mistake, and the Model T's were turned out with frames and bodies with dimensions that didn't match, which created a six months' delay in delivery.

What about the first nineteen years of Howard Hughes' life?

They need to be studied in order to understand more fully the unique character that he was. Some of the story can be found in the oft-repeated legends of his boyhood. But those tales have become time-worn as they pass from biographer to biographer. Although I didn't know Howard until he had achieved manhood, he often during our long association revealed glimmers of his youth. The following will deal with some of those revelations, as well as the familiar facts of the early Hughes.

I never knew Howard Hughes Sr. He died the year before I went to work for his son. From all Howard Jr. told me and from what I learned from the elder Hughes' friends and business associates, I concluded that father and son were much alike.

Both possessed mechanical skill. Both were plungers, men of whim and fancy. Both were partially deaf. And both had a fondness for beautiful women.

"Big Howard," as the Houstonians referred to the senior Hughes (his six-foot-three son was termed "Little Howard" or "Sonny"), was born in Lancaster, Missouri, in 1869, descendant of an American family. His father was a lawyer, and the son seemed destined for the law, too. He graduated from Harvard and took his law degree at Iowa State.

But Hughes Sr. wasn't satisfied with the dusty world of torts and briefs. When the huge Spindletop oil strike hit Texas, he left his Keokuk practice and headed south. He became a "lease hound," who negotiated leases for the oil companies as close as possible to big strikes. Some leases proved to be good, some not good.

During one of his moneyed periods he met and married Allene Ganò, a dark-haired beauty, daughter of a Dallas judge. He took her off to Europe for a lavish honeymoon, returned months later when his money was spent. Howard Robard Hughes, Jr., was born on Christmas Eve of 1905, when the couple lived in a modest rented house at 1402 Crawford Street in Houston. The Hughes luck was in a temporary decline; soon it would rise to unbelievable heights.

The senior Hughes continued his leasing ventures, with some degree of success. He observed drilling operations from the derrick floor and pondered over the fish-tail bits with one scraping edge, which scraped into rock until they blunted and became useless.

"There must be a better way," he muttered. "Why not get a number of edges down there in that hole. Also you can chip faster than you can scrape."

He hit upon an idea that proved as revolutionary as steam power or the incandescent light. I'm convinced that jets wouldn't be flying the skies nor cars crowding the freeways if it hadn't been for Hughes' invention.

Big Howard devised the idea of a bit with first two and then three cone-shaped devices, each with teeth that revolved freely. His partner, a Texan named Walter B. Sharp, was impressed with the idea, and they worked with an engineer to perfect the bit. It was patented in 1908, and the partners formed the Sharp-Hughes Tool Company to manufacture the cone-shaped bits.

Drillers came running. The news had spread about the new bit that could cut rock like cheese, and the demand was enormous. Hughes and Sharp cannily refused to sell their product. They leased the bits. Out of that decision came the millions for Little Howard to play with in years to come.

Sharp died in 1917, and Big Howard bought out the family's interest for $325,000. That sounds like one of the best buy-outs in financial history, in view of the later prosperity of the Hughes Tool Company. But the enterprise did not always flourish. After I took over the company in 1946, I found in the firm's old ledgers loans of $25,000 apiece from Shell, Humble, and the Texas Company. Big Howard had needed the money to meet his payroll.

Little Howard lived an affluent but lonely boyhood in Houston. He loved to tinker, and he and his pal, Dudley Sharp, son of his father's partner, put together a ham radio. Howard wanted a motorcycle, but he was too young. So he induced his father's engineer, Matt Boehm, to help him install a battery-powered motor on his bicycle. At night Howard sat alone in his bedroom, tootling on his saxophones.

Howard was sent off to the Fessenden School in West Newton, Massachusetts, where his father hoped his son might qualify for Harvard. But the gangly boy was shy and unhappy in the formal atmosphere of New England. In 1921 he was sent to the Thatcher School at Ojai, California.

A fateful move. Ojai was a mere fifty miles from Hollywood. And Hollywood was the stamping grounds for Howard's uncle Rupert Hughes, a novelist who had turned to writing for the screen.

Rupert Hughes took pity on his lonely nephew and sent a limousine to bring the boy to Hollywood on weekends.

Howard had started to notice girls. That was one of the reasons he was delighted when Uncle Rupert took him to watch movies being made on Saturdays. Howard was fascinated by the plethora of beauties who worked at the studios. He was also intrigued by the process of moviemaking itself.

He sat on the set like a scholar, a ten-cent pocket notebook on his knee. As he watched the director conduct the scene, he made notes in small, laborious script. Most of his notations were of things he believed he could do better than the director. (Later, on my first trip to Houston with Howard, he lost the notebook on a golf course. He was frantic. "You've got to find it, Noah," he told me, and I spent a thousand dollars advertising for the finder. No one ever claimed the reward.)

Big Howard also visited the movie sets.

Oil was booming in California, and Hughes Tool Company set up an office in Los Angeles. The company president visited California often, to oversee the operation and to visit his son. He also visited Brother Rupert, who was acquainted with all the famous stars of Hollywood. He introduced his brother to one of them, the lovely Eleanor Boardman, and a romance ensued.

In 1922 Allene Hughes became ill. On the night before she was to go into the hospital for an operation, she wrote a letter to her husband. Later I found the letter in a family safe which young Howard asked me to ship to California and clean out for him.

Mrs. Hughes told her husband that she knew of his fondness for Eleanor Boardman, but she forgave him. She had a premonition of death, and she wished that the family home would be given to her sister. Half of her share of Hughes Tool was bequeathed to her relatives, half to her son.

Howard's mother died on the operating table.

In 1924 Big Howard was conducting a business conference when he fell dead of a heart attack. Young Howard buried his father, then went off to Europe with his friend Dudley Sharp and Dudley's mother. When they returned, Dudley went off to Cornell. Howard's relatives pressured him to follow Dudley's example and enroll at a university. He would have none of it.

Howard began to demonstrate his famous independence. After long wrangling, he convinced his relatives to sell their shares to the Hughes Tool Company. The cost of obtaining 100 percent ownership was $325,000, another monumental bargain. He had already gone to court and had himself declared a legal adult at the age of eighteen—just in case some relative tried to take over.

The relatives still nagged him to go to college. "You'll never amount to anything unless you get an education," he was told.

"I'll show them I'm responsible," he vowed. "I'll get married."

But whom should he marry? Here again we see the coldness of his calculations. He thought about all the Houston belles he had dated. Which one was the nicest? He decided that the winner was Ella Rice, a sweet, dark-haired beauty of the prestigious Rice family—though not from the rich side of that family.

How to woo her?

His plan might have come from one of the corny movies that he watched being made in Hollywood. He feigned illness and had a doctor telephone Ella with the news: "Howard is in a coma, and he keeps calling for 'Ella.' Perhaps you'd better see him."

Ella hurried to the bedside of Howard. He made a miraculous recovery, and in three weeks they were married.

After he won total ownership of Hughes Tool Company, he lost interest in it—that was typical of his actions down through the years. Something else was involved. Hughes Tool Company had been created by his father, a hearty, extroverted man who bent his son to his will.

"The tool company was my father's success, and it always will be," he told me. Hence it interested him only as a source of revenue. He never evidenced the slightest interest in its operation. All he ever asked of me was: "How much is it making? How much can it make next year?"

Movies were Howard's big interest. Soon after the marriage, he and his bride packed up and left for Hollywood by way of New York City. Howard was never to make Houston his home again.

CHAPTER THREE

The $5,000,000 Toy

When I went to work for the nineteen-year-old Howard Hughes on Thanksgiving Day, I had no notion of the demands he would make on me. Throughout my business career I had been employed by executives who conducted their affairs according to conventional practices. Not Howard. His business methods reflected his life: impulsive, unorthodox, contradictory, and disorganized.

He and his bride were living in an Ambassador Hotel suite, sharing a bedroom with twin beds. He rented a room next door for me to use as my headquarters. I was to spend more time there than at my own home in Hollywood.

During our first conversation I had warned Howard that I would function neither as a secretary nor a chauffeur. However, I did chauffeur him, but for one purpose.

Howard had become intrigued with the millions that could be earned in the stock market. That appealed to his gambling spirit. He spent his mornings in a brokerage office in the Ambassador Hotel, studying the figures on the quotation board.

That didn't satisfy him. The board listed only the major quotations. He needed to know all the market figures as they came over the ticker.

So each morning I picked him up at the hotel at 6 A.M. and drove him downtown to a brokerage office, arriving at 7, in time for the opening of trading in New York. This went on for a few weeks until Howard became exhausted.

He was watching the stocks from early in the morning, playing golf every afternoon, then taking Ella out to Hollywood parties in the evening. The Hughes stamina began to flag.

"Noah, I want a stock ticker beside my bed," he told me. "Then I can just wake up at seven and start watching the market without all this trouble."

"A stock ticker at your bedside?" I asked.

"Yes. I want it—right now. Give up everything else you're doing and get it for me."

It was typical of thousands of missions I was to perform in future years. The pattern was always the same. Howard wanted it. He wanted it immediately. Noah, get it for me. No matter what it cost, no matter how hard it was to get.

I seldom argued. Howard wasn't interested in logic, nor would he accept excuses. He expected me to do the impossible. And I did.

Paul Williams was the Los Angeles manager for Western Union. He was a member of the downtown Rotary Club, and so was I. I told him about my boss's request.

"Sorry, Noah," he said. "We can't supply any stock market service beyond Figueroa Street. But I'll tell you— we're going to run a line out Seventh Street into Hollywood. It'll go right past the Ambassador."

"How soon will that be?" I asked.

"Eighteen months," he said.

Not soon enough. Howard wanted it now. My problem was how to run a Western Union line three miles past Figueroa Street to Howard's bedside at the Ambassador. The next day I was driving to the hotel on Seventh Street. I happened to notice that the poles carrying power for the trolley line had empty insulators on them.

I telephoned the superintendent of the Los Angeles Street Railway Company and explained my need of a private line from Figueroa to the Ambassador Hotel.

"Very simple," he replied. "All you have to do is join the Joint Pole Line Association. You can string your line for twenty-five cents a year per insulator."

That was the solution! Within a week I had a line strung from Figueroa to the Ambassador. Then I went to Paul Williams and told him of my plan.

"Highly irregular," he humphed. "I can't allow you to run Western Union stock quotations on a private line. It's against the rules."

He was one of those executives who operated by the book. Howard Hughes wasn't interested in rules; he only wanted results. I had to devise a different scheme.

I had the line from Figueroa to the hotel. Now all I needed was a hookup to the line. I rented an office on Sixth Street across the street from the Pacific Mutual Building. Then I told Williams to install a ticker in the office. It was all square and according to regulations.

On the following day the glass-domed ticker was busily tapping out the up-to-the-minute prices of Anaconda Copper and A.T.&T. in the empty office. Meanwhile, Howard was three miles away in his Ambassador suite, waiting for me to produce results.

A line was strung from the office to the trolley poles that carried the line to the hotel. I hired a friend with a knowledge of electricity to help my clandestine plan.

"Easy," he said. "I'll just install resistance, disconnect the ticker and take it out to the Ambassador and hook it up in your boss's bedroom. You stay here with the dome, and I'll phone you when the job is done."

He did his work and left. I sat down on the floor and waited for his call, pleased that I had satisfied the need of my new employer.

A knock came at the office door. I opened it and found two servicemen from Western Union. One of them explained: "We got a red light on our control board, which means that your ticker isn't working."

He peered over my shoulder into the vacant room. "Say —where is the ticker?" he asked.

I had to think fast. "Well," I said "a pal and I were fooling around and we knocked it over. He took it out to get it fixed."

He eyed me strangely. "That wasn't necessary," he said.

"We repair tickers, free of charge. No matter what happens to them."

"I'm glad to know that," I said. "I'll let you know the minute I hear from him."

"Okay," said the Western Union man. He took another glance at the empty office and left with his companion.

I quickly dialed the Ambassador Hotel and asked for the Hughes suite. I knew Howard would be out playing golf. My friend answered, and I told him: "Bring the ticker back right away."

"What the hell!" he complained. "I was just getting ready to install it in the bedroom."

"Don't ask questions. Just bring it back. I'll explain when you get here."

When he arrived, I told him what had happened. "Damn!" he said. "I must have reversed the terminals when I put in the resistance."

There was no way to clear myself but to call Western Union and ask them to re-install the ticker. The same repair man came. He inspected the ticker and said, "There's nothing wrong with this machine."

"That's good," I replied. "I'm glad we didn't break it."

Again the repair man departed, scratching his head. I was left alone with the ticker, which was busily tapping out closing prices on the New York Stock Exchange. The damned thing was useless to me, because it was three miles distant from where my boss wanted it.

The more I thought about it, the madder I got. Finally I shoved my hat on my head and stalked out the door. I charged into the Western Union office and stood defiantly before Paul Williams' desk.

"See here," I began, "I'm going to get that stock wire into the Ambassador, and I'm not going to play any more games! I've gone to a whole lot of trouble to string my own line from the hotel to where you provide service. Now if you don't give it to me, I'm going straight to the Railroad Commission and raise hell about your attitude. And if that doesn't work, I'll take you into court and sue you!"

The magic words were Railroad Commission. That was the State of California's regulator of public utilities. Neither Western Union nor any other utility enjoyed being hauled on the carpet in front of the Railroad Commission.

"Now calm down, Noah," Paul Williams said. "If it's so all-fired important to you, you can have your ticker at the Ambassador. We'll hook it up."

On the following morning, Howard Hughes was able to watch the rises and falls of his stocks without leaving his bed. And did he express his gratitude?

Hell, no. There was never a word of thanks. Not even an inquiry of how I had managed it. He simply assumed that it would be accomplished.

It was an expensive toy. During the next few years he lost $5,000,000 in the market.

CHAPTER FOUR

Texas, Taxes, and Saxophones

"Come on down to Houston with me."

It was not so much an invitation as a command. Howard wanted to return to Texas and wind up all his affairs in the state that provided his income. "I intend to come back to California and make motion pictures," he announced to me.

Characteristically he scheduled the trip at Christmastime.

I had no choice but to go along. And I must admit that I relished the challenge. After fifteen years of toting up figures and dealing with humdrum business types, it was exhilarating to be associated with a man who followed no established patterns, whose whims were a constant prod to my ingenuity.

So off we went to Houston—Howard and Ella Hughes, and my wife, two daughters, and I. Ella was happy to be back in Texas, Howard was less so. He paid a cursory call to the tool company and was satisfied that it was functioning. The rest of the time he spent in golfing, remodeling the family home, fiddling with a ham radio, and his saxophones.

We remained in Houston through the winter, and come March, I was faced with my first important financial task for Howard Hughes: preparing his and the company's income tax returns.

In 1925 the federal income tax was a great deal simpler than it is today. But even in those times Howard's income tax was a formidable challenge. That was because of the chaotic condition of his finances.

This was early in my dealings with Howard, and I made one great mistake: I presented him with two alternatives.

Later I recognized the wisdom of avoiding such an error. But I was new at the game of dealing with Howard, and I didn't realize that it was virtually impossible for him to make up his mind about two relatively equal propositions.

The issue was this: whether to file his income tax in Texas, which had long been his residence, or in California, where he had spent some time and intended to live. He could legally have established residence in either state. I studied both possibilities and concluded that Texas was the best place to file his tax. The reason was simple— Texas had a community property law which provided a more favorable rate for married couples (California had no such law until 1936).

Howard had been receiving $50,000 annually from the Hughes Tool Company, as well as a $75,000 dividend in 1925. If he filed in Texas, he and his wife could split the income and remain in the lower brackets. Income tax was not great in 1926, but Howard could have saved about $5,000 by filing in Texas.

"Which will it be—Texas or California?" I asked.

He pondered. And fussed. And fretted. He simply could not make up his mind. My arguments in favor of Texas seemed to affect him not at all. He seemed to think there were some hidden benefits for filing in California.

As the March 15 deadline grew closer and closer, I became desperate. I prepared two tax returns—one for Texas and one for California. I thought surely he would decide in plenty of time to file the one he chose.

But he didn't decide. March 15 arrived, and he still hadn't made up his mind.

"Howard, I must know!" I implored. "There's a twenty-five percent penalty for late returns."

"I know, I know," he replied. "But I'm still mulling it over in my mind."

He continued his deliberations as the midnight deadline approached. I finally made out two checks, one for the Texas return, one for the California, and I went down to the Houston tax collector's office. At 11:30 P.M., I telephoned him.

"I haven't decided yet," he replied. "Call me back in ten minutes."

I did. He needed ten minutes more. At 11:50 I called once more. We debated the issue on the telephone for five minutes. Finally I said, "Howard, in just five minutes you will be subject to the twenty-five per cent penalty. You will *have* to make up your mind!"

"All right," he said falteringly. "File the . . . California return."

I sighed deeply and hurried to the counter to hand over the California return. I went home for the first sound sleep I had known in nights.

My slumber was broken at 7 A.M. by a telephone call. I instantly recognized the querulous voice of Howard.

"Noah, I've been agonizing over that tax return all night," he said. "I've talked to my attorney, and we both agreed that I was wrong in going against your advice. I want you to get back that return and substitute the Texas one."

I could scarcely believe my ears. "Howard, you can't take back a tax return once it's been filed," I protested.

"Try," he said, and he hung up.

I shook my head unbelievingly. No, it hadn't been a bad dream; Howard actually wanted me to retrieve his income tax return. So I rose from my bed and decided I would try.

First I went to the tax office in Houston. I told the deputy that I had made a terrible error and I needed to exchange my employer's tax form for another one. He was sympathetic.

"But all of the returns have already been shipped to Austin," he said.

I bought a ticket for the next train to Austin. During the ride I planned my attack.

"I'm new in my job, and I made a terrible mistake," I

told the tax commissioner. "If I don't get that tax form back, I'll be fired. And I've got a wife and two small daughters."

To support my petition, I presented the Texas form, complete with the signed check. Fortunately the commissioner was a kindly old Southern gentleman, and he sympathized with my plight.

"We'll see if we can't find it for you," he said. He summoned his chief deputy and ordered a search of the mail bags for the envelope I described. It was found, and I switched the returns, offering my profound thanks.

As soon as I returned to the Austin hotel, I telephoned Howard with my triumph.

"Noah, I've been thinking," he said. "Maybe it wasn't such a good idea to file a Texas return after all. I want you to go back there and substitute the California return."

It was all I could do to avoid throwing the telephone across the hotel room. I controlled myself, and I explained to Howard that it was simply impossible to devise another story that would convince the tax people to make another switch.

"All right," he said poutingly. "Come on back to Houston."

Howard continued his aimless activities in Houston for another few weeks. He remodeled the house, although he had no intention of living in it. He assembled a large amount of radio equipment, which he would abandon. But one thing he wanted to take to California with him: his saxophone cabinet.

He had accumulated more than a dozen saxes, and he cherished them. So much so that during his youth he had ordered a special cabinet made for them, a massive piece of furniture constructed of walnut. Howard designed it himself, and the cabinet makers put it together in the family game room. It was built in two pieces, the base and a top cabinet.

When Howard decided to ship the cabinet to California, he made a disconcerting discovery: both pieces were too big to pass through the doors of the house. Or the windows.

Howard fumed over the problem. Finally I told him, "Howard, you'll either have to tear out a wall or cut the cabinet in half."

His decision was startlingly quick: "We'll cut it down the middle."

That was done, and the saxophone cabinet was shipped in four pieces to California. Howard followed soon afterward.

The cabinet was reassembled in Los Angeles, and the slice down the middle didn't seem to bother Howard. He continued blowing on the saxophones until, as with all his hobbies, he lost interest. The saxes rusted and ultimately they and the bifurcated cabinet were sold at auction.

Somewhere in Los Angeles, someone may own a curious, four-part walnut cabinet. If that person reads these words, he will now know what it is and to whom it once belonged.

During the early years with Howard, I became accustomed to handling a variety of personal problems for the eccentric young man. One of them had its genesis in early 1925, before he had married Ella and before I had joined him. Howard's romantic career was in full swing, and he had made the acquaintance of a number of young girls of charms and availability. He had also become acquainted with a young man who was a driver for the police department. We'll call him Bruce Davis, which wasn't his name.

Davis performed small chores for Howard, notably driving girls to and from the Ambassador Hotel, where Howard was staying. One night Davis was driving one of the girls home during a heavy rainstorm. His car skidded at the intersection of First Street and Beverly and slammed into a light pole. When the police arrived, they found the girl dead. All she was wearing was a mink coat.

Davis had the brains to convince his friends in the police department not to involve the young Texas heir in whose car the girl had been killed. Howard was grateful, and he told Davis, "Bruce, if there's anything I can ever do for you, just let me know."

The young driver drew a suspended sentence as a result

of the accident, and that might have been the end of the incident. Except that he got drunk one night and slugged his wife. He was arrested and sent to jail.

Davis made a plea to Howard for help. By this time I had joined Howard, and he told me, "Noah, I want you to spring him."

"Howard, in order to do that, you will have to guarantee his employment," I pointed out.

"I don't care. Spring him."

I found Davis a job, and he was released from jail. His power over the rich Texan went to his head, and he started making requests for a thousand dollars now and then for his "urgent needs."

One day Howard told me, "Davis wants me to give him five thousand dollars. What do you think I should do?"

"Howard, this is blackmail," I said. "You keep on giving this man money and he'll stop at nothing. I think you should have it out with him before it goes too far."

"You handle it, Noah."

Noah handled it. I summoned Davis and told him sternly: "What you're trying to do with Mr. Hughes is nothing more or less than blackmail. You can go back to jail for that, and this time you'll stay there. Now you seem like a nice young man—where are your parents?"

"In Kansas," he said. "They run a farm."

"Why don't you go back there and help them run the place. I'll tell you what I'll do. I'll give you enough money to buy yourself a caterpillar tractor, and you can rent it to other farmers, too."

He returned to the farm, bought a tractor, and apparently straightened himself out. Howard never heard from him again.

CHAPTER FIVE

Movies

When Howard Hughes returned to California in April of 1926, he plunged into the making of movies. During the next thirty years he visited the Hughes Tool Company only once.

Howard was determined to become an important movie producer. He had made one stab at it before I became associated with him. In 1925, Howard was very young and very impressionable. One of the Hollywood figures who attached himself to the rich young Texan was Ralph Graves, an actor. Graves had pretensions of being a director, and he convinced Howard to back him in a movie. The pictured was called *Swell Hogan,* and it was a disaster.

"I've got a great story, and I can make it for fifty thousand," Graves enthused. Howard agreed to go along.

But the story wasn't great—it was lousy. And Graves didn't make it for $50,000; he spent almost twice that much. When Howard showed it to company bosses in hopes of getting a release, they held their noses.

"It stinks," they said.

Swell Hogan never saw the light of day. It disappeared into the Hughes vault.

You might think that would have been a chastening experience for young Howard, convincing him he should leave the making of movies to experts. He didn't think that way. Failure was unconscionable to him. Besides, his relatives, headed by Uncle Rupert, tried to convince him of the folly of squandering his inheritance on such a foolhardy course. That was the worst thing they could have done. He was more determined than ever to prove his relatives wrong.

He was luckier on his next film.

This time he hired competent help. His director was Marshall (Mickey) Neilan who had amassed a record of successful films. The story was a sophisticated comedy called *Everybody's Acting*. And the cast was topflight: Louise Dresser, Ford Sterling, Betty Bronson, Henry B. Walthall, Raymond Hitchcock, and Lawrence Gray. Howard allowed Neilan to spend $150,000 on the picture, and it proved a success.

Everybody's Acting turned a modest profit, and it encouraged Howard to continue with his motion picture career. As his financial advisor, I didn't exactly approve. Having been schooled in strict cost accounting, I found the economics of the movie industry appalling. Money could be wasted in enormous amounts and never recovered.

But Howard was utterly fascinated with movies, and he couldn't be dissuaded. Not by his family. Certainly not by me.

His next film was even more fortuitous. Through his attorney, Neil McCarthy, Howard met John Considine, a young producer and son of the founder of the Sullivan and Considine vaudeville circuit. Through Considine, Howard met Lewis Milestone, a Russian-born director of uncommon talent.

Milestone directed *Two Arabian Knights,* a clever tale about a couple of American prisoners of World War I who escape the Germans and make a roundabout route to freedom, landing in Arabia. The stars were Louis Wolheim, a splendid actor with the face of a pug, and William Boyd, who later became famous as Hopalong Cassidy.

Two Arabian Knights was a sparkling success, and it earned Milestone the 1927-28 Academy Award for direction at the first Oscar ceremonies (he shared the honor with Frank Borzage). It was to prove the only time that a Hughes picture was to get within smelling distance of the Oscar.

Milestone made another movie for Hughes, *The Rack-*

et. Starring Wolheim, Marie Prevost, and Thomas Meighan, it capitalized on the public's fascination with gangsters.

Two hits in a row made Howard confident in his abilities as a moviemaker. Overconfident, you might say.

"I can direct as well as those other guys," he told me.

That was a sure route to calamity. As long as Howard made movies with strong directors like Lewis Milestone and allowed such men to exercise their creative talents, he was on safe ground. But the minute he started to take over and supervise the film himself, he was in dire trouble.

He was totally unsuited to be a movie director. The necessary qualities for a director include such things as having a sympathy for human problems, understanding emotion, maintaining a schedule, and, most of all, making split-second decisions—hundreds of them per day.

Those elements were lacking in Howard's makeup. But that didn't stop him from trying.

His next try was a whopper: *Hell's Angels.*

Howard was determined to make a movie involving his other hobby, flying. He acquired a potboiler script about two World War I aces who were both wooing a beautiful English society girl. This triangle was played against a backdrop of air warfare, including the attack of a Zeppelin on London. Howard hired a director who seemed ideal. He was Luther Reed, who had been aviation expert for the New York *Herald* before turning to screen writing and directing. Ben Lyon and James Hall were cast as the two heroes, and Greta Nissen, a voluptuous Norwegian, was assigned as their sweetheart.

I could see from the start that *Hell's Angels* was going to be a headache. Howard expected the picture to cost a million dollars, a huge sum for those Hollywood times. From the way he was spending, I knew the picture would cost much more. He was buying old war planes by the dozens and stashing them at airports all over Southern California to be rebuilt. He needed scores of aviators and thousands of extras for battlefield scenes.

I tried to temper his extravagance. But in 1927 when the film began shooting, I was still new to the Hughes operation, and I did mostly what I was told. My job was to find the money for Howard to pour into *Hell's Angels*. And, with the country still enjoying the Coolidge boom, the Hughes Tool Company was still supplying large profits.

Hughes and his director clashed from the outset of filming. Howard insisted he knew how the air dogfights should be shot; Luther Reed had his own ideas. When Reed found himself being shoved aside while Howard called the shots, he quit.

"I'm going to take over as director," Howard announced to me. "I'll keep a director on the set, but the decisions will be mine."

The director he chose was James Whale, an Englishman who later directed *Journey's End* and *Frankenstein*. He was new to Hollywood and was content to stand aside while Hughes did most of the direction.

I witnessed the chaotic nature of their collaboration one day when I was visiting the *Hell's Angels* set. The company was shooting the scene in which the Zeppelin was trying to escape back to Germany after the London raid. According to the script, the big dirigible was losing altitude and needed to jettison all ballast to elude the British fighter planes. Members of the crew agreed to leap to their deaths "for the Fatherland."

The big stage at Metropolitan studio (now General Service) was almost filled by the mammoth mockup of the Zeppelin. Huge wind machines blew smoke that was supposed to resemble passing clouds. The gondola was suspended above the floor of the stage, and Howard had ordered eighteen mattresses to be piled below the hatch. Thirty stunt men jumped onto the mattresses, one by one.

Howard ordered the scene taken over and over again. I stood there unbelieving as he totaled more than one hundred takes.

"My God, Jimmy," I said to Whale, "isn't that ridiculous? What the hell is he trying to achieve?"

"Damned if I know," said the director. "From that camera angle, you could take the best of his shots and the worst, and even an expert couldn't tell the difference."

But Howard kept ordering the Zeppelin crew to continue leaping "for the Fatherland."

The logistics of the Hughes air force would have done justice to a Balkan war. Howard had bought up Fokkers, DeHavillands, Sopwiths, Nieuports and every other kind of war plane he could lay his hands on. He conducted the filming just like a wartime operation. Unfortunately nature did not cooperate.

Howard sent two fleets of fighter planes into the sky to simulate dogfights between the Germans and British. But the planes encountered no clouds, and he wouldn't film unless he had the proper clouds. Once he sent a crew to Oakland to make flying scenes. The men and planes remained there six months before finding clouds that were cinematically effective.

For a scene requiring a Gotha bomber, Howard rented a Sikorsky twin-engine plane from Roscoe Turner, the famed speed pilot. It was camouflaged to resemble the German bomber, and a pilot agreed to undertake the stunt Howard wanted. The pilot's pay was $5,000.

He was to fly the Sikorsky to the highest altitude it could reach, put it in a stall, and nosedive toward earth. If he couldn't pull out of the stall, he was to parachute to safety.

There was a problem involved in the stunt. The plane was to be smoking at the tail, and there was no way the pilot could release the smoke from the cockpit. One of the set workers volunteered to ride in the back and set off the smoke pots. He was equipped with a parachute and given the same instructions as the pilot: if the plane didn't pull out of the stall, jump.

The two men took off in Roscoe Turner's plane, and it reached its highest altitude. The plane turned downward in the stall, then started spiraling toward earth. A parachute appeared in the sky—the pilot had decided the plane wasn't going to right itself.

The film makers scanned the sky anxiously. No other parachute. The plane continued twirling toward the ground, then strangely leveled out and crashed into an orchard. An inquest was held into the young man's death. He may have been knocked unconscious in the dive. Or he may have believed the pilot was going to control the plane. No one really knew the reason why he hadn't jumped.

Another flier was ferrying a single-engine Sopwith biplane for locations in Oakland. Midway in the flight he ran out of gas and landed in a field. He took off after refueling but couldn't rise above tree level. He crashed and died.

One of the *Hell's Angels* pilots was a veteran stunt flier who had barnstormed the country with his tricks. He took a plane up one day to show off to the movie crew. One of his stunts was to dive downward and straighten out just before he would have hit the earth. That day he didn't make it.

The fourth fatality on the picture was a pilot who was planning to take one of the old planes from Grand Central Airport in Glendale to Mines Field in Inglewood. His plane tangled in power lines as he was taking off, and he was burned horribly.

Howard visited the pilot in the hospital. If he was shaken by the man's accident, Howard didn't show it. He offered a few words of comfort, but he was phlegmatic, as he was about everything. The pilot died about eighteen hours after the crash.

During the making of *Hell's Angels,* the motion picture industry underwent the biggest revolution in its history. Until October 6, 1927, movies remained mute, dialogue being transmitted to the audience by way of titles. Then on that memorable date, Warner Brothers introduced spoken dialogue and song in *The Jazz Singer,* starring Al Jolson.

The industry underwent a convulsion. Some leaders including Irving Thalberg and Charles Chaplin, said talkies were a passing fancy, some claimed sound was here to stay. Howard Hughes plunged onward to conclude his all-silent *Hell's Angels.*

Halfway through shooting, Howard made his decision. "It's got to have sound. I'll make it over again."

My heart sank when I heard the news. He had already spent more than $2,000,000, and I wasn't sure that the

Hughes Tool Company could produce enough revenue to finance another film-making splurge.

But it wasn't as bad as it seemed at first. Most of the air battles were salvageable by injecting sound effects. Some of the dialogue could be dubbed and scenes reshot. But Greta Nissen was impossible. She couldn't possibly read dialogue in the retakes as an English girl; her accent was as heavy as a Norwegian maid's.

Howard hunted around for a substitute. Joe Engel found her. Joe had been president of Metro Pictures before it merged to become MGM, then had fallen from grace, becoming a gateman at one of the studios. Hughes had hired Joe as a kind of business manager for his film enterprises. It was Joe who suggested that Greta Nissen be substituted by Jean Harlow, who had been appearing in Laurel and Hardy comedies for Hal Roach. Howard agreed, and Harlow was hired at $125 a week.

Most of Harlow's scenes were directed by Howard, including the famed boudoir sequence ("Excuse me while I slip into something more comfortable"). With sound added, Howard continued tinkering with *Hell's Angels,* insisting that the aerial combat scenes be perfected. Despite all his expense on real-life dogfights, a large percentage of the scenes were actually miniatures.

The set workers grew accustomed to Howard's pace. They spent most of the day playing cards on Stage 5—sometimes all day, for days at a time. But when Howard drove his car through the studio gate, Stage 5 was alerted. The crew dropped their cards and swung into action. An overhead trellis carrying plane models dangled by string began to swing to and fro. A smoke machine pumped simulated clouds across the backdrop.

When Howard walked through the stage door, the aerial action of World War I was in progress. He made a cursory inspection of what was going on, then retired to a corner of the stage to read a book as the craftsmen did their work.

Almost inevitably, he was dissatisfied with what he saw in the rushes the next day, and he told the crew, "Try again."

For weeks, waste film filled ten barrels on the Metropolitan lot, all of it discards from *Hell's Angels*.

In the end, Howard shot an all-time record of 2,500,000 feet of film on *Hell's Angels*. The final film ran about 15,000 feet on the screen.

The picture required three years to complete. Total cost: $3,500,000.

During the long time that Howard was making *Hell's Angels,* he became very protective of the movie. Warner Brothers was also shooting a World War I flying picture, *Dawn Patrol,* starring Richard Barthelmess and Douglas Fairbanks Jr., with Howard Hawks as director. There was competition between Howard Hughes and Warner Brothers over the hiring of stunt pilots. From the reports Howard heard from the pilots, he became convinced that *Dawn Patrol* was copying *Hell's Angels*.

Howard was determined to catch Warner Brothers in the act of thievery. He assigned his screen writer, Joe Marsh, and an assistant director, Reggie Callow, to deliver a *Dawn Patrol* script to him.

The two men knew of a girl who worked in the Warner Brothers script department. They wined her and dined her and finally divulged the reason for their attentions. They offered to pay her $500 if she would give them a script of *Dawn Patrol*. She agreed to do so at her apartment the following evening. They appeared, handed over the $500, and received the script. And then two police detectives stepped out from behind a door.

Howard called me late that night.

"Noah, Joe Marsh and Reggie Callow are in jail," he said.

"What on earth for?"

He told me, then added, "I don't give a damn about Reggie, but I want Joe Marsh out of jail."

Fortunately I had a friend who was a superior court judge. I convinced him to get out of bed and start court proceedings early. At 5 A.M., Callow and Marsh were released without bail. The case was never prosecuted.

For a long time I feared Howard would never complete *Hell's Angels*. But at last in the spring of 1930, he indicated that he was ready for release, and he engaged two theaters in New York for the premiere. A half-million dollars was spent on advertising and exploitation.

The day arrived for Howard to leave for New York with two copies of the completed film. He had scheduled a train journey that would bring him into New York on the morning *Hell's Angels* was to open. If he didn't arrive in time, there would be no premiere.

Howard chose that day to have a financial conference with me. The meeting went on and on, and I reminded him periodically of his need to get down to the Southern Pacific depot to catch his train.

"Don't worry," he said. "I want to finish up these matters first."

Howard had utterly no conception of time, and finally I said to him: "Howard, if you don't leave now, there will be no New York opening. The train leaves in exactly fifteen minues."

"Jesus H. Christ!" he exclaimed. "Let's get going!"

We hurried to the studio parking lot, and he started to climb into the driver's seat of his spanking new $4,400 Packard.

"I'm too nervous to drive," he said. "You take the wheel, Noah. And if you get me to the station on time, I'll give you the car."

I slid behind the wheel and gunned the motor. It seemed an impossible task. The Southern Pacific station was ten miles distant, and it was city traffic all the way. No freeways then.

But one of the many things that Howard Hughes didn't know about me was that I had done some semi-professional race car driving. I inhaled the fresh new-car smell of the Packard and gazed down its long shiny hood. I was determined to get Howard to the depot on time.

Oh, what a dash that was! I cut through gas stations. I slid around the left side of street cars. I sped right through an intersection where a cop held up his palm for me to stop. When a jam of cars prevented passage, I put two wheels on the sidewalk and passed them in the gutter.

Howard said nothing through the flight. He pressed

both feet down on the floorboard and stared straight ahead, perhaps fearing this would be his last automobile ride.

But we pulled up before the depot with a minute to spare. He grabbed the film cans and started racing toward the train tracks.

"It's your Packard, Noah," he yelled as he left.

CHAPTER SIX

A Study in Paradox

During my early years with Howard Hughes I came to recognize patterns in his habits and behavior—patterns which have continued throughout his lifetime. At first his eccentric ways seemed amusing, and they added to the legend of an authentic and singular character. But as Howard grew older I could see his eccentricities become more pronounced and, eventually, disabling.

He was a paradoxical man.

Howard was a man of great physical courage; you need only review his achievements as a pilot to prove that.

Yet he harbored an intense fear of being robbed. That's the reason he never carried any money around with him, and the legends multiplied about how he paid taxi drivers with IOU's and borrowed dimes from friends for telephone calls. Howard fostered those legends.

"Goddammit, Noah," he said to me, "there are people in this country who will knock you off if they think you have five hundred dollars in your pocket. I want everyone to know that I don't carry any money."

Another paradox: Howard greatly feared kidnapers. Yet he also wanted no one to profit at his expense, and he instructed me: "If they ever grab me, Noah, don't pay any ransom. If you get notes from me pleading for money, ignore them. You'll know I wouldn't write such notes unless I was forced to. Don't give any of those crooks a goddam dime."

"But," I protested, "supposing you become convinced

that the kidnapers are going to kill you for sure if the ransom isn't paid."

He pondered over that point. "In that case, I'll write the ransom note and put 'PDQ' under my signature. That'll mean 'Pay Damn Quick.'"

Howard was a man who would let million-dollar airplanes rust unattended on airfields, because he couldn't bring himself to sell them. Yet he had utterly no concern for personal belongings.

One time when he was selling his house, he ordered me to auction everything in it.

"Everything?" I asked.

"Everything," he said.

"But what about the silver, Howard?" I asked. "It's monogrammed, and it should remain in your family."

"I don't want it," he said.

"Then why not give it to your aunts in Houston. They would want to keep the silver in the family."

"Auction *everything*," he declared.

On my own, I told his Houston aunts about the silver, and they came to California for the auction. But the bidding went too high for them, and the Hughes silver went to another party.

He was a man of great wealth, who could have done great good with his money. But his benefactions were nil. He gave away no money, and wouldn't even lend it to close friends. Whatever he gave was for a purpose: to win a girl's fancy, to achieve a business advantage, to seek political favor.

The Wall Street crash of October 1929 came during the filming of *Hell's Angels*. Ben Lyon was desperate for money to cover margin payments on his stocks. He went to Howard Hughes, who was a close personal friend as well as his producer.

"No, I don't lend money," he told Ben.

Howard's distrust stemmed from an experience that came early in his Hollywood days. He played golf every afternoon, seven days a week, at such courses as Bel-Air, Wilshire, and Lakeside. He always chose as his partner an expert player like the National Amateur champion George

Von Elm or Ozzie Carlton, who was state champion of Texas. Howard's team almost invariably won, because he was a two-handicap golfer himself.

Each afternoon Howard and his partner wagered on their game. Not thousands of dollars, but hundreds.

It added up. After a few months Howard was owed from $5,000 to $15,000 by three prominent Los Angeles golfers. They welched.

"Those sons of bitches won't pay me!" he complained. It was inconceivable to him, and he never again allowed himself to be in the position where people owed him money on a personal basis. Unless, of course, it was to his special advantage.

Howard never smoked. He didn't like people around him to smoke, although I never heard him say so. It didn't bother me, because I didn't smoke, either. Other associates quickly learned of his dislike of cigarette smoke—he never had ash trays on his desk—and prudently refrained from lighting up in his presence.

Once he granted another producer the privilege of using the private Hughes projection room. "But there's to be no smoking in it," Howard cautioned.

He drank very little liquor.

When he was traveling with the Hollywood crowd, there was pressure on him to have some bootleg booze. Howard took a few sips, but little more. He never really learned to drink.

Once when he acquired a supply of liquor, he said, "Noah, why don't you drop by the house each night after work and we'll try some of it."

I stopped at his house for a couple of nights, and he poured us a couple of drinks. We drank and talked, and it seemed obvious that he was trying to educate himself in how to become a gentleman drinker. I called the whole thing off. I saw little enough of my family, and I saw no reason to sit around in the evening with my boss while he tried to learn to drink. Besides, I clung to the old theory that familiarity breeds contempt. I was determined to keep my relationship with Howard Hughes on a business level only.

Howard would not tolerate drunks in his employ. If an underling telephoned him in an obviously drunken condition, that man was usually fired the next day.

"I can't have anyone working for me who can't control his tongue," Howard said. "That guy will get drunk and tell my secrets all over town."

Secrets, secrets, secrets. His passion for secrecy became a mania.

Howard pursued no other sport beside golf and skeet shooting. I never saw him with a tennis racket. He never rode horseback. He never fished or hunted.

He cared little for music. After he gave up the saxophone his interest in music diminished to background music for his films.

He never read for pleasure. His only reading was novels and short stories which might present possibilities for film subjects.

His vocabulary was limited. He was aware of his lack of education, and he chose his words carefully. He spoke in a rather high-pitched, nasal voice that was unmistakable on the telephone. Despite his boyhood in Houston, he hadn't a trace of Texas accent.

He never wrote letters. Unsigned memos to his employees, yes. But no letters.

"I don't want to go on record where they can pin me down," he explained to me.

The only letter that I ever heard him dictate was one he composed on the train to Houston the first time we visited there together. He had been playing golf on Los Angeles courses and had admired the bent grass on the greens. He wrote a letter to be sent to the two Houston golf clubs he belonged to, advising them on how they could improve their fairways and greens. The letters were never mailed.

Howard never raised his voice, but he could express his disfavor with someone by referring to him as "that bastard" or "that son of a bitch." His favorite expression of disdain was "that shitass." When I first heard him use it, I was amused; I hadn't heard the word since I was in grammar school.

Later I learned that whenever Howard referred to

someone as a "shitass," that person was forever banished from Hughes' good graces.

Howard loved to hear dirty jokes. I never heard him tell one, but he enjoyed listening to the latest jokes. He responded with a high, ribald laugh.

I can recall his telling only one joke during our long acquaintance. That was early in the game, and this was the joke:

A man went to a very fancy English party. He was an old chap who carried an ear trumpet so he could hear the conversations. The hostess was introducing him to one of the lady guests: "This is Mrs. Hefflefinger."

"What's that you say?" the old man asked.

"I said, this is Mrs. Hefflefinger," she said.

"I can't hear you!" the man said.

"THIS IS MRS. HEFFLEFINGER!" the hostess shouted.

"I don't understand," said the man. "It sounds like you're saying 'Hefflefinger.' "

Howard thought that one was a knee-slapper. It was a curious joke for him, because he never kidded about his own deafness. In fact he was extremely sensitive about it.

It was apparently a hereditary condition; his father and grandfather were deaf, too. The doctors told Howard it had something to do with thickening of the bone, and there was no way they could cure it by surgery. Howard rarely mentioned his deafness to others; his associates learned to raise their voices in his presence.

I always suspected that Howard Hughes used the telephone excessively because he was hard of hearing. That saved him embarrassment. And he could attach an amplifier on his phone so he would have no trouble with conversations. In later years a technician followed him everywhere with a couple of suitcases containing a telephone amplifier which could be used wherever Howard wanted to telephone.

On several occasions I purchased hearing aids for Howard to use. He refused to wear them. Vanity.

Howard usually had swimming pools at his houses, but he never swam.

He never played cards. He shot a little dice. Once when he was in Houston he fell into the hands of some professionals and lost $2,800 in a crap game in the Rice Hotel. That burned him, and he went back the next night with a man who was reputed to be one of Houston's best crap shooters. Howard lost again. I think that taught him a lesson.

His attire? When I first new him, he didn't dress as eccentrically as he did in later years. He wore tailor-made suits that had been made for him in Europe at $200 and $250 apiece. He would order twenty or more suits at a clip.

Later he realized he didn't need to dress to impress anyone. That's when he started wearing corduroys and plain shirts. He had formerly worn expensive shoes that had been molded to his feet. Once he ordered thirty pairs of them in several styles and made by a famous English shoemaker, but never wore them, complaining that they did not fit. They cost $35 per pair. Howard returned them and got $10 per pair as a refund. The famous sneakers came later, when he was troubled with a foot infection. He took plenty of baths, but he couldn't control the infection.

Only his closest associates could kid him about his clothes. One day Howard came on a movie set in sloppy dress and Pat DiCicco cracked, "Jesus, Howard, with all your money, why can't you dress decently? You look like something that crawled out from under a rock."

Howard didn't smile. "All right, Pat," he said. "You be the dude. I'll do the work."

He gave gifts only if he was seeking something in return. I recall when he went to Brock's, a jewelry store in Los Angeles, and purchased a half dozen $500 watches. He gave them to persons in the film business, but always with a view of having the favor returned.

When he was married to Ella, he did not lavish gifts on her. She had charge accounts at the better stores, so why should he bother?

Howard did proffer diamonds and furs to film beauties. But there again, he expected something in return.

He had no Christmas list of gifts to his associates. When any of us did receive a gift, it was in a most off-handed way. For instance, he had a $2,500 Zeiss telescope with seven lenses, which he had bought in Europe on his tour with Dudley Sharp. I doubt if Howard had ever looked through it. Once when he saw me gazing at it, he said "I don't want it—you can have it." He also gave me a pair of miniature binoculars that he had purchased abroad.

After Ella left him, he was throwing out some things. He came to a $350 English leather suitcase, beautifully sewn and fitted with everything for travel. It had been a gift from Ella.

"Here—like to have a suitcase?" he said. I used it for years until it finally wore out.

His eating habits were astonishing.

Throughout my association with him, I never saw him order anything but the same dinner: New York cut steak, medium rare; dinner salad; peas.

That's all. Steak, salad, peas. Preferably small peas. He would usually push the larger peas aside and eat only the small ones. For dessert: vanilla ice cream and cookies.

He was meticulous about how his eggs were cooked in the morning. They had to be scrambled exactly the way his family cook Lily had done them at home in Houston. He was insistent.

Shortly after I first went to work for him, he became upset over the way his eggs were served at the Ambassador Hotel. After giving instructions to the kitchen several times, he summoned the chef. The cook was instructed to bring a portable stove, eggs, milk, and a skillet. Howard then demonstrated exactly how his eggs should be scrambled. Milk was poured into the warm skillet—not too hot so as to scald the milk—then the eggs were cracked and scrambled.

Howard was lacking in the social graces. I sometimes had to instruct him that it wasn't proper to squeeze the last drop of juice out of his breakfast grapefruit.

He cared nothing about other people's hunger. On our first trip to Houston, I became acquainted with Lily, the Hughes' cook. She was a wonderful black woman who took good care of Howard's needs—she always had cookies and milk ready when he returned from the golf course in the afternoon. Lily was also solicitous of visitors. Often Howard and I would work into the evening at his house. Lily would be getting dinner ready, and she would chide Howard: "Aren't you going to ask this nice man to stay for supper?"

"Oh, yeah—sure," Howard would say blankly. "Stay for supper."

After he left the care of Lily, Howard lapsed into bad eating habits. He could get so wrapped up in cutting a movie that he would stay in the projection room two or three days at a stretch with scarcely a thing to eat. Then he'd emerge to eat three steaks.

Possibly because of his poor nutrition, he suffered chronic constipation. He spent an uncommon amount of time in the bathroom, and he kept a supply of magazines and books there to scout movie stories as he waited. He was always seeking remedies for constipation, and for a long time he consumed something called sylla seeds, which passed through the body without being digested.

Howard had a phobia about germs even early in our association. It was based on the fact that both of his parents had died early—in their fifties. He was haunted by the specter of an early death, and he took extraordinary precautions to avoid germs.

Again, the paradox. Here was a man who risked his life in flying feats, yet was terrified of microbes.

At first his behavior seemed no more unusual than that of the usual mysophobe. He avoided people with colds, gargled often, consulted his doctor. On some occasions he seemed oblivious of the dangers of contamination. Once I went to a music store where he wanted to try out the saxophones. He was playing one when he recognized a jazz musician. "Try this one," Howard suggested. Then he took back the saxophone after the other man had played it. Howard merely wiped off the mouthpiece with his handkerchief and played the instrument himself.

Later in his life the germ phobia took over completely. He would shake hands with no one and avoided close contact with most people. The fear of contamination became a mania.

CHAPTER SEVEN

The Hughes Steamer

Like most young men, Howard Hughes was fascinated with automobiles. Unlike most other young men, he could afford to indulge his whims. And he did.

When I first joined Howard, he was the owner of four remarkable driving machines. When he went to New York on his honeymoon, he bought two Rolls Royces, his and hers. His was a phaeton, hers a limousine. Both were shipped out to California by train.

Earlier, in Houston, he had become fascinated with steam cars. He enjoyed racing the other blades on Houston streets, and he discovered that the steamer could best any other automobile in a drag race; the steamer had as much power from a standing start as it did at full speed.

So Howard bought two steamers—a Stanley and a Doble. He had both shipped to California. He also owned a Cadillac, but he left that in Houston.

Like some of today's ecologists, Howard in 1926 was convinced that the steamer was the car of the future. No matter that they required a long time to work up steam. Or that they needed a water refill every sixty or seventy miles. Howard was convinced that those drawbacks could be cured by sound engineering.

And so he set himself the task of creating and manufacturing a revolutionary new automobile, the Hughes Steamer.

Where to start?

Howard decided to pilgrimage to that center of scientific knowledge, the California Institute of Technology in

Pasadena. He went directly to the president himself, Dr. Robert Millikan, the famed physicist who had won the Nobel Prize a few years before.

"I want to build a steam car which will be practical enough for general use," Howard announced. "I need engineering help—men who understand the dynamics of steam and can supply them to a workable automobile."

Dr. Millikan considered the problem of the brash young Texan and referred him to a couple of recent Caltech graduates, Howard Lewis and Bruce Burns.

Howard contacted the two engineers, and they were willing to work for him, especially when he mentioned the handsome salaries he was willing to pay. He outlined his challenge: "I want a steamer that will get underway in twenty seconds, starting from a dead stop. With the two steamers I've got, I have to wait two to five minutes to build up enough steam to make them move. Why, if I had a fire in my garage, I might not be able to get them out in time.

"Another thing—I want a steamer that will run from Los Angeles to San Francisco on one filling of water."

It was a large order—a steamer that would start operating almost as fast as a gasoline engine, and one that would travel four hundred miles without stopping for water. The two Caltech men seemed willing to tackle the task, and Howard installed them in a workshop on Romaine Street near the Sunset Strip.

Howard devoted himself to making movies and paid little heed to the two young engineers on Romaine. It was my chore to see that the Hughes Tool Company profits kept coming through to pay for both the steamer and Howard's movies.

Burns and Lewis started by buying a French car with a tubular frame and individual wheel suspension. They removed the motor, stripped the car down to the chassis, and used the shell on which to build the Hughes Steamer.

The whole venture seemed fallacious from the start, and I tried to tell Howard so.

"It's really sort of a hobby with me," he admitted.

"How many cars could you turn out a year?" I asked.

"I doubt if we could make more than twenty-five to fifty."

"How much would they cost?"

"Somewhere between twenty-five and thirty thousand."

"Who could afford to buy them at that cost?"

"Oh, I think some of my sportsmen friends would like to own them."

"And supposing they don't?"

"Well, then," he said, "at least I'll have a dandy new car every year."

There was no arguing with that kind of logic. So I continued pouring more of the tool company profits into the steamer. This went on for three years, and the bill mounted to $550,000.

Howard rarely paid a visit to the Romaine workshop. I couldn't understand his lack of regard for this expensive project of his. Later I realized that Howard reacted in two divergent ways to projects he initiated. Either he ignored the work and let the creative people proceed unhindered, or else he injected himself into the operation to a maddening degree, often fouling up the works entirely.

In this case, he ignored.

Meanwhile, Howard fell in love with another automobile. It was a Rolls Royce roadster which a Hollywood dealer had for sale. Howard insisted on buying it, not only as a runabout for himself; he thought the chassis would be ideal for the Hughes Steamer.

He had lost interest in the Rolls phaeton which he had purchased on his honeymoon, and sought to turn it in on the roadster. But the dealer would not meet the price that Howard wanted, so the phaeton was placed in the dealer's lot on consignment—if a customer came up with Howard's price, a sale would be consummated.

Howard was happy, but I was suspicious. We had paid for the roadster, but the dealer failed to produce the bill of sale.

I visited the dealer's showroom, and he gave me an adroit stall. He failed to take me in, and I noticed on his desk some correspondence from a bank. After I left him, I went to the bank and explained my concern.

"I really shouldn't tell you this," the banker said, "but that dealer has a seven thousand dollar loan on that roadster."

Returning to the dealer, I confronted him with the information. He acquiesced, and Howard received unencumbered title to the roadster. But now the dealer had possession of the phaeton, and it was nowhere to be found.

It was my business to protect my boss's interests. I made some inquiries at garages around Los Angeles. Finally I located the phaeton—it was at the Pacific Mutual garage in downtown Los Angeles. I quickly sent a couple of mechanics to the garage to put a chain and padlock on the front spring so the car couldn't be driven away.

But when I arrived at the garage to claim the phaeton, it was gone. The dealer had arrived before me and had raised enough threats to convince the garage men to file the chain and let him drive away.

I returned to my office and began contemplating my next move. A telephone call solved my problem.

"Do you represent Howard Hughes?" a voice asked.

"Yes."

"Well, I found a bunch of keys with his name on them."

I found out where he was and said, "Stay right where you are. I'll be there with a fifty dollar reward."

I sped to Hollywood Boulevard, claimed the keys, and paid the reward. Then I started driving in concentric circles, examining every garage and driveway until I located the phaeton. I put the key in the ignition and drove it away.

Another challenge mastered. Howard had his phaeton back from the crooked dealer. And he had possession of the roadster that was to be the base on which his Hughes Steamers were to achieve fame and prosperity.

Oh, yes, the steamer.

The two Caltech geniuses continued laboring away at the Romaine Street plant. Finally they issued the word: it's ready!

It was one of the few times that I saw Howard in a state of real anticipation. He and I went to the Romaine Street location and were ushered by Burns and Lewis into the presence of the completed automobile. It was truly handsome. But then, it should have been, considering the half-million dollars that went into its development.

The steamer was a five-passenger, open-top touring car, low-slung and more attractive than the big Stanley Steamer. Howard circled the car with a quizzical expression, then interrogated the engineers on its performance.

"It will travel four hundred miles on one load of water and can start almost as fast as a gasoline car," he was assured.

"Amazing," he said. "How on earth did you manage that."

They explained that it was a matter of water condensation. The body of the car was a network of radiators.

"You mean the entire body is composed of radiators, including the doors?" Howard asked.

Burns and Lewis nodded.

Howard thought for a moment. "Then supposing I'm driving along and some other car hits me broadside," he said. "What is the result?"

He failed to elicit a reply, and he continued with his logic: "I'd get scalded to death—right?"

"It's possible," one of the engineers admitted.

Without pondering further, he said, "Dismantle it, get some torches, and cut it up in pieces."

He walked out of the workshop, and I followed behind.

"Noah, you see to it that they cut it up into pieces," he said. *"Small* pieces."

CHAPTER EIGHT

Howard and His Flying Machines

Howard first learned to fly in 1925 at the time he was making a debut as a motion picture producer with the unreleasable *Swell Hogan*. His teacher was an early pilot named J. B. Alexander. He taught Howard how to fly in a Waco. The first plane that Howard bought was also a Waco.

He was still enamored with flying when I joined him, and he talked of buying a Fairchild. There was a national air show at Mines Field in Inglewood (now the site of Los Angeles International Airport), and I went out to see the spectacle. Astounding stunts were performed by four army planes, including flying past the grandstand at fifty feet—upside down. One of those fliers was soon to become famous: Charles A. Lindbergh.

The German ace, Ernst Udell, was part of the show, and he thrilled the audience by picking up handkerchiefs with a hook on his wingtip.

The plane that impressed me the most was a Boeing P-4. It was a little plane with a big motor, and it took part in a race from the field to a station ship 10,000 feet high, and return. That little Boeing left all the other racing planes behind.

When I returned from the air circus, I told Howard: "If I had your money, I'd put it in that Boeing P-4. It's a nifty plane."

Howard pooh-poohed the notion. But a short while later he bought a Boeing P-4.

Characteristically he wasn't satisfied with the plane as it

was. He sent it out to Douglas Aircraft at Clover Field to have it rebuilt. The P-4 was a two-seater aimed at speed, and Howard wanted it remodeled to provide more safety. He ordered the wings removed and rebuilt, and a leather-covered rubber cushion built around the edge of the cockpit.

On his way to the golf course every day, he dropped in at Douglas and inspected the latest changes on his plane. "No, that's not right," he would say time after time. "Tear it apart and do it differently."

The members of the Douglas crew were almost at their wits' end when Howard finally approved the changes. Then he received the bill. It was for $75,000. And the plane had only cost $45,000 in the beginning.

"My God, that's unreasonable!" Howard exclaimed. "I won't pay it. You take care of it, Noah."

I negotiated with the Douglas management; they wouldn't shave a dime off the bill. I knew I had to get results, and I took my petition to the headman himself, Donald Douglas.

The company president bristled at the implication that the bill had been padded. He called for the time sheets on the job, and I had to admit that the charges seemed reasonable. I relayed this information to Howard.

"Douglas is trying to cheat me!" he replied. "I won't pay those exorbitant charges."

Back I went to Douglas, and he agreed to make a small adjustment. That didn't satisfy Howard. The negotiations went on for six months until finally Douglas became exasperated.

"Dietrich, you take that bill back to Mr. Hughes and tell him to write his check for any amount he wants," Douglas ranted. "He can write it for five dollars, five thousand dollars, or any damn figure, and I'll mark the bill paid. And you can tell him this for me—I never want to do business with him again!"

I returned to Howard with the news, and he was delighted.

"Great work, Noah," he said. He wrote out a check for $15,000, a considerable saving over $75,000. I returned to Douglas and he receipted the bill. And he did do business with Howard Hughes again.

Here's another paradox about Howard: at the same time he was spending all that money to make the P-4 safer, he was needlessly risking his neck in other planes.

Even though he still owned the Waco, he wanted to fly somebody else's plane. One day he called Paul Mantz, the movie stunt flier.

"I need to fly up to Santa Barbara," Howard said. "What have you got?"

"I've got a Stearman here," Mantz replied, "but it hasn't been flown in thirty days."

"That's all right. Rev it up and I'll be there pretty soon."

So Howard flew the Paul Mantz plane of dubious safety to Santa Barbara to pick up a golfing companion. On the way back, he said, he ran out of gas and had to make a forced landing. It just happened that he landed on a fairway at Bel Air Country Club, where he was planning to play eighteen holes. The greens committee was very upset about this, and the plane was impounded.

"Take care of it, Noah," Howard said. I did—to the tune of a thousand dollars.

There were other times when Howard's air exploits did not turn out so harmlessly. During the filming of *Hell's Angels,* he wanted to film a special stunt with some Thomas Morse Scouts.

They were unusual planes, built in San Diego and flown in the latter stages of World War I. The unusual factor about them was that they had a radial engine that was attached to and revolved with the propeller.

Howard's flying instructor, J. B. Alexander, had rounded up nine of the TM Scouts for the movie. Howard wanted to film a low-altitude maneuver in which the planes swooped past the camera at an elevation of two hundred to three hundred feet, preformed a left bank, and returned, all in camera range.

The stunt fliers on *Hell's Angels* were among the best in the country, but they balked at such a stunt.

"It can't be done, Howard," one of them said. "You

bring that plane in on a left bank and it'll sideslip two or three hundred feet, sure as shootin'. We can do it at a thousand feet, but no lower."

"Ridiculous!" Howard replied. "You can't tell me that you can't counter-control the sideslip."

"Not possible, Howard."

"I'll show you it can be done," Howard insisted. "Which one is the best plane?"

No amount of persuasion could prevent him from taking up the TM Scout and attempting the stunt he wanted.

It happened just as the stunt flier had predicted. Howard went into the left bank and the plane slid inexorably toward the earth. It crashed in a cloud of dirt.

The entire company raced to the scene of the accident, and Howard was pulled unconscious from the wreckage. An ambulance rushed him from Mines Field to Inglewood Hospital. I hurried to see him there, and he didn't even recognize me.

After four days he was transferred to St. Vincent's Hospital in Los Angeles. Surgery seemed imperative to repair his crushed face. When he came back from the operating room, I talked to the surgeons.

"We made an incision and then sewed him right up," one of them told me. "There was nothing we could do. The cheekbone is crushed so badly there's nothing to put a pin or wires into. He'll just have to live with it the way it is."

Howard recovered, but his face was never the same. Where the cheekbone had once been, there was an indentation. The injury was to give him considerable pain in later years.

The TM Scout crash was the first of three serious airplane accidents that Howard was to experience. They affected him, both physically and mentally, and I believe they contributed greatly to the peculiar personality that Howard Hughes became.

CHAPTER NINE

The Golden Goose

"My first objective is to become the world's number-one golfer. Second, the top aviator, and third I want to become the world's most famous motion picture producer. Then, I want you to make me the richest man in the world."

This is what Howard told me one day in a moment of candor. He was still in his early twenties, and nothing seemed impossible to him. Indeed, he was to achieve three out of four of his wishes.

The golfing crown eluded him. He was a superb player and might well have gone on to championship competition. The high point in his golfing career came at the Del Monte tournament in the late 1920s. He was a low qualifier, but then he eliminated himself by a bit of horseplay.

Howard was celebrating his triumph in the club house the night before competition was to start. Spirits were high, and the men were indulging in a test of skill, as men sometimes do when they've had a few drinks. The party was sitting before a roaring fire, and someone suggested a contest of jumping backward to sit on the mantel.

Howard was certain he could do it, because of his height. He stood before the fire, leaped up, and cracked both his elbows on the mantel. The pain was so great that he couldn't play in the tournament.

He continued playing golf after that incident, but he gave up the idea of becoming the number-one golfer of the world.

He *did* become the world's most famous movie producer. Not because of his movies. They were generally roasted by the critics, and he lost $10,000,000 on them over the years.

Yet no one who produced movies was more famous than Howard. That was largely because of his legendary fame in other activities besides picture making.

What about the matter of becoming the richest man in the world? He did achieve it; some authorities claim that Noah Dietrich is the man responsible. I won't deny it.

The key to the Hughes fortune, as everyone knows, was the Hughes Tool Company. That was where it all began. But the company wasn't simply a money machine that poured forth unlimited cash. It had good years, and it had bad ones. Although it enjoyed a near-monopoly in its early history, the company was woefully mismanaged and was producing nothing close to the potential in profits that it was capable of.

When Howard inherited the Hughes Tool Company, its net worth was estimated for estate purpose at $660,000. A year or so later he bought out his relatives' quarter-interest for $325,000, hence the market value of the entire investment could have been placed at $1,300,000.

At the beginning of my employment by Howard, I had little to do with the tool company, except to prepare its annual income tax return. As time went on, I paid more and more attention to the company, always at Howard's behest. He wanted it to produce more and more income so he could indulge himself in the activities that interested him: movies, airplanes, women. Expensive hobbies.

My first acquaintance with Hughes Tool was in early 1926, when I accompanied Howard to Houston. I was appalled by what I saw at the factory. It had a dirt floor. There was no production line. Parts were carried by wheelbarrow from one production stage to the next. It was a mess.

There was little that I could do about improving the tool company operation as long as I was not a part of management. But within a year or two, Howard realized that I had management capabilities, and he gave me more responsibility. Anything I could do to step up Toolco income would be welcome.

So I began taking more trips to Houston.

One of the things that disturbed me was the multiplicity of models. I found we were producing almost a thousand different shapes and sizes of bits.

To an efficiency expert like myself this seemed idiotic. The bits ranged from two inches to twenty-four inches, with a different model for every eighth of an inch variation. There were different patterns, different teeth.

"Why do we make so many kinds of bits?" I asked one of the plant officials.

"We've got to," he told me. "Each driller wants his own particular bit. Those guys are superstitious, you know, and they think their own special bits are lucky for them."

I decided that superstition had no place in business. With the help of the government, which was pushing for standardization, I induced the management to cut down to three hundred models.

Despite this saving, Hughes Tool was not producing its potential profit. I could see this quite readily in the statements we were getting from our competitor, Reed Roller Bit Company.

Why would Hughes Tool be receiving statements from its arch-rival? That's an interesting story.

The elder Howard Hughes had employed a bright young engineer named Clarence Reed. Like many of young Howard's later employees, Reed became disgruntled over his lack of participation in the profits. So he decided to leave Hughes Tool and set up his own drilling-bit manufacturing company.

Big Howard sued the Reed Roller Bit Company for infringement of patents. The suit was brought by the Caddo Rock Bit Company, a Hughes subsidiary which owned the patents.

Reed admitted that he had taken Hughes blueprints when he left the company, but he claimed he did so only to be certain that he was *not* infringing on Hughes. The judge decided differently. Caddo was granted a $500,000 judgment—which young Howard put into his movie operation, Caddo Productions, after his father's death. Hughes Tool was also granted a fifteen percent royalty on Reed's gross sales.

The decision was a boon for Hughes Tool. Not only did it provide a steady source of income, with no outlay whatsoever. It also provided an inside view of the financial progress of Hughes' chief rival.

I kept a close eye on the Reed reports. In the early 1930s Reed gained on Hughes and then pulled out in front. I puzzled over this. Hughes Tool had a virtual monopoly in its field, yet it was being outdistanced by a competitor with a fifteen percent disadvantage.

"Howard, I don't like the looks of this," I said when the latest Reed statement appeared. "Something must be wrong at Toolco."

Howard took his mind off movies for a moment. "Okay, Noah, maybe you're right," he said. "Why don't you go down to Houston and look into it?"

This time I was going to Houston in a different capacity. I was no longer merely Howard's executive assistant; I was his personal delegate. Howard remained President of Hughes Tool Company, although he did little or nothing to exercise his position.

When I arrived in Houston, I realized that the management harbored resentment against the playboy president who did nothing for the company except to squander its profits on crazy schemes. I proceeded in a low-key manner, asking a lot of questions in a friendly way and making no comments.

I soon learned why Reed had pulled ahead. It was making a better drilling bit.

"Why is the Reed bit selling better than ours?" I asked the production engineer.

"Well, they've got a new model over there," he explained. "It combines roller bearings with ball bearings, and the drillers think it does a better job. But it's just a fad. That Reed bit won't hold up in the long run."

"The drillers seem to think so. They're buying 'em by

the carload, and passing up ours. What makes you think the Reed bits won't hold up?"

"Because we've experimented with ball bearings. They simply won't stand up under pressure. They crack and break. We've tried the hardest ball-bearings we could get. Under heat and pressure the balls crush, and it's like trying to turn an egg-beater in cold molasses."

"Have you heard any complaints about the Reed bit breaking up?"

"No," he admitted. "But I'm sure it will."

"Obviously they're doing something better than we are. Let's get a Reed bit and find out what it is."

We bought a Reed drilling bit and cut it open to see what was inside. What we found was amazingly simple. Instead of using the hardest ball bearings, Reed installed bearings that were almost as soft as lead. Under extreme pressure, the bearings lost their shape, but they didn't break. They still rolled.

And so the Hughes bit was converted to malleable ball bearings, and once more Hughes Tool Company was able to compete with Reed.

Before I left Houston on that trip, I was confronted with what had all the earmarks of a mutiny.

R. C. Kuldell, who was the head of the plant, acted as spokesman, and he appeared to have the support of the rest of the company executives.

"We've put our life's blood into this company, and we think we're entitled to some consideration," Kuldell told me. "Howard has made no contribution to Toolco; he's only interested in making movies. He's a spendthrift kid who's taking all the money out of this company and spending it on wild living in Hollywood."

He presented what he considered was a fair proposal both for Howard and for the company executives. They would give him $10,000,000 in cumulative preferred stock in return for all of his stock, and he would receive five percent annually. The executives would retain ownership and management.

"That way Howard will be assured of an income of five hundred thousand a year," Kuldell reasoned. "That's what

Toolco is earning in profits now, anyway, and I don't think it will ever earn more than that."

I listened respectfully and said I would transmit the proposal to Howard.

To most people, that would seem like a handsome opportunity. Howard would be assured of a royal income of a half-million dollars per year. "That's more than he can possibly spend," said Kuldell, and that indicated how little he knew about Howard.

When I returned to Los Angeles, I reported the offer to Howard. He tossed it aside without a second's hesitation.

"Those guys must be kidding," he said. "Hughes Tool is going to make a hell of a lot more than a half million a year. They must think I'm stupid."

"But Howard," I continued, "even if you think nothing of their proposal, I think you should give consideration to what inspired it. Those fellows are very restless back there in Houston. They think they're doing all the work, and you're getting all the gravy."

Howard pondered the issue and came up with a solution: "Tell those boys to relax. I'm leaving the company to a foundation when I die. There will be nine trustees, and each one of the plant leaders will be included. They'll be on life salaries of a hundred thousand apiece. And I'm going to make you the chairman, Noah, at two hundred thousand dollars."

I relayed the information to the Toolco officials and they were naturally elated. So was I. But that was before I realized that Howard hadn't the slightest intention of setting up a trusteeship.

The Hughes Tool Company executives finally realized it, too. But their dissatisfaction was allayed by a previously instituted plan by which they received fifteen percent of the profits. And profits began to climb precipitously—up to $3,000,000 in 1930.

There was plenty for everyone—for a while, at least.

CHAPTER TEN

Goodbye, Ella

The surprising thing about the marriage of Howard Hughes and Ella Rice is that it lasted as long as it did.

They remained married from 1925 to 1929, but in the later stages they weren't working very hard at it. I found that out—much to my chagrin.

At first they lived at the Ambassador Hotel. Then they spent those few months in 1926 at the Hughes home at 3921 Yoakum Street in Houston. They returned to the Ambassador, then Howard decided he wanted to rent a house. He assigned me to find him one.

I hunted around in the Wilshire district of Los Angeles and found a house which I thought would be ideal for Howard and Ella. It was a large two-story place, adjacent to the Wilshire Country Club, where Howard played a lot of golf. It was also convenient to the movie studios. The house was fully furnished.

"I'll take it," Howard said after he viewed the house. I considered the rent exorbitant, but Howard insisted on having it. After he had lived in the house a few months, he decided to buy it.

I opened negotiations with the widow who owned the house. She wanted $150,000 for the house and $35,000 for the furnishings. I considered this high, and I told Howard so.

"I think I can get her to come down," I said.

"Buy it at her figure," he said. "I want the house. I want it now."

And so Howard took possession of the only house he

ever bought. It was typical of him to say, "I want it now." In business negotiations he could drag out the proceedings for months, wearing down the other party until Howard got a bargain. But when he wanted something personally, he had no patience with haggling. He wanted it now. As the result of his impatience, the widowed landlady reaped a bonanza. When Howard sold the house many years later, it brought only $60,000.

The Muirfield house was not exactly a happy honeymoon home.

The union with Ella seemed to be exactly what it was: a marriage of convenience for Howard, who wanted to convince his relatives that he could be responsible. He displayed none of the affection you might expect from a young married man. Ella was a pretty girl and well brought up, but she was lacking in the qualities that Howard favored after his marriage; she was far from the extroverted, voluptuous actresses his name was later connected with.

Ella and Howard had separate bedrooms in the Muirfield house, and theirs seemed like a passionless marriage. He was forever occupied with his planes, steamers, movies, and golf. On rare occasions the Hugheses went together to a Hollywood party or a premiere.

I never heard Howard mention anything about wanting to have children, neither during his marriage to Ella or in later years. Providing an heir to the Hughes empire did not appear to be part of his planning.

Left alone much of the time, Ella sought her own diversions. Through salespeople in the exclusive stores where she shopped, she made the acquaintance of society people in Pasadena. She tried to interest Howard in attending some of their parties. He declined.

Ella was still determined to make a go of her marriage. She decided to try a social experiment: inviting some of her Pasadena socialites and some of Howard's movie friends to a dinner party at the Hughes home.

Throughout the previous week Ella cautioned, "Now don't forget the dinner party Saturday night, Howard. Cocktails at seven, dinner at eight."

Ella devoted all of her excellent taste to the preparations. She personally chose the flowers and decorations,
selected the menu and schooled the servants in how to
serve the meal. As Howard left for the studio Saturday
morning, she reminded him: "Cocktails at seven, dinner at
eight."

The guests began arriving shortly after 7 P.M. They
were an odd combination. The society swells in their
Pierce Arrows and Rolls Royces, dressed in tuxedos and
velvet. The movie crowd arriving in Duesenbergs and
Hispano Suizas, the men wearing sporty clothes and the
women with feather boas. The two groups clustered in
separate camps, sipping bootleg martinis as they eyed the
other side.

Ella was desperate. Not only were her guests behaving
like oil and water, there was no Howard.

At 8:30 the chef warned Ella that the dinner would be
ruined if the guests did not sit down. So she announced
dinner, and the two factions filed into the dining room.
Everyone discreetly avoided mentioning the fact that the
host was missing.

At 9 Howard stalked in. He was wearing rumpled corduroys and a soiled white shirt.

"Worked late at the studio," he said, sitting down at the
head of the table. "I'm hungry."

He ate ravenously, then pushed his plate forward. "Excuse me," he said, and he disappeared upstairs.

That was the end of Ella's efforts to integrate her
friends with Howard's. "You know, Mr. Dietrich," she
said, "I've tried. I've really tried."

A short while later, Howard told me Ella was going to
Houston for an extended visit. He instructed me to make
monthly deposits for her in a Houston bank.

Two weeks later, Howard fell desperately ill. The doctors diagnosed his case as spinal meningitis, and he grew
so weak that they feared he might not survive.

"Does he have any close relatives?" one of the doctors
asked me.

"A wife," I said. "She's in Texas."

"I think it may be prudent to send for her. I'm not sure he's going to be able to pull through."

I put through a telephone call to Ella. She wasn't in Houston. She had left for New York to meet her sister Lottie, who was the wife of W. S. Farish, chairman of the board of Standard Oil of New Jersey. Ella was about to embark with the Farishes on a tour of Europe.

"Howard is desperately ill," I told Ella. "I think it would be best if you would come home immediately." She hesitated, then agreed to come.

I met Ella and her sister at the Los Angeles depot and drove them to the Muirfield house. Before we arrived, Mrs. Farish asked me, "Do you think it will be safe for us to go to the house?"

Her question seemed odd. I assured her that Howard's illness had been proven to be something besides spinal meningitis, and there was no danger of contagion. Ella went inside and there was a restrained reunion between her and Howard. Very restrained.

I didn't find out until later what was going on. Ella stayed a couple of weeks until Howard seemed well on the road to recovery. Then she and her sister departed for Europe.

After they had gone, Howard gave me an assignment: "I want you to find out what son of a bitch asked Ella to come out here without my knowledge or consent. Drop everything until you find out who it was."

I was astounded at his vehemence. "Why, Howard, *I* was the one who asked her to come out," I admitted. "You were desperately ill, close to dying. What was so wrong with that?"

Then he told me the truth: when Ella left the first time, she and Howard had agreed to a separation. No one knew but the two of them. And Lottie. Now I understood the logic behind her question: "Do you think it will be safe for us to go into the house?"

It was safe—but just barely. At about the same time Ella was entering the front door, a beautiful movie actress was leaving by the back entrance. She had been comforting Howard during his illness. As soon as Ella left, the actress moved back in. Howard was to have a succession of such famous "house guests" over the years.

I was chagrined by my gaffe, but also angered.

"How was I to know you and Ella were separated?" I said. "You were terribly ill, so I sent for your wife. If you're not going to take me into your confidence on such matters, then you will have to endure the consequences."

"Okay, Noah, don't get excited," Howard said. "It's all right."

Ella divorced Howard in Houston, and Howard made a generous settlement—$1,250,000, payable in five annual installments of $250,000. She remarried happily and raised a family. I used to see her at social functions in Houston, and we talked cordially. But she never mentioned Howard Hughes.

CHAPTER ELEVEN

Hello, Billie

The next woman to play an important role in Howard's life was Billie Dove.

Oh, what a beauty! It's no wonder that Howard lost his heart to her.

Billie liked him, too. "I have such a motherly feeling toward Howard," she told me. "I'd like to take care of him in his old age."

It didn't work out that way. But for a time, theirs was a flaming romance. Also an expensive one for Howard.

Billie Dove, born Lillian Bohney, first dazzled New York at sixteen as a *Follies* girl. Her faultless beauty brought her movie offers, and she made her debut in *Polly of the Follies* with Constance Talmadge in 1922. Soon she was a leading lady; she starred opposite Douglas Fairbanks in *The Black Pirate*.

Billie was an important star when Howard met her in the late 1920s. He became enamored. It was his first real love affair, and he fell madly in love with her. Or as much in love as Howard would allow himself to be.

Howard's ingrained acquisitiveness took over, and he insisted that he wanted to guide her movie career. She had just finished a contract with First National, and he signed her to five pictures at $85,000 per picture. Unfortunately he was acquiring her services at the end of her career. Sound had come in, and she had neither the voice nor the acting skill to survive in the talkie era. But that was no great concern of Howard's. His infatuation precluded any sound analysis of her box-office potential.

Billie Dove and Howard became constant companions. They went to parties together. They flew in Howard's airplanes together. They even went yachting together.

This was a new interest for Howard—the sea. The first I knew about it was when Howard telephoned me and said: "I want you to find a yacht for me. Something that will cruise at thirty knots or better and have a comfortable cabin arrangement."

It was a new kind of assignment, but I had learned to be prepared for anything. I drove down to the harbor at San Pedro and scouted some brokers about a swift, well-appointed yacht. There seemed to be nothing available. Then one broker came up with a suggestion: the *Hilda,* a 170-foot craft that required a crew of eighteen.

Howard took a look at the *Hilda* and said, "It'll do."

I suggested that he test the yacht a few times to see if it really suited him. He agreed, and went cruising for three weekends in a row, with Billie Dove as his sole guest.

On the Friday before the fourth weekend, Howard called me and said he wanted to test the *Hilda* again. I telephoned the owner, Mrs. Hilda Boldt of Santa Barbara, widow of a steel magnate who had named the yacht after her.

"I think Mr. Hughes has had enough trial runs," she said. "I'd like to know whether or not he wants to buy the boat."

I asked her how much she wanted for the *Hilda.* Originally she had wanted $450,000. Now she was willing to let it go at $350,000.

Howard was waiting for my reply, and I told him what Mrs. Boldt had said. "I think if we hold out we can get it for two hundred and seventy-five thousand," I told him.

"But I want it this weekend," Howard replied. "I've already asked Billie to go on a cruise with me."

"Howard, Mrs. Boldt won't allow any more demonstrations. If you want to buy it, I suggest you hold off for a week or so, and she'll bring the price down. She hates the boat and wants to get rid of it."

"No," he replied. "I want it this weekend, Noah. Buy it."

Now it was late afternoon on Friday and the banks were closed. So I telephoned Houston and ordered the money telegraphed from the Hughes Tool Company so that Howard could have his weekend cruise with Billie Dove.

As owner of the *Hilda,* he took a few more weekend cruises with Billie and made a few short voyages. But he never really cruised with the *Hilda.* He used it mainly as a harbor hotel.

Howard never fished from the *Hilda,* nor did he ever fish, to my knowledge. But he did use a gun. On sea gulls.

When sea gulls landed on the rigging, Howard took pot shots at them. "I don't want those birds crapping on my boat," he explained. It was the only occasion I knew him to hunt.

A few weeks after Howard had acquired the *Hilda,* he called me in a state of agitation. He had lost a watch. This didn't seem too important, because he rarely wore a watch —in later years he disliked having one around.

But he had lost a special watch—a diamond-studded pocket watch that Billie had given him.

"Jesus, I'm in a spot," he said. "Billie keeps asking me where the watch is and why I never wear it. You've got to find it for me."

"I'll try, Howard," I said. "Can you remember when you last had it?"

"Yes. I remember having it on the boat."

I drove down to where the *Hilda* was docked, and I told the captain to line up the crew on the foredeck.

"Gentlemen, Mr. Hughes has lost his watch," I said to the crew. "It is a very special watch, and he wants it back right away. If anybody knows anything of the whereabouts of that watch, I suggest he come up with the information by noon tomorrow. Otherwise there will be an entirely new crew on the *Hilda.*"

I figured that would get results. Those sailors had a cinch job, working for a rich landlubber who rarely took the boat out to sea. Sure enough, the next day I received a call from the captain.

"A week or so ago I fired a seaman named Sutton," he said. "This morning one of the crew members told me that he saw Sutton pick up the watch in Mr. Hughes' cabin, and he took it with him when he left."

"Do you have any idea where Sutton went?" I asked.

"The boys tell me he's still around the harbor, looking for another ship."

"Thanks, captain. You can tell the crew that if this tip pans out, they don't have to worry about their jobs."

I reported the theft to the police and gave them a description of Sutton. Within a few days, they had both Sutton and the watch in custody. He had pawned it for a hundred dollars. Billie Dove had paid $3,500 for it.

Nothing upset Howard as much as learning that someone had stolen from him. He went down to the police station and signed the complaint against the hapless Sutton.

As the case neared trial, I noticed that Howard was getting nervous about it. "How much of a rap do you think the guy will get?" he asked me.

"The D.A. tells me it could run upwards of seven years," I said.

Howard pondered over this. "I don't like it," he said. "Think of what could happen. He could get out on parole in a few years and come to my house some night and shoot at me through the window. Tell the D.A. to spring him."

"But Howard—" I protested.

"Do it," he insisted. "And be sure the guy realizes that I refused to appear against him."

So I went downtown and relayed Howard's decision to the District Attorney, Buron Fitts. It was an open-and-shut case, and Fitts was furious about losing a conviction. But without Howard to testify against the man there was no case.

I made it a point to see Sutton after he was sprung and tell him that the man he had stolen the watch from had turned out to be his benefactor. Sutton seemed penitent, and I treated him to a suit of clothes, a railroad ticket to New York, and two hundred dollars.

End of story?

Not quite. The ungrateful bastard got off the train at San Bernardino, returned to Los Angeles, and filed suit against Howard Hughes for false arrest. I had to talk three lawyers out of handling his case before he finally gave up and left town.

There was only one trouble with Howard's romance with Billie Dove: she had a husband.

His name was Irvin Willat, and he was a director at First National, where Billie had been a star. They were separated when Howard became enamored of Billie. Naturally Howard wanted him out of the picture. Then he planned to marry Billie himself.

I discovered how serious he was when his lawyer, Neil McCarthy, telephoned me with the message: "Howard has talked to Willat, and Willat has agreed that Billie can get the divorce. Howard wants us to give Willat three hundred and twenty-five thousand dollars as a settlement. In thousand-dollar bills."

There was no reason for me not to believe McCarthy, but such a huge outlay required confirmation by Howard. I telephoned him and he said, "Yes, that's right; give Willat the money."

Now the question was: how did I acquire $325,000 in thousand-dollar bills?

No bank carried that many thousand-dollar bills. So I went to the place where I did the Hughes banking and got a cashier's check in favor of the Federal Reserve Bank. Then I went to the Federal Reserve headquarters in Los Angeles and obtained 325 thousand-dollar bills. You can bet I was nervous as hell when I traveled across town with $325,000 in my pocket. Any holdup man would have enjoyed a bonanza if he had knocked me over.

I breathed a sigh of relief when I reached Neil McCarthy's office safely. I handed the bills to McCarthy, and he delivered them to Willat. The transaction was completed.

Howard personally saw to it that Billie got the divorce. He flew her to Nevada in his own plane. Not to Reno or Las Vegas, where her arrival would attract publicity. She sat out her six weeks' residency in a remote town and was able to acquire a quiet divorce.

Now that Billie was free, Howard had big plans for her.

He put her in two pictures. The first was *Cock of the Air* (Howard loved that title). It co-starred Chester Morris, and Howard used some of the planes from *Hell's Angels*. But the box-office results were not the same. Next came a comedy, *The Age for Love,* equally unsuccessful.

Howard went off on his second trip to Europe, and Billie went along. He still seemed enthralled with her when they returned. But—and this was to be another pattern for the future—nothing ever happened of his plans to marry her. Eventually they had a falling out, and she never finished the five-picture contract with Howard.

Neil McCarthy had a contract settlement drawn up, and he showed it to me. The terms were that she would be paid the full price for the three unmade movies—$255,000. I was the secretary of the company, and it was my responsibility to conclude the arrangement. I stalled. It was the custom in the movie business to settle contracts for something less than face value, and I believed in following custom.

Howard never mentioned the matter to me. In time I negotiated to cancel Billie's contract for $100,000.

CHAPTER TWELVE

Bootlegging for Howard

I engaged in many bizarre missions for Howard Hughes, but none was more unusual than my task of transporting the family hootch from Texas to California.

It was unusual—and illegal. This was in 1930, when transporting liquor across state lines was a penetentiary offense. These were Prohibition times, and federal officers were on the lookout for anyone dealing in liquor, which was forbidden for ordinary use by the Volstead Act.

I wasn't much of a drinker at all. In fact, I never touched liquor—until after the 18th Amendment became law following World War I. Like many American citizens, I took an interest in drinking only after it was forbidden. There must be a natural human urge to try whatever is illegal.

Howard didn't drink much, either. But he had a rare sense of possession; if he felt something belonged to him, no one else could have it. That is why he delegated this mission to me.

My first inkling of it came when I was in New York in 1930 on business for the Hughes enterprises. He telephoned me and said, "I want you to go down to Houston. Got something I want you to take care of. Call me as soon as you get there."

During my five years with Howard, I had learned never to question him on such missions. For one thing, he was loath to discuss important business matters on the telephone. This was long before telephone tapping had become an art, yet he was concerned that his business and personal affairs might be spied upon through telephone intercepts.

Whether on the telephone or in person, Howard seemed to be addicted to a CIA brand of secrecy—and this was long before there was a Central Intelligence Agency. Part of this, I believe, stemmed from the difficulties his father had in preserving his drilling-bit patent, particularly in regard to former employee Reed, who took along blueprints when he left the company.

I finished my work in New York and went on to Houston. I telephoned Howard to find out what my new mission was to be. After he had ascertained that both of us were telephoning under circumstances which precluded overhearing, he told me what he wanted.

When Prohibition became effective in 1920, Howard's father had purchased the remaining stock of the Rice Hotel bar. The large stock remained at the Hughes home on Yoakum Street in Houston, hidden in a sealed vault. Howard now wanted it transported to Los Angeles.

"But, Howard," I protested, "there are laws against the transporting of liquor."

"I know, Noah," he said. "But you're resourceful. And besides, you're the only man I can trust."

It was nice to know that your boss placed such trust in you. But I had visions of myself joining moonshiners and bootleggers who had also defied the Volstead Act and had been sent to prison.

None of my protests made any impression on Howard. He was single-minded when he wanted something, and he told me, "I don't care about any problems, Noah. I want that liquor delivered to my house at 311 Muirfield Road."

Another Hughes mission. Somehow it had to be solved.

First I wanted to calculate the legal risks. I consulted a Hughes lawyer I felt I could trust. He told me that since the liquor had been legally acquired, it could be transported lawfully—except into California. It seems that Californians had embraced Prohibition earlier than other states and had banned importation of liquor, legal or illegal.

So the risk was there. But so was my boss's order, and somehow I had to satisfy it.

I paid a visit to the Hughes home, which was now occupied by Howard's aunt, Mrs. Lummis. I tramped down to the basement and found a rusted metal door which had not been opened since Big Howard died. The combination to the lock had been lost with his death, so I called a locksmith to drill open the door.

The view inside the vault was a tippler's dream. Row upon row of fine old scotches and bourbons, gins and rums, vintage wines and rare liquers.

There was no time to rhapsodize over the rare collection. I counted the number of bottles and plotted how best to package them for safe and clandestine delivery to the West Coast.

I engaged two Hughes aides I believed to be trustworthy. Together we packed the bottles into metal containers the size of an office desk. Each bottle was carefully placed on a rack, nestled in sawdust, and the metal containers were soldered shut. They were then encased in two wooden boxes and bound with metal straps.

But how to discourage anyone from inspecting the boxes? I hit upon an inspiration: each box was stenciled with the words "EXPOSED AND UNDEVELOPED FILM."

Oh, were those boxes heavy! It required four men to load them into vans. I instructed the Westheimer Storage Company to engage a freight car for shipment to Los Angeles. Then I took off for California to await the arrival of the *verboten* booze. In the meantime I ordered construction of a cement vault, complete with metal door and combination lock, in the basement of Howard's Muirfield Road house.

A week after I returned to California, I received a telephone call from the Southern Pacific freight office. The shipment of film had arrived. I felt relieved. At least my mystery cargo had passed the state line without being inspected. The worst was over. Or so I thought.

I ordered the freight car moved to the Pacific Electric yard at Highland Avenue and Santa Monica Boulevard, only a few blocks from Howard's house. My next plan was to hire a truck and transport the metal cases to the house one at a time. I planned to do that in the dead of night, just in case someone had learned what was inside those cases. They would have made a rich haul for hijackers.

"How long can I leave the freight car on the siding?" I asked the agent at the Pacific Electric yard.

"Ordinarily you could leave it here as long as you want, just by paying a daily demurrage charge," he told me. "But you've got a problem, Mr. Dietrich."

"A problem?"

"Yes. You see, that car from Houston was an old cotton car. The state of California requires that the car and its contents be fumigated. We've already notified the State Agricultural Department."

My heart sank. "Fumigated? What does that involve?"

"It's simple. Everything has to be opened up and sprayed."

"But—but, you can't do that!" I insisted. "That's *film*. My boss is a movie producer. That stuff in those cases is exposed film that's going into a picture. If it's exposed, the film will be ruined. And I'll be fired!"

"Sorry. But you should have thought of that when you chose that freight car. There's nothing you can do about it now. Law's the law."

Good Lord, I thought, has Dietrich outsmarted himself this time? By skirting around one law I had run smack-dab into another one—the law to protect California cotton from contamination.

Because of the boll weevil, Howard was going to have his precious liquor confiscated and I was facing a stretch in Leavenworth.

I hurried to my lawyer and told him my predicament.

"You're in deep trouble," he said—as if that was news to me.

"Supposing I did move trucks into the freight yard at night and removed the cases," I suggested.

He explained that I couldn't be jailed for hijacking my own property; the boxes were all consigned to me.

"But you have to break the seal on an interstate shipment. Federal law prohibits tampering with a sealed interstate shipment."

"What is the penalty?"

"Ten thousand dollars or a year in jail—or both. According to how lenient the judge is."

"Well, at least I know the risk now."

"What are you going to do, Noah?" the lawyer asked.

"I'm not sure," I admitted. "And I'm certain you'd prefer not to know."

Time was getting short. I had asked for a two-day extension of the fumigation order. At 10 the following morning the order would be carried out. I decided to seek expert advice.

Next door to the freight yard was the Hollywood Storage Company, which specialized in film shipments. I sought out the manager and explained my problem. Of course I didn't disclose the real contents of those cases.

"I've got to save that film!" I told him. "And I've got to do it by ten o'clock tomorrow morning."

"Maybe I can help you," he said.

"How? How?"

"Well, there *is* a way to remove a seal from a freight car and replace it without detection. I could do it for you—for two hundred dollars."

"You mean I could remove the cases and seal the car back up again?"

"That's right."

"But what happens when the inspectors come and find the contents gone?"

"Well, if the seal is still intact, nobody can prove anything. The only one who can file a complaint is the owner of the contents."

I smiled and handed over the $200.

That night I had two trucks and two crews waiting for me when I arrived at the freight yard at 11:30. The yard manager had taken his wife to a movie that night, so I believed I had nothing to worry about from him. I had just removed the seal from the freight car when the manager drove up. He had decided to stop at the yard to check on things.

He was startled to see me there at midnight and he blurted, "What the hell are you doing here, Mr. Dietrich?"

I had to think fast. "Well—you see—to be honest with you, I simply can't allow the contents of these cases to be exposed tomorrow morning." That much was true. Then I added: "If that film is exposed, I'll lose my job and I won't be able to support my wife and two daughters. I'm desperate. I'd be willing to pay a thousand dollars to move that film out of here tonight."

He eyed me as if I were a henchman of Al Capone. "I don't know what you're up to," he muttered, "but it smells fishy to me. I'm calling the police."

As he dashed off to a telephone, I replaced the seal and said to the truckers, "Sorry, boys, I won't be needing you tonight. I'll call you tomorrow morning."

They went off shaking their heads, and I made a quick departure in my car. I drove around for an hour, keeping an eye on the freight yard. The manager had carried out his threat. Police arrived, but since the suspect had flown and there was no evidence of foul play, there was nothing the officers could do. But they remained on guard, shotguns ready.

I spent a sleepless night frantically searching for a new plan as the deadline for fumigation neared. My mind was so fogged that I could think of nothing.

Bleary-eyed, I reported to the freight yard at 9:30 that morning. The yard manager still harbored suspicions about me, and he treated me coldly. He pointed to a young man in the yard and said, "That's the state fumigator." Then the manager returned to his office.

My last chance.

I took the fumigator aside and repeated my plaint about ruining exposed film, losing my job and starving my wife and two young daughters. To my happy surprise, he sympathized.

Perceiving a glimmer of human understanding, I continued: "I'm not really violating the law. The contents can't be contaminated, because they are packed inside airtight metal containers and double-packed in those wooden crates."

"Hmmmmm," he commented.

"If we open those boxes, it will be a disaster," I insisted. That was true enough, though it wasn't exactly the kind of disaster I had been describing. The real disaster would come when the headlines shouted:

HOWARD HUGHES' AID SEIZED
AS LIQUOR SMUGGLER

As that specter played before my mind, the inspector commented half-heartedly, "Well, I've got my job to do."

"Do you like your job?" I asked.

"Not particularly," he admitted. "This is just a vacation job. I'm working my way through school."

"If you weren't working, what would you be doing?"

"Why, I'd be up at Yosemite with my wife and son, enjoying a vacation."

"I see. And what would it cost you to be able to take your family up to Yosemite?"

"Six or seven hundred dollars."

I took a roll of bills out of my pocket and peeled off seven hundreds. I placed them in his hand.

"What do I have to do for this?" he inquired.

"Just let me take the boxes out of the cars."

"Why not? You remove the boxes and I'll fumigate the cars."

"Splendid idea!" I said. I ran off to telephone the trucker to send two crews to the freight yard immediately.

I was nervous as a cat while I watched the trucking men unload the box car and place the boxes into the trucks. I exhorted them to speed as I gazed nervously around for the yard manager or anyone who looked like a revenue agent. None appeared, and I gave the state fumigator a hearty handshake.

"Bless you, my boy," I said, then I yelled to the drivers: "Let's go!"

We pulled out of the freight yard like hijackers in a gangster movie, and I maintained lookout for any followers. When I was certain that we weren't being tailed, I directed the trucks to a warehouse. I still didn't dare to involve Howard by delivering the goods to his house.

A few days passed, and nothing happened. I ordered the boxes moved to a second warehouse, hoping to erase the scent for anyone who might be tracking the mystery shipment.

When I had convinced myself that no one was following, I had the boxes delivered to the Hughes home and unloaded in the new cement vault.

I telephoned Howard to tell him, "The bottles are in the basement. Not a drop was spilled."

"Great!" he said. "I knew if anyone could pull it off, you could."

That was all. He never asked how I had done it, and I didn't explain that it was accomplished at severe risk to my personal freedom. It was simply another affirmation of the Hughesian belief that "Noah can do it."

As with many Hughes stories, there is a sequel.

A few months after I had pulled off the big bottle switch, Howard asked me to come to his house. We went down to the basement, and he said, "I want to change the combination to the liquor vault. I don't trust the servants. And some of my guests have watched me turn the dial; they may know the combination. You're the only one I can trust. I want only you to know the combination to the vault."

Howard rarely expressed himself in such personal terms, and I felt complimented. As a matter of fact, Howard had little to worry about; I was a moderate drinker and could afford to buy my own liquor.

"Now let's figure out a combination we both can remember—I don't want it written down," Howard said.

We arrived at the idea of using multiples of seven. It was seven to the left, fourteen to the right, twenty-eight to the left, and fifty-six to the right. Open!

I had no occasion to open the liquor vault in the months that followed. I continued with my normal duties while

Howard vacationed One day he took off for Nassau, where he had anchored his new yacht, the *Southern Cross*. A group of his socialite friends joined him, and he took them on a cruise through the Panama Canal and up the coast of Mexico.

Howard telephoned me from Acapulco.

"Send the plane down for me; I'm coming home," he said.

"Aren't you going to come back here on the boat?" I asked.

"No, I'm tired of these goddam people. All they're interested in is drinking and screwing."

Before he hung up, Howard added some instructions: "Tell the servants I'm coming back—and get the liquor vault open. I'm bringing a few house guests, and I'll be doing some entertaining."

I dispatched a plane to Acapulco, then I stopped by the Muirfield House to inform the servants of Howard's return. I went down to the basement to open the liquor vault.

Multiples of seven, I remembered. Seven, fourteen, twenty-eight, fifty-six. Open? No, the door remained as tight as a bank vault.

Try again. Seven, fourteen, twenty-eight, fifty-six. Still it didn't open. Could my CPA mind have forgotten the numerals? Not possible. I tried the combination a score of times, and it wouldn't budge.

Howard had told me to open the vault, and there was only one way. I called a locksmith to drill out the lock and install a new combination.

After Howard returned from Acapulco, I told him of my curious experience with the vault combination. "Maybe the dampness in the basement rusted the dial," I suggested.

A sheepish grin came over Howard's face. "I'm sorry, Noah, it slipped my mind," he said. "After you left that night, I changed the combination to a different number." He poked me in the ribs and laughed.

Later I contemplated the significance of the incident. At the risk of imprisonment, I had rescued his liquor supply from confiscation. I was his closest associate, the man he trusted more than anyone else in the world.

But, when the chips were down, he could not bring himself to trust me, almost a non-drinker, with the combination to his liquor vault.

CHAPTER THIRTEEN

How to Become a Billionaire

"What would you do if you ever lost all your money?" I once asked Howard.

"I would take my plane out over the Pacific," he replied, "and fly it into the ocean."

Fortunately he was never faced with the occasion to test that resolve. As sole stockholder of the Hughes Tool Company, he was never impoverished. But there were times when he was short of cash. That's right—Howard Hughes short of cash. Anything was possible in the Depression years.

And anything was possible in the frantic finances of Howard Hughes. Hughes Tool Company was a golden cornucopia—most of the time. But even that remarkable moneymaker had difficulty keeping pace with the money-spending habits of its errant owner.

In the beginning, Howard was not an immensely wealthy man. Not by the standards of the Morgans, the Mellons, the Rockefellers, the Vanderbilts, and other great financial dynasties.

Then why, you ask, was Howard Hughes able to match their wealth and surpass it to become the nation's richest man?

I will tell you why.

The beginning of the story is in 1924, when an orphaned eighteen-year-old found himself three-quarters owner of a thriving company that manufactured and leased oil drilling bits. The young man would not be content until he owned one hundred percent of Hughes Tool Company.

He bedeviled his relatives to sell him their quarter interest. They didn't want to sell, but Howard persisted in his efforts to persuade them. He became obnoxious about it, and once his uncle Rupert grabbed him by his collar and the seat of his pants and ejected Howard from his house. But Howard returned. Finally the relatives acquiesced, simply to get rid of him.

Down through the years he fought off efforts to dilute his ownership of Hughes Tool, from his management team, from financiers, from potential buyers.

"I will not dilute my interest in the company," he told me over and over again. And he never has.

But total interest in the tool company would not have been enough to make him a billionaire. That was facilitated by some events in 1930.

First, you must understand the peculiar nature of the Hughes Tool Company. It differed from most other big manufacturers in that:

1. It was totally owned by one person, Howard Hughes.

2. It never paid any dividends.

Well, almost never. I knew of only one time when the company formally declared a dividend. That was shortly after Howard became president. He paid himself a dividend of $75,000 and established a salary of $50,000. Thereafter he took out no more than $50,000 per year from the company.

In 1930 the Federal Government took notice of the peculiarities of the Hughes Tool Company. The government had instituted a penalty against the unnecessary accumulation of surplus: it was a law aimed at forcing corporations to pay dividends or else plow the excess profits into expansion, rather than keeping the money out of circulation.

The penalty for failing to use the excess profits was stiff: 27½ percent for the first $100,000 and 37½ thereafter, based on the company's *net income,* not merely the amount of the accumulated income.

The Hughes Tool Company was slapped with a $5,000,000 bill for unnecessary accumulated surplus.

Howard was furious. Everybody hates taxes, but Howard hated them more than any man I ever knew.

"I'll be damned if I'll give the government all that money," he snapped. "How can I get out of it?"

"You can sue for relief from the penalty," I said.

"All right, I'll sue."

Howard took his case to the appellate division of the Internal Revenue Service, which acted more or less as a tax court. I prepared a great deal of material to prove that Hughes Tool Company was making plans for expansion. Howard hired a lawyer to present the case—and he won. The lawyer then presented a bill for $175,000. That seemed high to me, and I offered him $50,000. He refused it and sued Howard for the full amount. The judge looked at my material and the lawyer's and established the fee at $30,000.

Howard was pleased with his victory over the tax collectors, but he was concerned about the future. "How can we avoid having the government hit us for accumulated surplus again?" he asked.

I gave him the benefit of my experience with revenue agents. "I've found that when revenue agents look at fixed assets on a company's books, they are very critical of over-depreciation of machinery. But they rarely pay any attention to land values which are not depreciable.

"Furthermore, the government is not concerned with accumulated profits, as long as those profits are applied to expansion. A company must either plow its profits back into the business or else create and carry out a plan for future expansion and designate funds for that purpose."

Thus was established the pattern for the enormous growth of the Hughes empire. He avoided paying himself dividends, which would then be subject to income taxes. He also avoided penalties for excess accumulated surplus by expansion and by purchasing real estate.

Sometimes he spent the money unwisely: on flop movies, on unsuccessful stock market ventures, on impractical business enterprises, on an immense flying boat.

But other areas of business expansion provided undreamed-of profits for Howard. Included in that category are TWA and Hughes Aircraft.

Land became a principal asset for the Hughes empire.

Over the years Howard has purchased huge parcels of real estate, always with the professed purpose of using the land for plant expansion. Thus the land could be carried on books with the probability of no tax liability being levied.

Items:

1. Howard acquired about 1,200 acres for the establishment and operation of Hughes Aircraft in Culver City, California. When Howard was negotiating for the sale of Hughes Aircraft to General Electric in the early 1950s, it was stated that only 200 acres was necessary to plant operation, excluding the runaway; hence the rest of the property was not included in the package. Later, under threat of eminent domain, about 100 acres was acquired by the county of Los Angeles for the creation of the Marina Del Rey. No other use has been made of those excess acres.

2. Hughes Aircraft built a plant in Tucson for the purpose of manufacturing the Falcon missile, the plant to be turned over to the military when Congress appropriated funds. Howard bought seven sections adjoining the city. When the plant was transferred to the military, one section was included—Howard had tried to hold out for half a section. The six other sections were held by the company, purportedly for employee housing. No housing project developed.

3. In the early 1950s, Howard released publicity indicating that he intended to move Hughes Aircraft to Nevada (he never did). He began buying land near Las Vegas and accumulated 25,000 acres. Where did the money come from? It should be remembered that he had sold his interest in TWA for about $560,000,000. He then embarked on a shopping spree, picking up hotel casinos, ranches, and mining property.

Now you might ask: How can a man who pays himself only $50,000 and declares no dividends live like a pasha?

The answer to that one is simple: Howard charged everything to the company.

All his major expenses—planes, automobiles, houses, etc.—were paid for by Hughes Tool Company. Naturally the Internal Revenue Service went over his return with a fine tooth comb and disallowed whatever expenses were obviously personal. But it was hard to prove which were business expenses and which were personal.

So now you see how to become a billionaire. Easy, isn't it? Makes you wonder why more people haven't been able to do it.

CHAPTER FOURTEEN

How to Lose Millions in Three Easy Lessons

During my early years with Howard Hughes, he displayed no signs of becoming a billionaire. Far from it. I sometimes wondered if he would be able to maintain his millionaire status.

He had a habit of becoming enmeshed in the damndest losing enterprises. I've told you about the Hughes Steamer. About *Swell Hogan* and *Hell's Angels* and other deficit movies. About the bedside stock ticker that cost him $5,000,000 in wrong bets.

Howard managed to lose another $5,000,000 in the stock market. But this time he had a little help.

The first I knew about it was when Howard called me into his office and introduced me to a man who had a thriving insurance business in Los Angeles. Howard handed me a $20,000 check from the man and said, "Put that in my account, Noah."

I couldn't imagine why a stranger would be giving Howard Hughes a $20,000 check, and after the insurance executive left, I queried Howard about it.

He told me that the man had come to see him on the recommendation of a couple of friends. All three were members of an investment syndicate that included a famous family of automobile builders in Detroit.

"We've got a helluva syndicate going," the insurance man said. "We've been making a cleanup in stock after stock. Now the boys and I thought that Howard Hughes should be in on this, too. But we knew what a smart cookie you are and we wanted to convince you of what a good thing this syndicate is. So we included you in our last venture without telling you about it. Here's your share of the profits—twenty thousand dollars."

When Howard told me the story, I could scarcely believe my ears. I was amazed that he could be so naïve as to fall for such a con-man scheme, where the sucker is warmed up by receiving an undeserved profit.

"Why, Howard, it's absolutely transparent," I told him. "Those guys are out to hook you."

"No, you're wrong about that, Noah," Howard insisted. "They're being absolutely honest. Why else would they hand me twenty thousand dollars? That shows their faith."

I couldn't talk Howard out of it, and he plunged into the syndicate with his resources. And got taken. I found out later that his partners were unloading $300 General Motors stock on him at the top of the market; they had bought it much lower. When the Crash came, the stock plunged to $8 and Howard was stuck with enormous losses.

I was in New York in 1930 when the market took a second dip and Howard called me with the instructions: "Go down to Wall Street and talk to the bigshots there; ask them how they think the market is going to move."

I made some inquiries, and the counsel that seemed to make the most sense to me was from a broker, Rulof Cutten. He told me: "Tell Mr. Hughes to keep out of the market. This thing hasn't stabilized yet, and we may have a secondary shock."

The information was relayed to Howard. The next day Cutten telephoned me and said, "What the hell did you tell your man? He called this morning and placed orders for seventy thousand shares. Chrysler and a lot of other issues. He's in for trouble."

He was indeed. He had been playing the market on margin, and he needed a lot of cash to cover his wrong bets. The money came, as always, from the Hughes Tool Company. The company's profits couldn't keep up with Howard's investments.

The investment syndicate had been an expensive lesson and it reinforced Howard's basic distrust of other people.

The insurance man who had been so beneficent with the $20,000 ended up under indictment for fraud. He fled to China and committed suicide.

While he was making *Hell's Angels,* Howard went into the color-film business. In view of the later importance of color to the movie business, it seems like a wise move on Howard's part. Trouble was, he got into the field a decade early.

Rowland V. Lee and his father-in-law William Worthington, both important movie directors, came to Howard with a scheme to develop a process for color film. At that point in film history, color had been used only rarely. In the earliest years, films had been hand-painted to achieve a touch of color. Later, some movies had been given a single tint—blue for night scenes, red for fires, sepia for storms. Technicolor had been developing an all-color process, but it was still impractical and had no widespread acceptance.

Lee and Worthington introduced Howard to an English chemist named Crespinel, who had devised a system of dipping film into a series of solutions to acquire color. The system offered promise of a color revolution for pictures, just as Warner Brothers had revolutionized the industry with sound. All that was needed to make the system a success was money. Howard's money.

He decided to invest in the company, which was called Multicolor. Always looking to the future, I advised him to make the investment in the form of a loan, so that he would be listed as a creditor in case the company went broke. He followed my advice and acquired a 51 percent share of Multicolor for a nominal sum. At least the sum was nominal in the beginning.

The Multicolor operation was installed in a two-story Hollywood building at 7000 Romaine Avenue, which was later to become a famous address in the Hughes legend. We hired two scientists from Caltech to help in developing the process. An engineer from the Hughes Tool Company came from Houston to contribute his skill.

As was his custom, Howard become engrossed in other

matters and left me to oversee the enterprise. At this time his prime interest was Billie Dove, and he took off for a tour of Europe with her.

The Multicolor investment mounted alarmingly. Originally the budget for completion of the building and development of the color process had been $250,000. Now the management came to me and announced an additional $190,000 would be needed for completion.

I could see no value in continuing. I cabled Howard in Vienna and told him: "I don't believe there is enough demand for color pictures to warrant further investment."

Howard cabled back: "Give them what they need. I don't want people to think I'm running out of money."

And so the Multicolor investment climbed to a million and a half.

It was doomed to failure. In the first place, the process wasn't very good. One reel of a picture would be in beautiful color, the next one would be muddy and dark. The color wasn't stable at all.

Most damaging of all was the fact that theaters would not pay any more for color pictures than they did for black and white. It was an expensive process for producers—$125,000 per picture at a time when the average budget for an entire movie was the same amount. The public was not intrigued by color movies, and theater owners refused to pay premium prices for them. The exhibitors had recently gone through the expensive process of converting to sound, and they were not about to incur any added expense.

Howard finally acquiesced to my economic logic.

"All right, Noah," he sighed, "close it down."

Multicolor was liquidated. Now began a long and involved litigation in which the creditors claimed that Howard's investment in Multicolor was a capital investment and hence he was not entitled to any recovery. They offered the theory that the Hughes Tool Company was his alter ego, since he was the sole stockholder. That scared Howard.

He was even more scared one morning when he telephoned me with the news: "A process server is here at the house with two deputy sheriffs. They've got an attachment on the Duesenberg, and they're going to haul it away!"

"Stall them," I said. "I'll be right there."

As I sped toward Muirfield Road, I tried to devise a plan of attack. This was a new challenge for me. I had performed some bizarre missions for Howard, but never had I contemplated that I would be trying to prevent the impounding of his car by the sheriff. I realized how upset Howard would be over the seizure of his Duesenberg. It was among the most magnificent cars in the world, and he was excessively proud of it.

When I approached the Hughes house, I could see the sheriff's car in front. So I wasn't too late. I swung my Lincoln sedan into the one-lane driveway between the house and garage, thus sealing any egress for the Duesenberg. I closed the windows, pulled the brake, locked the car, and approached the three interlopers.

"What's going on here?" I demanded.

The process server showed me the paper. It was perfectly legal. This was during Depression times when sheriffs all over the country were enforcing foreclosures on farms and houses. The law also permitted disgruntled creditors to claim a millionaire's Duesenberg as pawn in a liquidation.

I was arguing with the process server and deputies when the tow truck arrived. "Move your car," ordered one of the lawmen.

I shook my head resolutely.

The tow truck driver was peering inside my Lincoln. "No problem," he said to the deputies. "The car isn't in gear. I can pull the linch-pin on the handbrake and haul the Lincoln out so we can get at the Duesenberg."

"Don't touch my car!" I warned.

The burly truck driver wasn't intimidated by my forty-year-old, five-foot-six physique. He slid under my car to free the brake. I was wearing a business suit, but I slid under the other side of the Lincoln and confronted him horizontally on the cement driveway.

"Don't touch my car!" I repeated.

The truck driver responded with a vulgar remark and

started to reach for the brake pin. Now there is very little that you can do in the way of offensive action while you are prone under an automobile. I chose the maximum deterrent, swinging my foot toward his most vulnerable part.

"Yowwww!" he yelled, rolling out from under the Lincoln. When I emerged, the deputies seized me by each arm and one of them said, "We're going to book you for interfering with the law."

They started marching me to their car when Howard appeared in the doorway of the house and said, "Just a minute, officers."

When the deputies explained my offense, Howard told them to delay arresting me while he called his attorney. He returned and offered to post a bond for the value of the Duesenberg. That seemed to satisfy everyone. Everyone but the truck driver, who departed muttering threats.

The near-loss of his beloved Duesenberg was enough to convince Howard to settle with the Multicolor creditors. He did so by giving them all the net current assets. He kept the liabilities and the mortgaged building.

The Multicolor creditors realized only 25 cents on the dollar. A few years later when the Hughes enterprises were thriving, I suggested paying off the creditors in full.

"It would be a great thing for your reputation," I argued. "The whole thing would cost a half-million dollars."

Howard looked at me as if I had become addled.

"To hell with that," he said.

Howard Hughes, theater magnate.

That was another role that Howard assumed during his pursuit of losing enterprises. I learned about it one day when Howard asked me to come into his office. He introduced me to Harold Franklin, a well-dressed, smooth-talking man who was president of the Fox West Coast theater chain. I soon learned what the conference was about.

"I'm stifled over there at Fox West Coast," said Franklin. "Those people are a bunch of fuddie-duddies. No vision. No imagination. Why, for a cup of coffee I can throw together a chain of theaters that will put Fox West Coast out of business."

That appealed to Howard. As an independent producer, he had suffered at the hands of the big theater chains, which were controlled by the major studios. Those companies always gave the best playing time to their own pictures and handed crumbs to independents like Hughes (a couple of decades later the government made the film production companies divorce their theater chains).

I did some investigating about Franklin on my own. I had a friend who was a CPA at Fox West Coast, and he told me, "That guy Franklin is being thrown out of the company. He has committed Fox to deals that will ruin us." Later Fox West Coast did go bankrupt.

Howard was unimpressed when I told him what I had learned. He had faith in Franklin and was aiming to proceed with the theater chain. It turned out that Franklin needed more than a cup of coffee. Howard contributed $1,250,000 for controlling interest in what became Hughes-Franklin Theaters.

Franklin started building the chain. He sent a man out on the road to buy up theaters. I didn't trust Franklin, nor his agent. So I sent my own man on the road to follow—a detective.

The agent went to Billings, Montana, and bought a theater there. He traveled to Kansas City and bought a group of little theaters. Then he went down to Texas and bought a whole chain. The detective returned to me with the information that the agent was not only charging the company a commission on sales, but the theater owners as well. I told Howard about this.

"This guy made eighty thousand dollars on that Texas deal alone," I said.

Howard grabbed his hat and started to leave.

"Where are you going?" I asked him.

"To Franklin's office," he said.

"What for?"

"I'm going to have it out with him about that agent."

"But, Howard, why don't you wait until the guy comes back? He's undoubtedly going to split with Franklin, and we'll trap them both."

"No, I'm not going to wait."

Howard rushed over to Franklin's office on Hollywood Boulevard and confronted him with the duplicity of the traveling agent. Franklin expressed surprise, and the agent was fired.

It couldn't have been a worse time to go into the theater business. The Depression had struck, and people had no money to spend on entertainment. Soon Hughes-Franklin Theaters were losing $25,000 a week.

I told Howard that we couldn't continue sustaining such losses.

"Okay, Noah, shut them down," Howard said. "Close the doors and salvage what you can."

And so the Hughes-Franklin chain folded. As with the Multicolor fiasco, the creditors wanted their money. The most troublesome was the American Seating Company. Howard had designated me to salvage what I could, and I went around the country divesting Hughes-Franklin of theaters. The terms under which Franklin had bought the theaters were: book value plus three and a half times the last year's net income—one-quarter down and the rest in installments. I offered to give the theaters back to the previous owners for a cancellation of the obligation. They accepted.

That was the end of Howard's adventures into new business enterprises—for a while, at least. He had learned some costly lessons, most of which he quickly forgot.

CHAPTER FIFTEEN

Girls, Girls, Girls

"I'd like to get married again, Noah. But when I marry I want it to be with someone who isn't in the picture business."

Howard made that remark to me one day, and I have since reflected many times about how typical that was of him. He wanted to marry someone who wasn't an actress. But he didn't date anyone who wasn't. The Hughes logic.

I know of only one affair that he had with a non-actress. She was a society girl and, even in that case, he told her he was going to groom her to be an actress. The daughter of a prominent diplomat, and she was on the voyage when Howard brought the *Southern Cross* from the Atlantic to Acapulco. He brought her to the Muirfield place and set her up as a "house guest." But then her parents came out from the East and hustled her home.

Howard's preoccupation with actresses stemmed from an obsession he had. He claimed he was searching for "the perfect woman," both in face and figure; when he found her, he would establish her as the greatest star in movies.

Well, Howard never really succeeded in that ambition. He tried—many times. Maybe to him the fun was in the searching.

He was strange about his dates. Here was a noted la- dies' man, famous figure who escorted the most beautiful and famous women in the world. Yet he couldn't make the first date. Someone else had to ask the girl if she would like to go out with Howard Hughes (not many declined).

How do you explain that? Shyness? Fear of rejection? I'll leave it to experts to psychoanalyze.

The Hughes dates followed the same pattern, at least in the early years. He took the girl out to dinner—usually a dull experience, because Howard was no conversationalist; the girl had to do most of the talking. Sometimes, during the years when he was still partaking of the social scene, he went to a Hollywood party. I believe he really tried to be convivial at such affairs, but it was impossible for him to be convincing at it.

Often he took a girl to his private projection room to view movies. This could also be a dull experience for the girl. There was never any hanky-panky in the projection room; Howard was more interested in what was on the screen.

What happened after the parties and the movies were over, I don't know. That was Howard's business. I'm bringing up these matters because no account of Howard Hughes' life can be complete without mentioning his relationships with women.

Despite the multitudes of beauties who passed through his life, I don't believe he was oversexed. As a young man, he had a normal man's interest in conquest of the opposite sex. Being rich and handsome, he had more opportunities than the rest of us mortals.

Women liked him. Not simply because he was a millionaire and could make them movie stars. They were taken by his boyishness, his seeming helplessness.

"I'm an orphan," he told them. "I went away to school when I was twelve, and I never really knew my mother after that."

The girls swallowed that routine, hook, line, and sinker. They wanted to mother him, and Howard enjoyed the mothering.

Hughes' biographers have sometimes assumed that all of the actresses whose careers Howard fostered were automatically inamoratas. Not true. It certainly wasn't true in the case of his first discovery, Jean Harlow.

If it had been true, I would have known about it. Be-

while away the time, he kept a supply of magazines and books on a large marble table and read from them in search of screen properties.

On this particular night, he became so engrossed in a novel that he forgot all about the lady in the bedroom. She was noted for her fiery temper, and after a forty-minute wait she put on her clothes and stalked out of the house. She returned to her apartment house, the El Royale, a few blocks away.

Later Howard came running out of the house. He asked his watchman frantically, "Did you see a lady leave?"

"Yes, sir," he replied. "She walked that way."

Howard leaped into his car and tried to overtake her. But she had already reached home, and she wouldn't talk to him. End of romance.

Since I was the closest associate of Howard Hughes, I became involved in all of his affairs, both business and personal. On the personal side, I performed some very strange missions. Very strange indeed. Three of them stand out in my mind.

The first concerned Katharine Hepburn. I was in Houston when I received a telephone call from Howard. He was calling from Kansas City, and he asked me to join him immediately. It was in the middle of winter, and I packed my heavy clothes and flew off to Kansas City.

I arrived and then waited two days for him to call me. I went to his hotel and Howard told me that he was planning to sell his yacht, the *Southern Cross*. He wanted me to fly to Bermuda immediately. I wondered to myself why he didn't tell me that on the telephone, instead of summoning me all the way to Kansas City. Now I was equipped with my heaviest clothes—for a trip to the balmy Caribbean.

"Something else I want you to do," Howard added. "I want you to arrange for two dozen yellow roses to be sent to Katie every day."

So then I discovered the real reason for my summons. Howard had been accompanying Katharine Hepburn while she was touring in a play. So I had flown 650 miles to place a florist order.

The second strange mission occurred in Los Angeles.

One evening I received the usual telephone message: "Noah, come over to the house right away. It's urgent."

I raced to Muirfield Road to learn the latest urgency. Here is what Howard told me: his latest "house guest" was a dramatic actress who had only recently broken up housekeeping with a well-known agent, later a Broadway producer.

"This guy is coming over to the house tonight," Howard said. "He's got a play I might buy, and he wanted to talk business here. And I don't want him to know that she's living with me."

"Well, can't you just send her out for a drive while he's here?" I suggested.

"That's not the problem."

"What *is* the problem?"

"The couch."

"What couch?"

"The couch in the library, in front of the fireplace. It's hers. She had it in *his* house when she was living with him. He'll recognize it."

I called in a couple of servants and together we lugged the heavy divan out to the garage for the duration of the conference. Later the actress returned, and so did the couch. And I added furniture-moving to my duties for Howard Hughes.

The third incident is the most bizarre of all. And the most revealing.

Again, the hurry-up summons to Howard's home. He told me: "I want you to get six canvas bags—big ones, the kind they carry mail in. With drawstrings. They must have drawstrings. And hurry!"

I drove to an army and navy store and purchased the six canvas bags. When I handed them to Howard, he took them upstairs to his bedroom and began stuffing his clothes into the bags. Everything he owned went in—suits, shirts, ties, socks, overcoats. He even packed the bathroom towels and rugs. When he had finished, he told me: "Now I want you to take those bags to a vacant lot and burn them. I want you to stay there and make sure they're all burned up."

I thought it weird, but he offered no explanation, and I raised no questions. I packed the bags into my car and took them off—to the Salvation Army. I saw no sense in destroying perfectly good clothes that could be used by someone in need.

Try as I might, I couldn't make any sense of Howard's action. I knew about his germ phobia, but what could have happened to make him want to destroy everything that came in contact with his body?

Later I found out. From bits of information that trickled to me and from my closeup observation of the Hughes idiosyncrasies, I pieced together what had happened.

Howard had been living with a beauteous actress. She was a sensuous lady who was sometimes free with her charms. One day at the studio she fell in the embrace of a golf professional, a man who often played golf with Howard. The golf pro had the misfortune to be carrying a mild case of what in those times was referred to as a social disease. The actress caught it, and Howard found out.

Another romance terminated, along with Howard's entire wardrobe.

CHAPTER SIXTEEN

Additional Data Concerning the Peculiarities of H. Hughes, Esq.

The work habits of Howard Hughes were unorthodox, to say the least. The older he got, the more unorthodox he became. Most working people function on a 9-to-6 day. Not Howard. He could work all night and sleep all day.

I had to become accustomed to his nocturnal habits. I was his fixer, his get-things-done man. When he got an idea in the middle of the night, he automatically reached for the telephone and called me. I kept the telephone by my bed and I trained myself to waken immediately and answer the ring with "Yes, Howard."

One of his early morning calls amused me, in a resentful sort of way. He called with a message for one of his subordinates; it was nothing urgent, but Howard had to let me know immediately, so he wouldn't forget it.

"And say, Noah, don't call the man until nine in the morning," Howard added. "I don't want to disturb his sleep."

"But what about me!" I said.

My protest seemed to surprise Howard. "Oh, you're different," he said.

Earlier in our association, I tried to standardize work routine. In the beginning, his suite at the Ambassador Hotel was his office, and that was chaotic. I was pleased when he moved his operation to the Metropolitan Studio, where we had offices and he could function more efficiently. But a studio office was no place to run the farflung enterprises that he was engaging in, and I convinced Howard to let me establish headquarters in the Taft Building on Hollywood Boulevard.

I spent a lot of money to make the new offices look fitting for the operation of an important young tycoon. Wood paneling, carved moldings, built-in cabinets. Howard's office was plush and spacious. And he never used it. After two years in the Taft Building, I decided it was impossible to persuade Howard to pursue normal business practices. I closed down the office.

Next I created a special office for Howard at United Artists Studio (now Goldwyn), where he was making a series of pictures. He was growing more secretive about his affairs, and I fashioned the office to fit his desires. His office was insulated throughout, with a thick door to complete the soundproofing. Not that he was disturbed by outside noise—he was partially deaf and couldn't hear them. He wanted the soundproofing to prevent others from overhearing what went on *inside* the office.

I had a garage door built into the building next to his office. Howard was able to pull in from Santa Monica Boulevard, park his car and enter his office without encountering anyone.

Later, Howard spent much time at 7000 Romaine, which had been the Multicolor laboratory. We had rented it to a brewery for a time, but the brewery went broke. Howard had his cutting room and film library at 7000, and I built him an air-conditioned, soundproofed printing room for $65,000. He insisted that his film should not be contaminated by dust, and so the printing room had two doors. The inner door would not open until the outer door was closed. Before entering the room, you were supposed to stand between the two doors and clean your clothing with a hand vacuum. The corridor was also equipped with three different filters to purify the air.

Howard could spend two or three days in that printing room when he was making prints of a movie. Then he would stagger out, bleary-eyed and starving, and sit down to a huge meal.

He had a peculiar attitude toward possessions, his and

other people's. One night his Packard was stolen, and he was greatly upset about it.

"But Howard, you don't have to worry," I said. "The car is fully insured."

"Yes, but I want it back! I left some magazines in it, and I was reading a serial. Now I won't be able to finish the story."

He thought nothing of borrowing things from me and never returning them. He came to see me one evening at my hotel in shirtsleeves. It was a chilly night, and I said, "Howard, you're going to catch cold. You'd better take my overcoat." An overcoat for a five-foot-six man looked rather silly on someone who was six feet, three and a half inches, but he took it.

Several weeks passed, and Howard made no mention of the coat. I went to Howard's house one afternoon and told the houseboy to get my coat. The houseboy said he wasn't allowed in Mr. Hughes' room.

"Give me the key," I said.

He was reluctant. "I have a key, but I don't know if Mr. Hughes knows I have one."

"Look—I'm your boss. Your checks come from me. Give me the key."

He handed it over and I claimed my overcoat and left. A couple of weeks later, Howard said to me, "Noah, I'm really embarrassed. I borrowed your overcoat, and now I'm damned if I can find it. Somebody must have stolen it."

"Me," I admitted. "I claimed it."

That was all that was said. He didn't wonder how I had entered his room. He never criticized me—not once in the thirty-two years we were together. It's not that I was so perfect; he simply wasn't a critical kind of person. He assumed that I would get things done and he didn't want to discourage me with criticism.

Another borrowing story.

It was in the 1930s, and I had just bought a new Buick that I was very proud of. One day Howard called me at the studio and asked, "Noah, can I borrow your car?"

"What's the matter with yours?" I asked.

"Well, I need another car."

"Look, Howard, my Buick means as much to me as your yacht does to you. And I doubt if you would lend me your yacht!"

"Noah, I promise I'll have it back to you in four days, and nobody else will drive it."

"But it's only got a few hundred miles on it!"

"Don't worry, Noah. I promise." Howard could wheedle like a little kid when he wanted something, and I gave in and loaned him the Buick.

Four days passed. No Buick. I telephoned Howard's house and spoke to one of the maids. She told me Howard was out.

"Have you seen my car?" I asked.

"Yes, Mr. Dietrich," she said. "It's been sitting out in the courtyard."

"Is it there now?"

"No, sir."

"When is the last time you saw it?"

"About an hour ago. Mr. DiCicco drove it away with three girls in it."

So that was it! Howard had borrowed my Buick for Pat DiCicco to chauffeur girls in. I put two and two together and figured that they were headed for Howard's yacht. I telephoned the parking lot at the yacht basin and learned that my Buick was indeed parked there.

Next, I went to a car dealer in Hollywood and bought a new Dodge, paying for it with a Hughes Tool Company check. I drove it down to the harbor and exchanged it for my car, using a spare set of keys. I sent Howard a cablegram telling him the Dodge on the dock was his.

When he returned from the cruise, he was full of apologies. He kept that Dodge for years and then gave it away to an underling.

During one period in the early 1930s, Howard decided he needed a bodyguard. This was at a time when there was a rash of kidnapings in the country, and he feared he could become a victim.

"I think I should have someone live in the house; he could use the apartment over the garage," Howard said.

"All right, Howard," I said. "I'll find someone for you."

"I want a Texas Ranger," he added.

"A Texas Ranger?" I was surprised to see the Texan come out in Howard.

"Yes, the Rangers have a good reputation, you know."

If Howard wanted a Texas Ranger, I was going to get him one. I telephoned a friend of mine in Texas, Judge Andrews—he wasn't really a judge, lawyers call themselves judges in Texas. I asked him to find me a Ranger who was a bachelor and had all the qualities that Rangers were supposed to have.

Judge Andrews interviewed several Rangers and picked one to go to California and protect Howard Hughes. When he arrived, I was somewhat taken aback. He didn't look like a Texas Ranger. He was only five feet five and stocky. But he had had long experience in the Rangers, and so I installed him in the apartment over the garage.

At the end of the first month, he came to my office and I paid him his salary, $400. I told him he could cash it at our bank across the street. He came back in a few minutes and said, "They won't cash it because I don't have any identification." I sent a note to the bank assuring that he was a Hughes employee.

A half hour later he telephoned and asked if he could borrow fifty dollars.

"What the hell did you do with the four hundred?" I asked.

"I don't know," he replied blankly. "I remember I put it in my pocket. Then I got on the streetcar to go downtown, and there were three guys who kept bumping into me. They couldn't decide whether they wanted to get off the streetcar."

"That's where the money went: you had your pocket picked."

The Texas Ranger continued his job without incident until one night when Howard was home alone in his library. He heard a shot and rushed out into the courtyard. Then he heard a moan. Howard found the Texas Ranger sitting on the ground in pain. He had been practicing quick draws and shot himself in the foot.

We hospitalized him for a few days, then he returned to work. A few weeks later a wife and four children arrived from Texas to live with the supposed bachelor.

That's when Howard decided he could dispense with the services of a watchman.

CHAPTER SEVENTEEN

More Movies

Howard continued making movies until the early 1930s. The pattern was always the same: when he hired a talented and independent director and allowed the man to make the picture himself, he had a hit; when Howard himself interfered with the filming, he lost money. Unfortunately he usually followed the latter course.

For a man who prided himself in being a shrewd operator, Howard could sometimes be taken.

Once a Paramount executive made a proposal to Howard. Paramount had two pictures remaining on Thomas Meighan's contract. If Howard would take over the two obligations, Paramount would assure him a minimum of $400,000 in film rentals from each picture.

"I can't lose, Noah," Howard told me.

But he did. The two films, *The Mating Call* and *The Racket,* cost more than a million dollars, and Howard didn't get his money back. What he didn't realize was that Meighan's popularity was at an end, and Paramount was eager to dump him. Howard was the sucker in this case.

Howard's ambitions to be a movie producer hit a snag in 1931. He ran out of money.

He had placed all his hopes—and $3,500,000—into *Hell's Angels*. The picture did do excellent business for those Depression times. But it wasn't enough to pay off the investment, and he lost $1,500,000 on *Hell's Angels*.

Then to his dismay the Hughes Tool Company stopped laying those golden eggs. The Depression had struck the oil fields, like every place else in America, and Toolco showed a loss for the first time in its history.

Howard had entered into a contract with Joseph Schenck to deliver five movies in 1931 to United Artists. Howard was determined to make those movies, largely because two of them were to star his current flame, Billie Dove.

As usual, it was up to Noah to find the money.

I had to scramble. The tool company couldn't provide. Howard's $3,000,000 in securities had depreciated 60 percent. Toolco had owned a good portfolio of securities, but the Australian Government bonds that he had bought at $100 were now selling for $38. There was only one solution: Howard would have to borrow some money to make those movies.

First I went to Houston and discussed the matter with the tool company management. They claimed they had spoken to the local banks and had been turned down; I suspect they wanted to discourage such a loan because of Howard's unprofitable operations.

So I went on to New York and began negotiations with the City Bank Farmers Trust Company. The terms were stiff. The bank wanted a ten percent discount, so Howard was actually getting only $2,700,000. Then $700,000 had to be placed in a reserve fund, to be used only for certain purposes. That left Howard only $2,000,000 to finish the five movies.

The loan still hadn't been approved by the bank. The man I was negotiating with said to me one day, "You know about those stag films?"

"You mean dirty movies?" I said. "I've heard about them."

"Dietrich, you get me a stag film and I'll see that you get your loan."

I returned to California and located an early classic titled *Gozinta,* which featured all kinds of bedroom activities. At considerable risk—the pornography laws were strict in those years—I shipped it to the banker in New York.

Howard got his loan.

He made the five pictures, and the pattern was the same. He fussed over the two Billie Dove pictures, and they were expensive failures. He had little more success with *Sky Devils,* which starred Spencer Tracy and William Boyd and made use of the *Hell's Angels* planes.

The other two pictures were successes—because Howard employed strong directors who wouldn't allow him to interfere.

Lewis Milestone directed *The Front Page,* from the hit play by Ben Hecht and Charles MacArthur. It starred Adolphe Menjou as the city editor Walter Burns and a newcomer from the stage, Pat O'Brien, as the star reporter, Hildy Johnson.

Howard Hawks was the director of *Scarface,* which made stars of Paul Muni and George Raft and became the classic gangster movie. It also marked Howard Hughes' first big confrontation with film censors.

Hawks had thrown a lot of brutality into *Scarface*—bodies being riddled by machineguns, cars crashing, etc. The Hays Office, the film industry's censor, objected strenuously. Howard was ordered to tone down the brutality and have Muni hanged at the end, instead of being mowed down by rival gangsters. The Hays Office insisted on legal retribution for Scarface's sins.

Howard cut out some of the more violent shots but he wouldn't budge on the ending. The Hays Office gave him a seal of approval, but *Scarface* ran up against censorship boards in New York and other states. He fought them, garnered a lot of publicity for *Scarface,* and eventually won.

He had given in on the violence, but he managed to sneak into *Scarface* an element that was strictly forbidden by the industry's Censorship Code. Howard wanted to establish a hint of incest between Scarface and his sister, played by Ann Dvorak. Hawks went along with Howard's notion. The incest was portrayed so subtly that no censor spotted it. But it's there.

Scarface marked the end of the first phase of Howard's moviemaking career. It is astonishing but true: Howard Hughes had simply run out of money. Cash, that is.

For two or three years after 1932, my job was relatively quiet. I remained caretaker of Howard's interests while he spent much of his time in the East. During four years the Hughes Tool Company reported small losses, and money was short. On one occasion I had to use $2,000 of my own money to meet the Hollywood staff payroll.

Howard spent his time with society friends on Long Island and in Florida. He wanted a place where he could headquarter in New York, so I rented him an office in one of the skyscraper buildings. My own secretary went to New York to staff the office. He was rarely there. He used the office as a message center, a practice he was to develop later at 7000 Romaine.

Those were strangely quiescent years for him. But, being Howard Hughes, he would not remain idle for long.

CHAPTER EIGHTEEN

"I Want to Be the Greatest Aviator
in the World"

Howard Hughes was a man of many ambitions. More than once he expressed to me his desire to surpass the achievements of all other aviators. And indeed he did achieve worldwide fame with his flying feats and was rewarded with a ticker-tape parade down Broadway and a medal from the President.

He was a very good but reckless flier. The fact that he had undergone—and miraculously survived—three major crashes indicates to me that he took unnecessary chances in the air.

I flew with him only once. This was at a time when I had my own private planes, and as I sat with him in the cockpit I remarked, "My pilot doesn't keep the manifold pressure that high."

Howard put his finger to his lips. "Don't tell anybody about that," he said. He was always pushing his airplanes to the limit of their capacities. Usually they responded. On three occasions they did not, and he nearly killed himself in the attempts.

With his moviemaking career temporarily suspended, Howard turned in the 1930s to his other hobby, airplanes.

I knew Howard had been flying in the East. He never mentioned it to me, but I was told that he had made an emergency landing in a field on Long Island because of an engine failure. Naturally I wasn't pleased to have the President and sole owner of the Hughes Tool Company risking his neck in airplanes, but there was nothing I could do. I was in no position to advise him to lead a more safe and sane life. And even if I had been, he wouldn't have heeded me.

Although I knew about Howard's ambition to excel as an aviator, I didn't fully realize how intent about it he was. The first inkling I had was when Howard bought himself an amphibian and started to modify it at the Lockheed airport in Burbank. Since the Hughes Tool Company was starting to regain its health, I was able to pay the bills.

The alterations of the amphibian were typical of Howard. He was never satisfied with the planes he bought; he always thought they could be improved. That had begun with the Boeing plane which he had Douglas rebuild. It continued with the amphibian and planes to follow. This restless search for improvement helped win him a host of speed records. But it also became a mania, as we shall see later.

Howard took a leisurely trip across the country in the amphibian, accompanied by Glen Odekirk, a young pilot and mechanic he had met in Burbank. In January of 1934 Howard entered an air race for amateurs in Miami and won. That set him off on a quest for air glory that was to take him around the world.

Racing airplanes had gotten into Howard's blood, and he returned to California with the intention of building his own speed plane. He was tired of fixing up other people's planes.

He established his headquarters in a hangar at the Lockheed airport. He called on the services of Richard Palmer, a brilliant aeronautics engineer just out of Caltech. The second member of the team was Odekirk.

Their assignment: to build the H-1, the fastest airplane in the world.

For eighteen months the three men labored over the H-1 in typical Hughes-imposed secrecy. Again, the lesson learned from the stolen blueprints at Hughes Tool: Howard insisted that research be conducted behind locked doors.

Howard was involved in his usual social activities, but

he paid periodic visits to the H-1 hangar. At times he could display an incisive knowledge of aerodynamics and an eye for important detail.

"You know," he remarked to the plane builders one day, "anything that disturbs the air flow on the wings and fuselage would interfere with the lift of the airplane. That includes bolt heads and rivets. Why can't we flush-rivet the entire skin and cut down on that interference?"

Flush-riveting had been developed at that time, and it was applied to the H-1. Another innovation was landing gear that retracted when the plane was in the air. These two developments may have been devised by other plane makers, but I believe Howard was the first one to make widely publicized use of them. Both were important advances toward the modern airplane.

By standards of the time, the H-1 was a strange-looking aircraft. The body of the plane was exceptionally streamlined, and the size of the wings were cut to a bare minimum, requiring high-speed takeoffs and landings.

Howard was as happy as I ever saw him while the H-1 was a-building. He enjoyed creating mechanical things, and he was never more at ease than when he was around a hangar. He felt comfortable with other airmen; to them he was a flier, and not Howard Hughes, millionaire. He couldn't cope with the small talk of social gatherings, but he could chatter for hours about propellers and motors and air fuel. When he was in the air, he was an entirely different man from the one that people knew on the ground. He seemed greatly at ease with nothing to concern him but weather and engines and maps.

When the H-1 was finally wheeled out into the sunlight one summer day in 1935, Howard announced that he was going to be the first pilot to take it up.

This was not what I would have liked. It also concerned Odekirk and Palmer. They were well familiar with the revolutionary nature of the H-1. No one could say for certain that it would fly successfully. But Howard insisted that he was going to be the one to find out.

It performed beautifully. And fast. Faster than any of

the observers had ever seen an airplane travel. Howard decided immediately that he would try for the land-plane speed record.

The test was scheduled for September 12, 1935, at Martin Field at Santa Ana. Howard invited me down for the event, and I had my usual queasiness watching him fly. He made a try at the record that day, but darkness fell before he could finish the four runs. The test was postponed until the following day—Friday the 13th.

Fliers of those days were a superstitious lot, and some of Howard's fellow aviators tried to dissuade him from a Friday the 13th flight. Howard had phobias galore, but no superstitions. Friday the 13th was just another flying day to him.

The device for timing Howard's flights was complicated. It had been developed by Western Union and it featured two electrically timed clocks a mile apart, connected by wire. Two cameras were aimed at the clocks and tilted so they would also photograph the plane passing overhead. The plane had to be flown at 200 feet so that the identifying number on the wing would show in the photograph.

Howard took off in the H-1. Circling overhead to observe his feat were two friends, Amelia Earhart and Paul Mantz, the movie stunt flier. Howard pushed the H-1 to the extreme in four passes over the course, and all of us watching him realized that he was breaking the record.

He wasn't satisfied. He wanted to test the utmost capacity of his plane, and he zoomed up to 12,000 feet, then nosed downward and hurtled toward the earth.

My heart was in my throat as I watched that little plane speed relentlessly toward the ground. He pulled out of the dive just as he reached the timing course and streaked past the observers.

Then the engine conked out.

The plane was speeding away from the landing field at low altitude. I saw it zoom up to 1800 feet and then dip down to earth.

Everyone leaped into cars and headed for the bean field where the plane had disappeared. We arrived to find Howard stepping jauntily from the H-1. He had scarcely a scratch, and the plane suffered little damage.

His feat made headlines around the world: a new land-plane speed record of 352.39 miles per hour, almost 40 miles per hour faster than the previous mark.

After the record flight there was speculation in the press about the cause of the crash. One report declared that a piece of steel wool had been discovered in the fuel line, and there were hints of sabotage, Not true. Howard had simply run out of gas. He had gone up with a minimum load to limit the plane's weight. Odekirk had warned him to keep a careful eye on the gas gauge, but Howard had forgotten to.

For his next record flight, Howard wanted to try a Northrup Gamma. The only one that was available was owned by the famed aviatrix, Jacqueline Cochran. I arranged a lease from her, and Howard took it over and made extensive changes. He flew the Gamma from Burbank to Newark on January 13, 1936, establishing a new coast-to-coast speed record of nine hours and twenty-seven minutes. He also established new records between New York and Miami and between Chicago and Los Angeles.

Later the Gamma was destroyed by a fire, and Jacqueline Cochran was angry for years about it. I remember seeing her at a Washington party where one of the guests remarked that Howard was a genius. "No part of Howard Hughes was ever a genius," Miss Cochran snapped.

In January of 1937 Howard was awarded the Harmon Trophy for his contributions to air progress. He went to claim the trophy in the revamped H-1, breaking the trans-continental flight record again with a time of seven hours and twenty-eight minutes.

Howard had flown across the country at an average speed of 332 miles per hour. After he had landed in New York, he received a telephone call from General O. P. Echols, commander of Wright Field at Dayton, Ohio.

"Mr. Hughes, the army is very much interested in your H-1," the general said. "You flew almost double the speed of our fastest interceptor. I wondered if you could stop at

Wright Field on your way back to California so that we can have a look at it."

"I guess I could do that," Howard said.

"Fine! I'll telephone Washington and have the top brass here to greet you. They are all fascinated with your plane's performance."

General Echols assembled a gathering of high-ranking army officers to welcome and inspect the H-1. Howard never arrived.

He flew past Dayton and stopped at Chicago to refuel, then continued on his way to California. General Echols was stuck with the chore of making some explanation for why the invited guest failed to show.

I chided Howard about the snub. "Hell, Noah," he said, "I just forgot I was supposed to stop at Dayton."

Knowing the Hughes mind, I knew he hadn't forgotten. He simply didn't want those generals snooping around his plane and stealing his ideas. Later events proved that it had been an expensive snub for Howard.

Eventually Howard lost interest in the H-1 and sold it to the Timm Company for the relatively minor consideration of $125,000 of Timm stock. The company went broke before the plane went into production, and the H-1 found a resting place in the Smithsonian Institution.

It also ended up at Pearl Harbor on December 7, 1941. Somewhere along the line, the Japanese apparently got their hands on the H-1 specifications. They made a similar model that proved to be a superior airplane—the Zero.

CHAPTER NINETEEN

Around the World in 91 Hours

The first I knew about Howard's plan to fly around the world was when he invited me out to his hangar to look at the Sikorsky amphibian he had bought. He had removed all the seating arrangements and had installed two rows of large gas tanks. These tanks extended from the roof to the floor and held about 200 gallons each. Howard said he was going to use the plane to circle the globe.

"How fast will it cruise?" I asked.

"One hundred and forty-seven miles per hour," Howard replied.

That didn't seem to me fast enough to break the record that Wiley Post had set in a solo flight in 1933. I pointed this out to Howard.

He picked up a ball and circled it with his finger.

"Noah, Wiley Post went around this way," he said, indicating toward the center of the ball. "I'm going to go around up here." He pointed toward what would have been a polar route.

Later he decided the Sikorsky wasn't fast enough, and he bought a Lockheed Lodestar. Again he had the plane stripped down to its shell and fuel tanks were installed. He devised a new fuel system, coating the tanks with neoprene to make them self-sealing.

Howard had first wanted the Sikorsky amphibian because he wanted to be able to land safely on earth or water. The Lodestar was a land plane, but Howard devised a means which would allow it to float.

"I've put eighty pounds of Ping-pong balls in every recess of this plane," he told me. "So even if I rip off a wing landing in the ocean, it'll still float."

Howard picked his crew with great care. Harry Connor had been co-pilot and navigator on a famous flight in 1930 from Montreal to London. Thomas Thurlow was a U.S. Army Air Corps lieutenant who was a navigation expert at Wright Field. Radioman Richard Stoddart was an engineer for the National Broadcasting Company.

Glen Odekirk was originally scheduled to go along as engineer. He backed out at the last minute, and his place was taken by another mechanic at the Hughes hangar, Ed Lund.

Howard left absolutely nothing to chance. He took along everything that he might possibly need—a shotgun in case he crash-landed among unfriendly beasts; a solar still to convert sea water to fresh; a kite to fly a radio antenna; parachutes with small radio transmitters. He carried ethyl to mix with ordinary fuel in case he couldn't find the kind he needed along the route. He even tested thirty different breads for nutritive value, to be used in the crew's sandwiches.

An important figure in the planning of the flight was Al Lodwick, a vice president of the Curtiss-Wright Corporation, which supplied the engines. He took care of all the details on the route, which had been worked out by Howard and his meteorologist, W. C. Rockefeller. Lodwick arranged for landing sites and flight permits and planned fuel supplies to be ready for the plane's arrival.

Lodwick was a straightforward man who had the nerve to correct Howard Hughes' manners. When Hughes was visiting executives at the Curtiss-Wright headquarters, Lodwick pointed out to him: "You shouldn't just walk out of offices and ignore the secretaries. You should tell them goodbye, too." Howard took the advice to heart, and he was saying goodbye and even bowing to each secretary as he left.

The Lodestar was ready for takeoff from Floyd Bennett Field on July 10, 1938. Howard had made a tie-up with Ney York officials and had named the plane *New York World's Fair, 1939*. There were departing ceremonies with speeches by Mayor Fiorello La Guardia and Grover Whalen, the famed greeter and president of the World's Fair. Howard was happy when the speeches were over and he could climb in the Lodestar and take off.

He almost didn't make it. Sagging under its heavy load, the plane rumbled down the runway and into a field— Howard had prudently ordered the fence removed. Finally the Lodestar rose above the cloud of dust and nosed eastward.

The Lodestar touched down at Le Bourget field in Paris sixteen hours and thirty-five minutes later, a new record. But now Howard faced a maddening eight-hour delay. He had damaged the tail wheel assembly in the takeoff from New York, and it had to be repaired.

Howard and his crew took off for Moscow, where they received a tumultuous reception. Then on to Omsk, where he had to mix his own fuel, using the high-grade ethyl he had brought along. Always methodical, he insisted that the gasoline had to be filtered through copper screens before going into the Lodestar's tank. But where were the screens? When a search failed to produce them, Howard radioed Odekirk in New York over his high-powered short wave set. Odekirk located the screen for him.

Again, the Hughes luck. The delays at Paris and Omsk probably saved the *New York World's Fair, 1939,* from crashing into a mountainside.

Howard's original schedule would have placed him over Siberia in the dark of night. He studied maps of the terrain past Kakussk and the mountains were listed at 6,500 feet. He had planned to fly through the night at 8,500 feet, which should have provided plenty of clearance. But when he arrived at the mountain range by daylight, he could see that the peaks rose as high as 10,000 feet! He zoomed upward and on to Alaska.

The whole world was keeping track of the *New York World's Fair, 1939,* as it flew over the Bering Sea and landed at Fairbanks. There he was greeted by Mrs. Wiley Post, widow of the flier whose record Howard was beating.

The Lodestar flew on, bypassing the scheduled stop of Winnepeg because of a storm and landing in Minneapolis.

The last leg of the flight was the most hazardous. The plane ran into a hailstorm, and the wings shook under the bombardment of hailstones. Howard lowered the speed almost to the point of stalling and managed to escape the storm without damage.

A huge crowd had assembled at Floyd Bennett Field by the time the *New York World's Fair, 1939,* touched down. The reception led by Mayor LaGuardia and Grover Whalen dissolved into chaos as the idolatrous mob clamored for the handsome young air hero, Howard Hughes.

Howard was accorded the traditional hero's welcome of the parade along Broadway amid clouds of tickertape and confetti. His triumphal return was handled by Al Lodwick, the Curtiss-Wright vice president, who had also planned the details of the flight. The tour included parades and receptions in Chicago, Los Angeles, and his home town of Houston.

All kinds of honors were given to Howard. The National Junior Chamber of Commerce designated him as one of the outstanding young men of 1938, along with William O. Douglas, John Steinbeck, and Thomas E. Dewey. He was named aviator of the year by the National Aeronautics Association.

Collier's magazine named Howard for its coveted trophy for the aviation achievement of the year, and the presentation was made at the White House by President Roosevelt.

How do you figure all this?

Hughes the recluse, the shunner of public places, the devout loner, allowing himself to be lionized, paraded before millions, subjected to civic oratory. Why?

You must remember Howard's ambition: "to be the greatest aviator in the world." For that brief period in aviation history, he was. The parades and banquets were public recognition of his status.

Still, you'd think that such public exposure might have been punishing for Howard, reputedly an extremely shy man. I don't think it bothered him at all. His arteries pumped ice water. I never knew a man who was so totally devoid of emotion.

CHAPTER TWENTY

Keeping an Eye on the Golden Goose

My duties for Howard in the mid-thirties were minimal. He was out of movie production and spending much of his time in aviation research, which required little attention from me. With little to keep me busy in California, I shifted my headquarters to Houston, where I could keep a closer eye on the Hughes Tool Company. It had recovered from its slump, but still was not performing up to its capabilities. The timing for the move was right for me. My two daughters had married, and my own marriage had ended in divorce. It seemed like a good time for a change.

I moved to Houston in 1936. The conditions that I had observed at Toolco ten years before still prevailed. Production was archaic. Sales efforts were weak. Plant morale was low because of the absentee ownership.

Executives and workers alike felt that Howard viewed the tool company only as a source of revenue to sustain his expensive hobbies. They were right. And this kind of realization was damaging to a multi-million-dollar enterprise.

When problems arose at the Hughes Tool Company, they usually went unresolved. There was no use in seeking an answer from Howard. It was impossible to focus his attention on difficulties at Toolco. He was only concerned when it stopped pouring forth money, as it did during the first part of the 1930s.

The tool company was beginning to return to its profitable status when Howard suggested I move to Houston and keep a closer eye on operations.

"I'll get along without you here," he said. "Go on down there and sit on the problem and analyze it."

It didn't take long to discover what was wrong. Not only antique production methods and listless management, one of the top executives was making a killing at Howard's expense.

A CPA is a financial detective, and hence I was ideally equipped for my sleuthing work. The first hint I had was in looking over the brewery operation.

Beer had been a recent enterprise for the Hughes Empire. When Prohibition seemed destined for repeal, the Houston management suggested that beer would be a worthy sideline for Hughes. Howard agreed. A brewery was constructed on the property of the tool company, and the Gulf Brewing Company was established as a fully owned subsidiary. The company made Grand Prize beer —so named because it was based on the same formula that had won a prize in a Belgium exposition. The son of the original brewer was hired to supervise the operation. It wasn't a very good beer, but it earned $2,300,000 for Howard in a peak year.

In looking over the comparative cost study of the brewery's beer hauling, I noticed that our long-haul costs were far higher than our competitors'. I soon discovered why.

Gulf Brewing had amassed $200,000 worth of trucks, but had hired a trucking contractor to supervise the operation. He also exacted a hefty fee for each mile of hauling. The contractor was drawing a huge sum for doing something we could have performed ourselves. We paid all expenses.

I asked this certain executive about the matter. He had a ready answer: "Well, you see, our trucks are overloaded most of the time; this guy keeps the state inspectors off our necks."

It seemed odd to me, and I made some inquiries at the other breweries. They were sending out overloaded trucks, too. But they didn't pay a contractor to do their hauling. All you needed was a good lobbyist at Austin.

I decided to hire my old employers, Haskin and Sells, to perform an audit. They made some interesting discoveries.

A byproduct of the brewing process is barley mash, which is retained after the beer is poured off and can be sold as cattle food. The ranchers backed up their trucks to breweries and hauled away the barley mash at a fixed price per pound.

The books showed no income whatsoever from barley mash. I investigated further and discovered that our mash was being delivered directly to the ranch of the executive in question.

Not only that. He also had the guts to have the deliveries made in company trucks!

The audit showed that the same man was taking money out of the employees' welfare fund and handing it over to a Fort Worth doctor, who in turn was buying blooded cattle for the executive's ranch. And the executive had even given himself an exclusive contract to supply milk to the company cafeteria.

You had to admire the man's audacity. He was stealing from the welfare fund to buy cattle, which he fed with company mash, and then sold the milk to the employees. Even Billy Sol Estes couldn't have devised such a scheme.

That wasn't all.

The man had first look at the incoming mail before it went to the factory distributing office. If he came across a non-recurring item—a lawsuit settlement or an insurance rebate—he banked the money in his own account. One of the checks was for $11,000, and he had the confidence to endorse it with his own signature and deposit it to his own account in the First National Bank of Houston.

The height of his larceny indicated his expensive taste. He had bought $20,000 worth of oil paintings at a New York art gallery and charged them to the Hughes Tool Company.

Where were the paintings? I asked all around the plant. Nobody knew. I told the auditor to ask the executive where the paintings had gone. The answer came back: he had loaned them to the Houston Country Club. I called the country club. No paintings. I called the Riveroaks Country Club. No paintings.

Finally I confronted the executive himself.

"Well, Dietrich," he smiled, "those paintings are actually out at my house. But I intend to loan them to the country club."

I had learned enough. I went out to California and told Howard: "This man is stealing you blind." I outlined his perfidies and Howard said, "Noah, I see your point."

Then he asked me, "How much do you figure he is stealing per year?"

"Approximately two hundred and fifty thousand."

Howard thought for a moment, then said, "Hell, Noah, I'd be a goddam fool to throw him out. He's got good standing in the oil community. He has spent my money cultivating friends in the big companies. If I throw him out on his fanny because he steals two hundred and fifty thousand a year, his friends will be sore. They'll all go over to Reed Roller Bit Company and buy their equipment there, because they figure I abused the guy. I could lose four million. So I have to weigh the two hundred and fifty thousand against the four million."

I was astonished at his reaction.

"I don't see it that way at all, Howard," I argue. "He knows we're onto him, but he doesn't know how much we've learned. If he sees us doing nothing to stop him, he's got a license to steal!"

Howard cut the argument short. "That's the way I want it. Just see that he doesn't steal more than two hundred and fifty thousand a year."

There was nothing I could do but return to Houston and follow his orders. A couple of weeks later, I was visited by the trucking contractor who supervised the brewery trucking. He threw a bundle of his canceled checks on my desk.

They were all payable to the thieving executive. More than $100,000 was involved.

"Why are you doing this?" I asked the trucker.

"Because that son of a bitch is trying to put the arm on me for another twenty-five thousand dollars, and I'm not going to give it to him," he said. "He has threatened to cancel my trucking contract and the tire contract, too—I sell a lot of tires to Hughes Tool. I'd rather go to jail than pay him another dime."

I thanked the man and said I would look into the matter. I called the other members of the board and told them, "You know what's been going on, and so do I. As far as I'm concerned, I'm not going to take it any longer."

They all agreed. We were united that Howard would have to choose between that crooked executive or us. I telephoned Howard and put each board member on the wire. Each told the same story.

When I got on the telephone, I didn't have to repeat the spiel. "All right, Noah," Howard said, "ease him out. Keep him on the payroll and then announce his resignation—or let *him* announce his own resignation."

"There's more to it," I said. "The Treasury men are going to want us to pay taxes on the mash sales and everything else that should have gone to the company. *He* should be the one to pay."

"No, *we'll* pay for it," Howard said.

So I kept the man on the payroll for a few weeks and then called him in and said, "You're through." That's all. He walked out scot-free, and Hughes Tool Company ended up paying taxes on what he stole.

Again, Howard Hughes the paradox. He refused to part with one-half of one percent of his ownership, yet he stood still while an executive looted the treasury. He could have recovered the money and sent the man to jail. But he didn't. You figure it out.

I had plugged up the hole in the moneybags, but I still couldn't make Hughes Tool perform up to its capabilities. Howard stuck to the policy of promoting men from the ranks, and the Peter Principle prevailed. We had a succession of plant managers, and all were unsuited for such responsibility. Howard refused to heed Toolco's chronic illness. He was far too busy with his other pursuits.

CHAPTER TWENTY-ONE

Is This Any Way to Buy an Airline?

One day in 1937 I was in my Houston office when I received a telephone call from New York.

"Mr. Dietrich, you don't know me," said the voice on the other end. "I'm Jack Frye, president of the Transcontinental and Western Airways. Could you please tell me when that check will go through to Lehman Brothers?"

I was mystified by his inquiry. "What check?" I asked.

"The check on the TWA transaction," he said impatiently.

"Mr. Frye, I don't know anything about a TWA transaction. Perhaps you had better tell me what this is all about."

Frye was momentarily stunned. "Mr. Hughes has agreed to buy a hundred thousand shares of TWA stock held by Lehman Brothers. He's paying ten dollars a share, and he told me that you would provide the check through the Hughes Tool Company."

"This is all news to me, Mr. Frye," I told him. "I'll have to speak to Mr. Hughes and call you back."

"I don't understand this," said Frye worriedly. "I thought that everything was all arranged. It's very important to me. I've got a stockholders' meeting coming up, and my position is involved."

Later I learned the cause for his concern. Frye had become president of TWA only a year before. He was a colorful figure, a onetime mail pilot who continued to pilot routes for TWA even though he was president. Frye wanted to expand the airline, but he couldn't convince the stockholders to finance his plans. He had become acquainted with Hughes, who once borrowed a DC-2 from TWA to experiment with. Hughes was Frye's hope to forestall a move to oust the ambitious president. Frye wanted Howard to buy the 99,293 shares of common stock held by Lehman Brothers for some of its clients. That would have been enough for control.

I telephoned Howard and asked him what was going on.

"Oh, Christ, Noah!" he said. "I forgot to tell you!" He explained his intention to purchase the controlling stock in TWA.

"If that's what you want, Howard, I'll send the check right away. Frye is more than anxious for it."

"Wait a minute, Noah," Howard added. "I've been thinking about this. I gave Frye an oral commitment to buy the stock at ten dollars a share. But I know that TWA is in trouble. I think I can get it for eight dollars. Try it. Fix up some story to cover for me. You be the bad boy. I don't want to offend Frye."

Noah the fixer went to work. I telephoned Frye in New York and told him: "The Board of Directors of Hughes Tool conferred on this matter. This is a corporation, and we function as a corporation. We looked up your rating in Standard and Poor's, and we came to the conclusion that ten is too high a price to pay for TWA stock at this time. We will offer you eight."

"Eight!" Frye exclaimed. "But Mr. Hughes agreed to ten!"

"I am aware of that. But all company decisions are subject to board approval, and the board members feel that eight is the proper price. Now you can take this matter up with Mr. Hughes, if you like. But I will tell you this: I have never known Mr. Hughes to overrule his board."

There had been, of course, no board meeting. And even if there had been, the members would have followed Howard's bidding. But Frye didn't need to know that.

Frye called back the following day. "Can I get eight and a quarter?" he asked plaintively.

"I'll take it up with the board," I said.

I waited twenty minutes, then called him back. "The board approves," I said.

By reneging on his agreement with Frye, Howard had saved $200,000. But he also established me at the very outset of the TWA investment as Frye's enemy. Frye was convinced that I was the ogre who had interfered with Howard's promise to buy the stock at $10. Well, I grew accustomed to playing that role. Whenever Howard wanted to go back on a promise, fire a top aide, exact a tough deal, or deny a request, he let Noah do the dirty work. Then, when the victim complained, he could always sympathize and say, "That Noah is a tough guy to deal with."

On at least one occasion a complainant said to Howard: "Why don't you fire that hard-hearted son of a bitch?"

"Fire Noah?" Howard replied. "I can't. He knows more about my business than I do."

Jack Frye would have danced in the streets to see me fired. At Howard's insistence, I went on the TWA board of directors immediately after his purchase of the controlling stock. I was thoroughly unimpressed by Frye's management of the company. The slogan of TWA at that time was "An Airline Run by Fliers." It should have been run by businessmen. TWA suffered from chronic deficits, and I believed the blame belonged to Frye and his inept management.

Frye and I had no open quarrels, but I reported to Howard my criticisms of the TWA operation. And I expressed myself frankly in board meetings.

After I had been on the board for a couple of years, Howard called me and said: "Noah, I don't know how to approach this, but you know you're very critical of how Frye is running the airline. I told him in the beginning that I'd give him every opportunity to operate TWA the way he thinks it should be. He complains you're a disturbing factor."

"And he wants me off the board—right?" I said.

"Well, yes."

"Howard, I'll be goddamned happy to get off that board. It takes up too much of my time, anyway."

"That's great, Noah," said Howard, and I could tell he was relieved. "But I want you to continue studying and analyzing TWA's problems."

I left the board of TWA, much to Jack Frye's delight. But I continued to receive regular reports on the airline operation, and I reported to Howard my findings.

Frye was an imaginative man, and he possessed an accurate vision of how air travel would proliferate to cover the globe. But his business sense was poor, and he was forever overreaching the limited financial means of TWA. On one occasion when added funds were desperately needed, Howard bought another $1,500,000 worth of stock. He refused to allow a public stock offering as long as he controlled TWA. This followed his lifelong policy of no dilution of ownership.

As with most other airlines, TWA's fortunes began to improve with the advent of war. Transportation was desperately needed, and all air carriers were jammed—so much so that seating priorities had to be established for servicemen and other important travelers.

Just before the war, Howard had wisely purchased six Boeing Stratoliners through Hughes Tool Company. He kept one for himself and put the other five into use for TWA. He had bought the first six models off the Boeing assembly line.

The Stratoliner was a remarkable airplane in its time. It was the first four-engine, internally pressurized commercial plane, and it could accommodate forty passengers, compared to twenty-three on the DC-3.

After the Pearl Harbor attack, the war wasn't going well, and air transportation was needed badly. The Stratoliners, which were the commercial equivalent of the B-17, were the only planes available which could fly non-stop across the ocean. The army needed the Hughes Stratoliners to ferry top personnel to Africa and Europe. But Howard had offended the brass on several occasions, and the generals didn't want to ask him for the planes.

They chose Jesse Jones for the job.

The tough-minded Jones was serving as Roosevelt's Secretary of Commerce. The brass figured that Jones, a fellow Texan and a distinguished American, could persuade Hughes to part with his Stratoliners.

I had become good friends with Jesse Jones during my years in Houston; in fact, he made me a director of his National Bank of Commerce. He called me to explain the army's proposal.

"The military really needs those planes, Noah," said Jones. "I recommend that Hughes establish himself as a patriot by saying, 'Gentlemen, those planes are yours; name your own terms.' That would do him a lot of good with the army and he'd be helping his country, too."

I told Howard of Jones' suggestion, and he replied, "It sounds great. I'll talk to Frye and he'll arrange it."

But when Howard called me back, he said: "Frye thinks we shouldn't hurry into this. We'll have to replace those Stratoliners with DC-3's, which have almost half the capacity. He thinks we ought to be assured of enough DC-3's to double the lost seating capacity. Besides, TWA has applied for some new routes, and we should get assurance that they'll be approved."

"Is that really the way you want it, Howard?" I asked.

"Sure. Frye's right. We should get something in return."

With grave misgivings, I arranged for a meeting with Jesse Jones and Jack Frye at the Department of Commerce in Washington. Frye wasted no time in reciting his conditions: "If TWA can get double seating capacity replaced by enough DC-3's and if we can get approval of all of our route applications, you can have the planes."

I could see Jesse Jones stiffen. "Mr. Frye, would you please step outside while I speak to Mr. Dietrich?" he said icily.

After Frye had left, Jones said to me, "Noah, I wash my hands of this. I want no part of it."

Even though I was a Hughes emissary, I could do nothing but sympathize with him. Frye was called back in, and Jones announced: "There will be no deal. Good day, gentlemen."

I quickly telephoned Howard the results of the conference. He was abashed.

"God, Noah, I made a helluva mistake," he said.

"You're right about that, Howard," I said.

"Go back to Jones. Leave Frye out of it. Tell Jones the government can have the planes on any terms."

I returned to Jones, but he was adamant. "I'm through with the whole deal," he said. "I've already told the army that. *They'll* have to deal with him. I don't want to waste my time with that kid's antics."

The army finally requisitioned the Stratoliners at its own price. TWA won no special preference in route applications and no extra seats for its lost planes. The government got only five Stratoliners. Howard held on to the one he used himself, using the excuse that he was engaged in important research with it. He did put larger engines in it.

There was an interesting sequel to the Stratoliner story.

Hughes continued experimenting with the Stratoliner through the war and afterward. In the early 1950s, he was flying the plane to Las Vegas with another fabulous Houstonian, Glenn McCarthy. The millionaire speculator was buying a lot of things in those days. When he admired the airplane, Howard said, "Do you want to buy it?"

"Sure," said McCarthy. "How much do you want for it?"

"Half a million."

"I'll take it."

Howard insisted on flying McCarthy to Houston and making delivery there. He had nothing in writing on the deal, just McCarthy's word.

Months passed, and no money was forthcoming from McCarthy. I kept reminding Howard about it, and finally he allowed me to see McCarthy and at least get something on paper. I went to McCarthy's headquarters in Houston, not without some misgivings; he had the reputation of being able to jump on top of his desk and kick you in the teeth if you said something he didn't like to hear. And I was arriving on the unpleasant mission of reminding him of his $500,000 obligation to Howard Hughes.

McCarthy was by no means pugnacious, and I walked away with his note for $500,000.

Howard never collected.

Nor did he get his plane back.

McCarthy had commissioned expensive changes in the Stratoliner, and he wasn't able to pay for them. His roller-coaster fortunes had taken another dive. The liens on the plane would have made it impractical for Howard to reclaim it.

Was he upset about the loss of the half-million? Not at all.

"Too bad about that poor bastard McCarthy," he shrugged. He turned to other affairs with the same ease he had demonstrated when he dropped the half million on the Hughes Steamer.

CHAPTER TWENTY-TWO

The Outlaw and Jane Russell

By 1939 Howard had been out of the movie business for seven years, and he was itching to get back in. I learned about his intentions during one of my periodic visits to California from my base in Houston.

"Noah, I realize I told you once I never would make another picture unless I could produce it for less than seventy-five thousand," he said.

"Yes, Howard," I replied, expecting the inevitable.

"Well, I've found a story that is simply too good to resist," he continued. "It's about Billy the Kid. A great story. And I'm going to make it not for seventy-five thousand—that's too impractical—but for two hundred and fifty thousand. No more."

"No more?"

"Absolutely. Do you think you can raise the money?"

"I think I could probably raise that much. Who's going to direct the picture?"

"Howard Hawks."

Hawks had done a fine job for Howard with *Scarface,* so I wasn't too much concerned. I visited the director and asked him how much he figured he could shoot the Billy the Kid feature for.

He showed me his budget: $440,000.

I returned to Howard and confronted him with Hawks' figure. "That means a half-million, Howard," I said. "Every picture seems to go over budget in Hollywood."

"Oh, no," Howard replied. "Don't worry about it,

Jean Harlow got her first starring role in one of Hughes'
early pictures. **THE BETTMANN ARCHIVE.**

Jane Russell—Howard Hughes made her a star. When he found her she was a 19-year-old receptionist in a dentist's office. Her fabulous equipment made her the famous GI pin-up.

Billie Dove—The dazzling Ziegfeld Follies girl and movie star he almost married after spending $325,000 on her divorce. SPRINGER/ BETTMANN FILM ARCHIVE.

Terry Moore—She divorced football star Glenn Davis to marry Hughes. But her plans to get Howard to the altar fell through. THE BETTMANN ARCHIVE.

Faith Domergue— Howard Hughes changed her name and her life. CULVER PICTURES.

Jean Peters—
The second
Mrs. Hughes.
She made him
keep his promise.
CULVER
PICTURES.

Katharine
Hepburn—One
of Hughes' long-
est romances.
She was the only
one of his girl
friends who
spoke up to him.
THE BETTMANN
ARCHIVE.

Ida Lupino—
Howard saw her
in a Palm
Springs restau-
rant and fell
hard . . . for a
little while *(left)*.
THE BETTMANN
ARCHIVE.

Elizabeth
Taylor—She
turned him
down *(right)*.
CULVER PICTURES.

Howard Hughes and his Boeing plane in which he won a race
at Miami, Florida, in June 1932.   WIDE WORLD PHOTOS.

Ginger Rogers—She dumped him when she caught him cheating. It was the only time anyone saw Howard Hughes cry. UPI

Hughes with New York Mayor La Guardia. Hughes was given the keys of the city and a Broadway ticker-tape parade after breaking the round-the-world flight record in 1938.

NEW YORK DAILY NEWS

Howard Hughes' flying boat, built of plywood at a cost exceeding $50,000,-000, flown only once and then with Hughes himself at the controls. First tested in 1947, this plane was actually larger than today's giant "747" plane.
UPI.

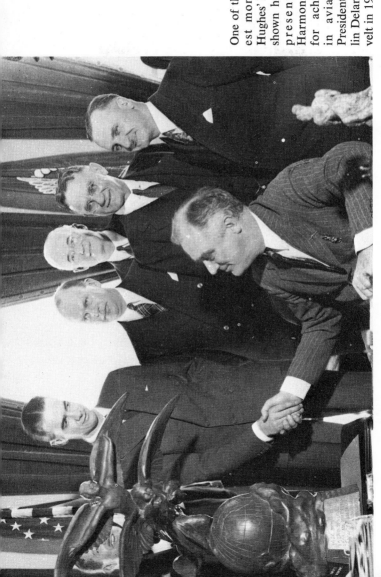

One of the proudest moments in Hughes' life. He is shown here being presented the Harmon Trophy for achievement in aviation by President Franklin Delano Roosevelt in 1937. UPI.

Loretta Young chats with Howard Hughes at a dinner part after a movie premiere.
UP

The wrecked fuselage of Howard Hughe F-11 experimental plane which crashed in residential area at Beverly Hills, Californi in 1946. The plane struck several house before it hit the ground and burned. Hughe was critically injured and it was thoug he would not live. WIDE WORLD PHOTO

Hughes pilots radar-equipped plane. The first passenger plane equipped with radar flown in demonstration May 1, 1947, by Howard Hughes and co-pilot R. C. Loomis over Culver City. UPI.

Ava Gardner—Howard and Ava at ringside during heavyweight title bout. Sometime later, Ava kayoed her escort with a piece of bronze statuary and their "torrid romance" ended abruptly. UPI.

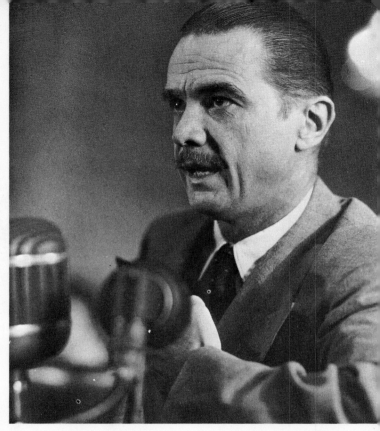

Howard Hughes tells the Senate War Investigating Subcommittee in Washington, D.C., that the testimony of Senator Owen Brewster "is a pack of lies and I can tear it apart if I am allowed to cross-question him."

Noah. I'll hold the costs down and bring the picture in for a quarter-million. You get the money."

The Outlaw ended up costing $3,400,000.

Howard needed a leading lady for his movie, a personality he could elevate to stardom, as he had done with Jean Harlow in *Hell's Angels*. But this time he was determined not to let his star get away.

One day I found Howard in a state of high excitement.

"Today," he announced, "I saw the most beautiful pair of knockers I've ever seen in my life."

He had been to the dentist, and the remarkable bosom belonged to the receptionist, a nineteen-year-old Van Nuys girl named Jane Russell. Howard signed her to a contract and designated her to play Rio, the girlfriend of Doc Holliday. For Billy the Kid, Howard chose another unknown, Jack Buetel, who was submitted by the non-performing Marx Brother, Gummo, a talent agent.

Howard wisely backed the two amateurs with two accomplished actors, Walter Huston and Thomas Mitchell.

Filming of *The Outlaw* started on location in Arizona. Each day's shooting was flown to Hollywood in a special plane, and Howard viewed the film in his private projection room. His old instinct for interference began to assert itself. After a week he flew to Arizona and watched on the set as Hawks directed the movie. Howard was full of suggestions.

This kind of kibitzing infuriated Hawks, a fiercely independent director. After the third week he turned to Howard and said, "If you think you can do a better job, why don't you take over the picture yourself?"

Howard did. Hawks left *The Outlaw* and went to Warner Brothers, where he made *Sergeant York*. It was one of the biggest moneymakers of 1941 and won an Academy Award for Gary Cooper.

Meanwhile, Howard Hughes was directing *The Outlaw* at his own pace. Slow. He drove Walter Huston and Thomas Mitchell to distraction with his countless retakes and limitless shooting schedule. Buetel and Jane Russell were entirely new to films; they thought that was the way all movies were made.

Howard was determined to make the best possible use of Miss Russell's most obvious assets. One of the key scenes came when the wounded Billy was suffering chills in an isolated cabin. Howard took shot after shot of Jane leaning over Billy's bed until he achieved the exposure he was seeking. That was the sequence that caused a soldier at the premiere to shout "Bombs away!" and convulse the theater.

Howard was delighted with a line of dialogue that was devised in a scene in which Billy explained away his borrowing of Rio from Doc Holliday. After all, Doc had borrowed Billy's horse. "Tit for tat," Billy commented.

Such suggestiveness and the exposure of Jane's epidermis would be laughably tame today, when anything goes on the movie screen. But in those times Will Hays, through the Breen Office, still censored films with an iron hand, and wholesale cuts were demanded in *The Outlaw.* As with *Scarface,* Howard decided to strike a blow for freedom of the screen—and incidentally, to stir up reams of publicity for *The Outlaw.*

His press agent was Russell Birdwell, the irrepressible idea man who had conducted the Search for Scarlett O'Hara and other notable stunts. Birdwell accomplished the remarkable feat of making Jane Russell a star before the public ever saw her on the screen. He flooded the newspapers and magazines with provocative poses of Jane, and GI's all over the world adopted her as their pin-up girl.

Howard fiddled and fiddled with *The Outlaw,* spending night after night in his projection room and recalling the entire cast and crew to film added scenes he believed to be necessary.

He was cutting *The Outlaw* right up to the last minute, literally.

The world premiere was scheduled for the Geary Theater in San Francisco in February of 1943. A trainload of Hollywood personalities and press had gone northward for the occasion. Howard was holed up in the St. Francis Hotel, sick in bed. His cutter, Walter Reynolds, was in the projection room at the theater. Just before the movie was to begin, Walter received a telephone call from Howard: "Bring Reel Three over to me."

Walter was puzzled, but he hustled over to the St. Francis with Reel Three. "I want to make a cut in it," Howard explained.

Gazing around the hotel room, Walter saw no projector. "For crissake, Howard," Walter said, "Reel One is running right now."

Howard was unconcerned. "Take the reel out of the can," he instructed. He held up a pencil and drew the film over it, peering at the image and humming the musical score.

"Cut here," Howard said. He continued running over the film, humming all the while.

"Cut here," he said. Twelve feet had been removed from the picture. There was a splicing machine in the room, and Walter hastily made the cut, then raced back to the theater. He arrived just as Reel Two was concluding. Remarkably, Howard had made a perfect cut, the musical score bridging the gap without a lapse. He had memorized the entire score.

The Outlaw was roasted by the critics, but Howard wasn't disappointed. He withdrew the picture from release and stepped up the publicity campaign, focusing on Jane Russell's bosom and his own fight against censorship.

"The longer I wait, the more valuable the picture will be," he told me. "I'm building up the public's desire to see *The Outlaw*."

He tried to create the illusion that he was spending a great deal of time combatting the censors. In truth, he put *The Outlaw* aside and devoted himself to other interests.

During this period Howard asked me to contact Cardinal Spellman in New York and see if he could use his influence to remove the Catholic Legion of Decency's condemnation of *The Outlaw*. I had several cordial meetings with the cardinal, and we became warm friends. One day he called me and said, "Noah, I got your picture passed."

Howard finally released *The Outlaw* nationally in 1946. All the years of buildup were not enough to insure success. The critics still found the picture corny, and audiences laughed in the wrong places. *The Outlaw* did pretty good business, largely on curiosity value, but it wasn't enough to pay off Howard's investment.

Because of her position as a Hughes protégée, many people presumed there was a romance at one time or another between Howard and Jane Russell. Not true. Jane had been in love with the football hero of her high school, Bob Waterfield, who later became a college and pro star. They were married in 1943.

As with Howard's other sex-symbol star, Jean Harlow, there was no romance. But unlike Harlow, whom Howard didn't like, there was mutual respect between him and Jane. He appreciated her straightforward and untemperamental manner. She was grateful for how he had nurtured her career.

Howard was proprietary of his important star and insisted that she get the best possible treatment when he loaned her to other producers. His own supervision of her career was thorough. How thorough it was can be seen in a remarkable memo which Howard composed in 1950, while Jane was starring in *Macao*.

The memo was addressed to the man I had installed as studio manager of RKO, C. J. Tevlin. Howard began with a single-spaced page of instructions about the dissemination of the memo: to the producer, Sam Bischoff; the publicity chief, Perry Lieber; to the wardrobe woman Lieber had designated for this delicate chore.

"I want these two copies of the Russell wardrobe notes returned to you and thence to me, because I do not want these notes lying around in the files anywhere," Howard cautioned.

He added that he wanted Lieber to make sure that the wardrobe girl "reads several times and digests thoroughly my notes with respect to Russell's bosom, but I do not want these notes taken out of Lieber's office by the wardrobe girl as I do not want any possibility of her inadvertently allowing someone else to see them."

Here is the text of Howard's memo:

I want [cinematographer] Harry Wild notified that I feel the photography of Jane Russell's nose was disadvantageous to her, and the defects of her nose which I discussed with him were quite apparent in this test.

I think Russell's wardrobe as displayed in this test is Christ awful. It is unrevealing, unbecoming, and just generally terrible.

There is one exception, and that is the dress made of metallic cloth. This dress is absolutely terrific and should be used, by all means.

However, the fit of the dress around her breasts is not good and gives the impression, God forbid, that her breasts are padded or artificial. They just don't appear to be in natural contour. It looks as if she is wearing a brassiere of some very stiff material which does not take the contour of her breasts.

Particularly around the nipple, it looks as though some kind of stiff material underneath the dress is forming an artificial and unnatural contour.

I am not recommending that she go without a brassiere, as I know this is a very necessary piece of equipment for Russell. But I thought, if we could find a half-brassiere which will support her breasts upward and still not be noticeable under the dress or, alternatively, a very thin brassiere made of very thin material so that the natural contour of her breasts will show through the dress, it will be a great deal more effective.

In addition to the brassiere situation, it may be that the dress will have to be retailored around the breasts in order that it will more naturally form to the proper contour.

Now, it would be extremely valuable if the brassiere, or the dress, incorporated some kind of a point at the nipple because I know this does not ever occur naturally in the case of Jane Russell. Her breasts always appear to be round, or flat, at that point so something artificial here would be extremely desirable if it could be incorporated without destroying the contour of the rest of her breasts.

My objection to the present setup is that her breasts do not appear realistic in any way. The over-all shape is just not realistic and at the nipple instead of one point, which would be very desirable and natural, there appears to be something under the dress which makes several small projections, almost as if there were a couple of buttons on the brassiere or under the dress at this point.

One realistic point indicating the nipple, if it could be incorporated realistically into the brassiere and show through the dress, would be very fine. The trouble with the setup now is that where her nipple is supposed to be there is more than one projection and it looks very unnatural. Also, the balance of her breasts from the nipple around to her body appears to be conical and somehow mechanically contrived and not natural.

This is difficult to explain, but if you will run the film I think you will see what I mean.

What we really need is a brassiere of a very thin material which will form to the natural contour of her breasts and, if possible, which is only a half-brassiere, that is to say which supports the lower half of her breasts only.

This brassiere should hold her breasts upward but should be so thin that it takes the natural shape of her breasts instead of forming it into an unnatural shape. Then, if something could be embodied in the dress itself at the point of the nipple to give it just one realistic point there (which Russell does not have) and if this could be accomplished without putting anything into the dress which will disturb the contour except right at the point of the nipple, this would be the ideal solution.

You understand that all the comment immediately above is with respect to the dress made of metallic cloth.

However, the comment is equally applicable to any other dress she wears, and I would like these instructions followed with respect to all of her wardrobe.

Regarding the dresses themselves, the one made of

metallic cloth is OK, although it is a high-necked dress, because it is so startling.

However, I want the rest of her wardrobe, wherever possible, to be low-necked (and by that I mean as low as the law allows) so that the customers can get a look at the part of Russell which they pay to see and not covered by cloth, metallic or otherwise.

In the test, both Jane Russell and Joyce MacKenzie were played chewing gum. If this was inadvertent and Russell merely did so because she considered it a wardrobe test, I suppose that is of no consequence.

But, if [director Josef] Von Sternberg intends to play these girls in the picture chewing gum, I strongly object as I do not see how any woman can be exciting while in the process. Incidentally, even in a wardrobe or make-up test, I can certainly tell better what the girl looks like without this indulgence. . . .

Howard, you can see, was ever the amateur engineer, whether he was rebuilding the Lockheed Lodestar to fly around the world or redesigning Jane Russell's brassiere.

When Jane's contract was expiring in 1955, Howard couldn't bring himself to part with her, even though he was phasing out his motion picture production. After all, he had made her a star, and he didn't want other producers to be cashing in on what he had created.

He asked me to conclude an arrangement by which Jane would be committed for five pictures and would be paid at the rate of $1,000 a week for twenty years.

At first the deal sounded excessive, but Howard explained: "I'm paying her a million dollars for five pictures —two hundred thousand per picture for a star of her status is not bad at all. But by paying her over a twenty-year period, I'm using the theory you taught me about 'present worth.' I'm really paying her only half a million, because I can invest the money and get back a half-million in interest."

Howard's contract for Jane was excellent in theory. But then he never made another picture with her. She was paid a thousand dollars a week for doing nothing.

Her contract continues until 1975. She still remains loyal to him. When I met her many years after I arranged the contract, she told me: "I'd still like to make a picture for Howard. And even though the time limit has expired, I'd do it for nothing."

CHAPTER TWENTY-THREE

Beginnings of Hughes Aircraft

When did it all start?

With Howard's motor-driven bicycle back in his Houston childhood? Or when J. B. Alexander taught him to fly in the old two-seater Waco? Or with the remodeled Boeing P-4 that drove Donald Douglas to distraction?

Perhaps the beginning of Hughes Aircraft should be dated from the first airplane that Howard built, the H-1. But Howard gave me no indication at the time that the H-1 was the start of an aircraft empire. Throughout his lifetime in business, he never had a long-range plan for anything—the tool company, movies, aircraft, or anything else he touched his hand to. He acted on instinct, caring only for immediate results. What happened in the future mattered nothing to him.

Sometimes this philosophy worked magnificently well. Sometimes it produced only chaos. But the Hughes luck usually prevailed, and the good results outbalanced the bad.

When the European war started in 1939, the United States started building up its defense potential, and the government was looking for airplanes to match the German aircraft that had blitzed Poland. Howard decided to try his hand at landing a government contract for airplanes, and he developed a mockup of a proposed twin-boom fighter—a radical design with double fuselages and a cockpit in the center. As usual, he and his little band of plane makers worked in complete secrecy in the Hughes hangar at Lockheed Airport.

It was so secret that even the commanding general of the U.S. Army Air Corps couldn't get inside.

Word of the twin-boom interceptor reached Washington, and General Henry H. (Hap) Arnold decided to go out to Burbank to see it and to determine if Hughes had the facilities for manufacturing aircraft. The Arnold party arrived at the gate to the Hughes operation and were met by an armed guard.

"Sorry, no one is admitted without a pass," the guard said.

"But this is General Arnold, commanding general of the United States Army Air Corps," an aide protested. "He wants to inspect the new plane."

"Sorry, no exceptions," the guard insisted. "Mr. Hughes says to let no one in without a pass."

And so Hap Arnold and his party were turned away at the gate. Howard claimed later that he was abashed by the incident, that no one had told him Arnold was coming. But I wonder. It would certainly fit the Hughes pattern if he deliberately had applied his no-snooping edict to the head airman himself.

Naturally Howard's affront to Hap Arnold didn't make him any points with the air corps. He faced competition for the interceptor contract with Lockheed and Weddell-Williams of New Orleans. Weddell-Williams went out of business before the contract was awarded. Howard was passed over with the excuse that he lacked production capacities. The contract went to Lockheed, and the result was the P-38, one of the fastest and most effective fighter planes of World War II.

The P-38 bore a close resemblance to Howard's twin-boom model, and he was bitter about it.

"Dammit, I'm going to shut down my plant so tight that no snooper will be able to get close to it," he vowed. "And I'm going to develop a plane so damned good that the air corps will come begging for me to make it for them."

It hardly seemed possible, but the security at the Hughes plant became even tighter than before. Under the direction of Glen Odekirk, the plant worked on a design for a twin-engine medium bomber which Howard called the D-2. Also under manufacture was a feed chute that would load 20mm airplane cannon.

In 1940 it became apparent that the Hughes operation in Burbank was bursting at the seams. The need for a bigger plant was urgent, and Howard sought large acreage in the Los Angeles area for a location. He and Odekirk went up for a flight one day to scout two locations, one in the San Fernando valley, the other near the ocean in Culver City. Howard preferred the Culver City site, and he paid $400 per acre for the first parcel. Eventually he acquired 1,200 acres.

The new plant was under construction in early 1941 when Howard sent for me. "We're going into the war, and we're going soon, Noah," he told me. "Roosevelt is going to get us in, come hell or high water. There's no reason why we shouldn't get some of that war production business. They can't turn me down this time because I don't have a plant. I'll have one at Culver City."

I left for Washington and arranged a meeting with General Oliver P. Echols, chief procurement officer for the U.S. Army Air Corps. I approached the meeting with trepidation, remembering how the general had been stood up by Howard, who had promised to display his speed plane at Wright Field.

My fears were correct. The general bristled at the name of Howard Hughes.

"That son of a bitch will never get a dime's worth of contracts out of me as long as I'm in this office," Echols ranted.

I tried to argue that personalities should not be considered during a time of national emergency, but I made no headway. The general's antipathy was too deep.

So, with the help of Jesse Jones I went over his head. I made an appointment with William Knudsen, former General Motors production chief who had been appointed head of the Office of Production Management. He was more sympathetic to my proposal for the use of Hughes factories, both in Houston and Culver City, for defense contracts.

The Hughes Tool Company received contracts for

struts for the B-25 bomber. Another contract was for centrifugal cannons, which the army badly needed. They were being made only at the Watertown Arsenal. Two years were required for the laborious process of building layer on layer.

We sent our top production men to the Watertown Arsenal to study how the cannon was being made. The process had been developed in France, and it involved pouring hot metal into a mold and turning it at 1,500 revolutions. The speed threw the heavy material out and the slag remained in the center, then was bored out.

At first the Army hesitated giving Hughes Tool the contract for the cannon, arguing that we had no experience in armament production. I called my friend Jesse Jones, and he and I visited Bill Knudsen and convinced him that Hughes Tool could do the job.

We bought the site in Houston and had the buildings constructed before the appropriation came through. Soon the plant was turning out cannon barrels in thirty days—the same cannons that required two years to cast and bore under the old process.

Another important contribution to the war effort was made on the West Coast. The air corps awarded Hughes a contract for the machinegun feed chutes, which had been developed by a young engineer at the plant, Claude Slate. The former Multicolor plant at 7000 Romaine was converted into a factory, and it produced nearly all of the 20mm machinegun feed chutes on American bombers during World War II.

Howard was still determined to develop a bomber that would fly faster than any other. He poured $3,000,000 of his own money into the design of the plane he called the D-2, only to have it rejected by the air corps as impractical.

Hughes Aircraft was a problem child in the beginning, not only because of Howard's obsession with the D-2. He was also involved with *The Outlaw,* devoting excessive amounts of his time and attention to the filming of Jane Russell's bosom and fighting with censors.

Much of the travails of the new aircraft plant stemmed from lack of strong management. Howard appointed his flying buddy, Glen Odekirk, as first general manager of the Culver City factory. Glen was a good friend of mine and a fine fellow, but I had to tell him, "Glen, you've gotten in over your head."

I told Howard that, too, and he finally agreed. Then Hughes Aircraft had a series of managers, all appointed by Howard, but none worked out. The problem was not merely with inadequate management; the nature of the new plant itself precluded any efficient operation. Over at the Lockheed hangar, Howard and his small, secretive group of plane makers had been hand-crafting individual aircraft. The exigencies of an all-out war called for mass production, and Hughes Aircraft wasn't geared for that. While great industrial accomplishments were being made by management and engineering teams, Howard remained the inscrutable loner. He couldn't seem to understand the difference between producing masses of airplanes for saturation bombings and fashioning a single speed racer to break the cross-country record. Technology had moved beyond the point where a single, eccentric tinker could prove effective.

During the early war years I kept hammering these points at Howard. Finally in 1943 he said to me: "I admit that we have not had the proper management at the aircraft plant. My idea of the best man to get for the head job is the person who is responsible for delivering the most airframes to the air force at the least dollars."

I made some inquiries in the industry and found that the company that had established the best production record was Consolidated Vultee. The engineer who appeared to be responsible for the company's performance was Charles Perelle.

Howard then began one of those clandestine operations that he seemed to enjoy. He flew to Dallas, where Perelle was headquartered. Negotiations were conducted between Howard and Perelle in cars on the streets of Dallas and Fort Worth.

In this case, Howard had more than his usual motive for secrecy. The aircraft industries had a wartime agreement against the proselyting of each other's executives.

Word of Howard's wooing of Perelle reached the board room of Consolidated Vultee, and the management was outraged. The negotiations were summarily ended.

Then in 1944 Perelle called Hughes and said, "I've made up my mind that I'm going to leave Consolidated Vultee. So if you still want me, I'm available."

He didn't tell Howard what had really happened. Tom Girdler, who had been loaned to Consolidated Vultee by Republic Steel Corporation, had finished off his term and was returning to his original company. He told Perelle that he was leaving and that he could no longer protect Perelle from his enemies in the company. Perelle, who was a controversial figure, then decided to jump on the Hughes bandwagon.

I was in Los Angeles at the Chancellor Hotel when Howard heard from Perelle. He came over to explain the situation to me.

"Will you go along with me on hiring Perelle?" Howard asked.

"Howard, I will go along with anybody you bring in," I said, "up to the point where I don't believe he is doing the job for you."

"Well, I want you to think it over and tell me tomorrow morning how you feel about it."

I called him the next morning and said, "Howard, I feel this morning the same way I felt last night. I will cooperate with anybody you want to bring in—until I believe that he is not the man for the job."

Howard sent Neil McCarthy down to San Diego, where Perelle was headquartered at the time, and a contract was signed. At last Hughes Aircraft was aimed in the direction of competent management. Or was it?

CHAPTER TWENTY-FOUR

The F-11

Howard couldn't understand why he couldn't land a big plane contract from the government. He didn't seem to realize that he had done just about everything possible to antagonize the military, including the barring of Hap Arnold from the Hughes plant and making an enemy of General Echols.

After Howard had lost out to Lockheed on the P-38, he stubbornly went ahead with his own version of a twin-engine medium bomber. He called it the D-2, and he assigned a large staff of engineers to work on it in utter secrecy. When he finally unveiled it, the military was something less than overwhelmed. There was no interest in buying it.

Howard never gave up. If the frontal approach failed, he would try more devious means. No one was more expert in that than he.

The man he hired to seek favor for him in high places was the hail-fellow expert, Johnny Meyer.

Johnny was a plump, pleasant man who had a glad hand and a smooth line for everyone. And why not? He had been trained to ingratiate himself as a movie press agent.

He was glamorizing the stars at Warner Brothers when Howard discovered how useful Johnny could be. In his constant search for "the perfect beauty," Howard had located a young beauty who fascinated him. She was a dark-haired young actress named Faith Dorn. Unfortunately she was under contract to Warner Brothers.

Johnny Meyer was in charge of the junior talent program at Warners. He somehow managed to have the girl's contract assigned to Howard Hughes. Jack Warner heard about the shenanigans and was furious. He fired Meyer, and Howard was obliged to hire him.

Meyer was put on the payroll at $200 a week. His title was public relations, but his duties went beyond that. Howard instructed him to ingratiate himself in high places of the government with the aim of securing important contracts for Hughes Aircraft.

I felt that this was a fallacious enterprise, and I told Howard so. While such friend-buying might produce immediate results, I argued that it would ultimately be self-defeating and destructive.

Howard wouldn't listen. If he couldn't gain admittance through the front door, he was going to enter from the rear.

And so Johnny Meyer embarked on his spending spree. From 1942 to 1946, he managed to spend $170,000 in entertaining bigwigs from coast to coast. Johnny certainly knew how to please the tired politician or general, and he was lavish with hotel suites, fancy dinners, champagne, and caviar, not to mention $100-per-night beauties. You'd be surprised how many senators, governors, and generals partook of his largesse.

Despite his obviousness Johnny Meyer produced results for the Hughes enterprise. The most important VIP that he snared was Elliott Roosevelt.

The President's son became an important figure in Howard's ambition to snag military contracts. Elliott had been an aviation buff before the war, had learned to fly, and had written about air matters for the Hearst syndicate. He entered the air corps as a captain and served with distinction in the early phases of the African and European campaigns. His specialty was air reconnaissance.

The combat commands began complaining about the poor quality of reconnaissance planes, compared to those of the enemy. A crash program to improve air reconnaissance was instituted, and General H. H. Arnold assigned

Elliott Roosevelt, by then a colonel, to investigate ways to help the situation.

Enter Johnny Meyer.

"Like many combat veterans, Elliott Roosevelt needed rest and recuperation, and Johnny Meyer had all the facilities. He arranged a date with an actress he had known at Warner Brothers, Faye Emerson. The date blossomed into a full-fledged romance. When Elliott Roosevelt took Faye Emerson as his bride, Johnny Meyer not only acted as best man—he picked up the tab for the wedding and the honeymoon as well.

During the course of his assignment to research possibilities to improve air reconnaissance, Elliott Roosevelt inspected a proposed plane by Hughes Aircraft, the F-11. He liked it. He gave it a strong recommendation to Washington. Others were not as enthusiastic, notably Howard's old sparring mate, General Oliver P. Echols of plane procurement. He argued against the F-11, particularly since it was of plywood construction. Howard, on the other hand, reasoned that the British had done well with a plywood Mosquito and that the use of wood would relieve the overburdened metal supply.

Elliott Roosevelt's opinion prevailed, and in late 1943 the Hughes Aircraft Company was awarded a contract for one hundred F-11 reconnaissance planes at $700,000 apiece.

Johnny Meyer was making an important friend elsewhere.

Major General Bennett Meyers was a regular army man who had risen to the influential post of assistant chief of the Air Staff, in Materiel, Maintenance and Distribution. Johnny Meyer sought the general's friendship, and it was forthcoming. General Meyers came out to California as the guest of Howard Hughes and was accorded all the benefits of luxury living, as promulgated by Johnny Meyer.

Howard was impressed by the resource of the important general. What Howard didn't know was that General Meyers had already advised against the government's entering a contract with Hughes for the F-11.

But Meyers then changed his tune and became one of Hughes' staunchest supporters. But he had in mind something more than Johnny Meyer's steak dinners and hotel suites. General Bennett Meyers was thinking big.

He came to Howard with a proposal. Meyers wanted to buy government bonds on margin and turn over a quick profit. The scheme was foolproof—and legal, he said. All he needed was the capital. That's where Howard came in. Meyers wanted to borrow $2,000,000 from Howard on a short-term, no-interest loan. Meyers would buy the bonds on margin and hold them. If the price went up, he would make a fast profit. If the price went down, then he expected Howard to make up the difference.

Despite the baldness of the scheme, Howard did not reject it. He felt that Bennett Meyers could do him a lot of good in Washington, where he sorely needed friends. I wanted nothing to do with the enterprise, and Howard assigned Neil McCarthy to negotiate the details.

Neil went east to deal with General Meyers. Something went wrong, and the scheme was aborted.

Howard was furious. "Fire McCarthy," he told me. "I want him fired right away."

This was one occasion when I didn't follow Howard dictation. Neil McCarthy had been Howard's trusted attorney since 1925, and it seemed senseless to end his services summarily. Especially when he had failed in a mission which I felt was foolishly dangerous. Neil remained on the payroll for another year.

CHAPTER TWENTY-FIVE

The Flying Boat

Its official name was the HK-1, or the Hercules.

Newspaper reporters referred to it flippantly as the Spruce Goose, or the Flying Lumberyard.

To the men who labored on its construction, it was known as The Jesus Christ.

There was a reason for such blasphemy. One of the workers told me the origin of the name: "When people walk in the hangar for the first time, they are staggered. They just stand there with their mouths open and stare up at the top of the plane. Then they say, 'Jeeeeezuzz Keeristt!'"

Indeed, on the many occasions I saw the Hercules I never ceased to be astounded at its size. Its wings are slightly longer than a football field. Its tail is the height of an eight-story building. It is leviathan in every way.

Many citizens were overwhelmed by the size of the 747 when it was introduced. The capacity load of a 747 is 490 persons. Howard's plane was designed to carry 700.

The flying boat can claim any number of superlatives. The biggest airplane in history. The most money spent for one aircraft. The longest period under construction.

I would give it another distinction: it was Howard Hughes' biggest folly.

It all started, of course, with Henry J. Kaiser. The plump, provocative, publicity-minded industrialist had drawn attention to himself by his feat of mass-producing needed cargo ships during the early phase of World War II. Kaiser enjoyed cutting through red tape and conventional thinking with his imaginative solutions to vexing problems.

One of the nation's gravest problems in early 1942 was the marauding of its convoys in the Atlantic by German submarines. In some instances more than 50 percent of the shipping was being sent to the bottom of the ocean by the elusive U-boats. The situation caused frightful loss of human life, drained desperately needed maritime resources, and endangered the supply of manpower and materiel to the fighting fronts.

Kaiser proposed an elemental solution: why not build airplanes capable of flying troops and supplies over the oceans in large quantities?

He attracted headlines with his proposal, but little encouragement from the powers in Washington. The government officials were not convinced that an airplane the size that Kaiser proposed would be flyable. At any rate, they argued, Kaiser had no experience in aircraft manufacture. Hence entrusting him with such a project would be risky.

Such rebuffs could not dissuade a man like Kaiser. He was determined to find someone with plane-building experience who could help him realize his dream. He found his man in the St. Francis Hotel in San Francisco one August day in 1942.

Howard was off on one of his periodic disappearances, which he made when business and personal matters pressed down too heavily on him. He had suffered a siege of pneumonia, and he had dropped everything to fly to San Francisco to hole up and recover in a St. Francis suite.

One day he was hurrying through the lobby when Henry Kaiser happened along—not by chance, I suspect. The two famous men recognized each other, Howard invited Kaiser to his suite, and Kaiser began his pitch. The two millionaires talked off and on for two days.

Kaiser's proposal appealed to the adventurer in Howard. It was a bold, brash, seemingly impossible task—building the biggest airplanes to escape the menace of the Nazi subs. The impossibility of it intrigued Howard. Also the fact that the air corps brass was opposed. Howard was determined to show up that antagonistic band of generals he called the Hate Howard Hughes Club.

Hughes and Kaiser reached a tentative agreement to combine their resources on the big planes, and Kaiser rushed into print with the announcement of "the most ambitious aviation program the world has ever known."

I was against the program from the very start. The military's opposition to the scheme seemed enough of a deterrent—and the brass would be even more antagonistic with Howard Hughes in the picture. Most of all, I knew Howard's dilatory habits. There was absolutely no way of achieving Kaiser's promise of delivering the airplane within ten months.

But Howard was intent on building the big plane, and I did nothing to talk him out of it. As it turned out, the meeting in the St. Francis lobby was an expensive one. The ultimate result was $50,000,000 out of Howard's fortune.

The partnership of Henry Kaiser and Howard Hughes was doomed from the start. I realized that when they had their first meeting after the agreement in San Francisco.

The meeting was set for 10 A.M. in my office on Romaine Street. Kaiser arrived promptly at 10. No Howard. I made conversation until noon, when I took Kaiser out to lunch. I also took him to dinner. He was getting redder and madder, and I had run out of explanations on why Howard was so late.

Finally Howard arrived at midnight, full of apologies and explanations. Howard had a very naïve manner when he got into such situations, and he was usually able to placate the offended party. Again he was successful, and Kaiser accepted his apology in good spirits.

The Kaiser-Hughes Corporation was established for the production of the 500 huge airplanes, and Kaiser returned to the military to seek support. Expectably he received none. But Kaiser knew his way around the Roosevelt Administration; he was one of the few industrialists who had supported the President. With a nudge from the White

House, the Defense Plants Corporation authorized a contract with Kaiser-Hughes for three flying boats at $6,000,000 apiece, for a total outlay of $18,000,000.

There were additional benefits from the government. The Defense Plants Corporation built the monstrous 800-foot hangar in which the HK-1 was constructed; after the war Howard bought the place for a fraction of its original cost. Some of the plane's equipment, including the eight huge engines, were Government Furnished Equipment.

And so work on the huge plane began. Kaiser sent a production team to Culver City—the same engineers that had devised ways to turn out Liberty Ships in large numbers. After weeks of frustration they returned to the Kaiser headquarters in Oakland. Henry Kaiser made several valiant attempts to plan how he and Howard could combine operations to mutual advantage. Nothing worked. The deadline passed for the ten-month period after which Kaiser had promised delivery of the flying boat. The plane was still on the drawing boards.

Ever the pragmatist, Henry Kaiser saw the impossibility of the project and bowed out.

That left Howard, alone against the scoffers. They were saying that Hughes would never finish the plane, that the laminated wood (used because of wartime limitations of metal) of the exterior was impractical, that the Hercules was a colossal boondoggle that would never fly.

Naturally Howard was more than ever determined to carry on with the flying boat in the face of such criticisms.

Construction on the Hercules continued long after the U-boat menace had abated, even after the war itself was over. The government tried to abandon the project, but Howard persisted. He wangled another $2,000,000 appropriation, and also made use of GFE—Government Furnished Equipment. When the taxpayers' money was shut off, Howard paid the bills himself.

The bills were immense. By the time Howard was ready to start testing the Hercules, he had lavished $7,000,000 of his own money on it.

The gargantuan size of the undertaking captured everyone's imagination. To transport the huge plane from Culver City to the Long Beach Harbor was a monumental undertaking. The Hercules had to be divided into three parts, and overhead wires along the route were severed so the plane could pass along the way.

When the Hercules was assembled in a temporary hangar at Long Beach, Howard made a sobering discovery. The plane was so immense that no pilot could operate its controls manually. So he put the engineers to work on hydraulic controls. This advance—similar to power steering in our cars today—may well have been an important contribution to aeronautics. If so, I suspect it was the *only* contribution made by the Hercules.

The flying boat, with all its enormous and seemingly insoluble problems, might have been abandoned by Howard, just as he had turned his back on the Hughes Steamer and Multicolor.

But events in Washington conspired to make him stiffen his resolve to make the flying boat fly.

CHAPTER TWENTY-SIX

Howard Burns His Clothes Again

It was during the war years that Howard began to evidence behavioral patterns that I found disturbing.

Heaven knows, he was not your ordinary run of millionaire. His eccentric dress, his excessive secrecy, his daring adventures and extraordinary enterprises had set him apart and created a living legend. But the oddities that made him so fascinating could eventually become disabling, and that was what I feared was happening to Howard as the pressures bore down on him.

He was attempting too much and doing it in such a helter-skelter manner that nothing was really accomplished. He was pushing the F-11, although there was a growing belief on the part of the military and his own staff that the plane would be of no value. He was obsessed with the flying boat, which was becoming the world's largest white elephant. He continued to promote *The Outlaw* and the dual charms of Jane Russell. He kept an occasional eye on the operations of TWA. All the while he was maintaining one alliance after another with some of Hollywood's most famous stars, from Olivia DeHavilland to Lana Turner.

A large order for one man. And not an entirely well man, either.

Howard still bore the effect of the *Hell's Angels* plane crash. He was also involved in a serious auto accident during the war. He was driving my car along Beverly Boulevard and started to make a left-hand turn onto Rossmore when a car headed east smashed into him. The steering wheel broke and Howard struck his head against the wind-shield.

He was dazed, but he managed to have himself taken to his Muirfield house, which was a few blocks away. The doctors examined him there, and so the story was kept out of the newspapers. I visited Howard and found him inco-herent and semiconscious. That condition lasted a couple of days.

My car was a total loss, so I went out and bought an-other one, charging it to the company.

Howard was involved in one other car mishap that I knew of. That was in 1936, when he was driving a girl home one night in his Duesenberg. As he headed west on Third Street, an elderly tailor stepped off the streetcar at Lorraine Boulevard. The Duesenberg struck him, and the old man was killed instantly. Howard put the girl on the next streetcar that came along, handed her some money and told her to go to Santa Barbara and hide out.

Howard told police that he hadn't seen the old man step off the streetcar. Howard was cleared, and we managed to keep the incident out of the newspapers. The tailor had no family, only some brothers and sisters; we settled with them for $20,000.

The car and plane crashes seemed to have no lasting ef-fect on Howard, but in retrospect I believe they must have taken a toll. The strains began to show.

I realized the extent of Howard's disability during one terrifying telephone conversation in 1944. He and I were talking business, as we had hundreds of times before. Howard said: "Noah, I want you to look into the matter of. . . ." and he mentioned a minor bit of business for me to investigate.

A minute later he remarked, "Noah, I want you to look into the matter of. . . ."

He repeated the same instruction. Then he did it again and again. I sat there unbelievingly; it was like a night-mare in which words are repeated over and over.

I had a pencil and pad in front of me, and I checked off the number of times that Howard had made the same re-mark. After a half-hour I interrupted him.

"Howard, I don't believe you realize what you're doing," I said.

"What do you mean?" he said defensively. "I always know what I'm doing."

"You've said the same thing to me many times while we've been talking," I said.

Howard was indignant. "What the hell are you talking about?" he demanded.

"I think you ought to see a doctor. I made a tally on a pad. You repeated the same sentence thirty-three times. You've been repeating yourself a great deal lately."

Howard was silent for several moments. "Seriously, Noah, have I been doing what you say?"

"You really have, Howard," I said. "There must be something wrong."

He telephoned me the next day.

"I'm glad you spoke up, Noah," he said. "I saw the doctor, and he said that I'm on the verge of a nervous breakdown. He told me I've got to drop everything and get away from the pressure or I'll really crack up."

"Well, take care of yourself, Howard," I told him. "And don't worry about things here."

"I won't," he said. "Hell, you're running the show, anyway."

"Where are you going?" I asked.

"I'm not going to tell you. And I don't want you trying to find me, either. I'll come back when I'm ready. And while I'm gone, there are just two things I *don't* want you to do."

"What?"

"Don't fire Jack Frye and don't fire Chuck Perelle. Outside of that, it's all yours."

Howard realized that I had scant regard for Frye as president of TWA and was growing less impressed with Perelle at Hughes Aircraft. He wanted them kept in office until he returned.

And so Howard disappeared. I felt anxious about him, particularly in view of his upset state of mind. But I kept my promise and made no attempt to locate him.

A few uneasy weeks passed; then I received a telephone

call from Howard's aunt, Mrs. Loomis. She was in an agitated state because she had been trying to call him from Houston, and she couldn't reach him.

"Do you know where he is, Mr. Dietrich?" she asked.

"No, I don't," I replied. That was the truth. But I saw no reason in upsetting her further by telling her the full story.

"I'm very worried about Howard," Mrs. Loomis said. "Sometimes I've had to wait a few days, but I've always been able to reach him before."

"I'll look into it, Mrs. Loomis," I assured her. "I'll call you when I find out something."

I checked with the servants at Howard's house. They said that he had driven off in his station wagon, but he had left no message as to where he would be. I called Howard's headquarters at 7000 Romaine. The office had heard nothing from him. The airport reported that the Hughes station wagon was parked there and the Sikorsky amphibian was gone.

When I relayed this information to Mrs. Loomis, she was unbelieving. She began making accusations: "It wouldn't surprise me if poor Howard had died and you're hiding his body and running things yourself."

No amount of reasoning could calm her hysteria. There was nothing I could do but try to assure her that I had told her everything I had learned and, as far as I knew, Howard was still alive.

A few days later I had gone from Houston to Los Angeles for a meeting. I was at 7000 Romaine when I received a telephone call from a man named Long who was in charge of the Hughes Tool office in Shreveport, Louisiana.

"Sit down and brace yourself, Mr. Dietrich," he began, "because you are not going to believe this. Mr. Hughes has been in jail."

I did exactly as he said: I sat down and braced myself. Then he poured out the story:

Howard had flown to Louisiana in the Sikorsky and had encountered some mechanical trouble. He docked the plane at Shreveport and wandered into town. He was unshaven and wore rumpled clothes and sneakers, and he carried a bottle of milk in a paper bag. He made some inquiries about directions, always speaking in a hushed tone as if he didn't want to be overheard. He talked of renting a car and driving to Florida. The gas station men became suspicious and called the police. The cops found $1,200 in cash in his pockets—and no identification. He was booked as a vagrant.

"I'm Howard Hughes," he said.

"Sure, sure," said the cop.

"But I *am* Howard Hughes," Howard insisted. "If you don't believe me, call my assistant, Noah Dietrich."

The policemen huddled in a corner and one of them said, "You know, supposing he *is* Howard Hughes. He looks like him."

"He's a bum," another cop said.

"Better not take a chance. Call the local Hughes Tool office and see if they know anything about it."

Our man in Shreveport received a telephone call from the police station: "We got a hobo down here says he's Howard Hughes. You want to come down and take a look for yourself?"

Long hurried to the police station, but he was in a quandary. The idea of his famous boss turning up in a Shreveport police station dressed like a tramp was inconceivable. At any rate, Long had never set eyes on Howard Hughes during his eighteen years of service with the company. How on earth would he be able to recognize Hughes?

"Well, he *looks* like Howard Hughes," said Long as he viewed the suspect, "but I can't really tell because of the beard."

"Goddammit, I'm Howard Hughes!" Howard said angrily.

Long calmed him down and said, "May I ask you some questions about the company, sir?" Howard agreed, and Long made some inquiries about company operations which only an insider would know.

"Yes, this is Howard Hughes," Long announced.

The police released him immediately, and that's when Long telephoned me. "What shall I do?" Long asked.

"Don't do anything," I told him. "Just leave him alone." Those had been my instructions from Howard, and I intended to follow them unless it appeared certain that he was incapable of handling his own affairs.

My next contact with Howard was even more curious.

A man telephoned from Florida. He was an early friend of Howard's, and Howard had stopped at his home to stay a few days.

"I don't know what to do about him," the friend said. "Howard showed up here looking like a bum. Then he went out in the backyard and burned all his clothes."

My thoughts went back to the incident of the canvas bags a dozen years earlier.

"Howard has been under a terrible strain," I told the Florida man. "He has been on the verge of a nervous breakdown, and his doctor advised a long rest. I suggest you buy Howard some new clothes and have him see a doctor, if you think that seems necessary. If you need any help, call me back."

I didn't hear from him again, so I presumed that the problem with Howard was worked out.

No word came from Howard until his return, six months after he had disappeared. He offered no explanation about his travels, and I asked him nothing. But I telephoned his aunt as soon as he arrived home and assured her that Howard was unharmed. I didn't want her to continue believing that I was running the Hughes empire while I kept her nephew in the Deep-freeze.

CHAPTER TWENTY-SEVEN

Changing Patterns
in the Hughes Phenomenon

When I was visiting a general in Houston one day during the war, I noticed a wood-carved motto over his door. It read: "In an emergency, any quick, common-sense decision is preferable to delay in search of the ideal solution."

The general gave me a replica of the motto, and I carried it to California on my next trip. When I saw Howard, I presented the plaque and said, "Here's something you might find useful."

He stared at the words, and without a smile he dropped the plaque into the nearest wastebasket.

It would have been asking too much, of course, to entreat him to change his ways. Howard Hughes was Howard Hughes, and nothing would change him.

As he was reaching the end of his thirties, his erratic demeanor began to solidify into certain patterns—patterns which intensified as he grew older.

The germ phobia became worse. He had satisfied himself that he did not have his father's bad heart. Once he had undergone extensive tests at St. Vincent's Hospital, including the running up and down of three flights of stairs. The doctors told him there was nothing wrong with his heart.

Then he believed that his only chance to avoid emulating his parents' early deaths was to shun contamination by noxious germs.

He declined to shake hands with anyone, unless he

could not possibly avoid it. He was deathly afraid of crowds, and his public appearances were becoming fewer and fewer.

His hypochondria sometimes took strange forms. Once he was convinced that something bad was happening to his throat. For a week he uttered not a word; he communicated with those around him by writing notes. When his throat improved, he started talking again.

But how do you reconcile his germ phobia with his constant pursuit of movie beauties? Surely he must have realized that girls carry germs, no matter how lovely they are.

His attitude toward money was also paradoxical.

He could spend millions pursuing some will-o'-the-wisp, and then quibble over a few dollars. During the filming of *The Outlaw,* he directed a table scene over and over again. Each day the prop man ordered a chicken from the Gotham delicatessen. Howard found out about it, and he was upset.

"Why the hell do you have to order a chicken every day?" he demanded of the prop man. "Why can't you put it in the ice box and use it the next day?"

When *The Outlaw* budget was getting out of hand, I cautioned Howard about it. He agreed to have a meeting with me, and he and I went over the expenses, item by item. Howard ran swiftly over most of the figures. Then he came to one that he questioned. It was 65 cents for a month's subscription to the Hollywood *Citizen-News.*

"What the hell does that have to do with the making of a motion picture?" he demanded. I had to talk him out of firing the production manager over it.

Howard displayed little consideration for those who worked for him. When he went on one of his three-day projection room binges, he expected his cutter, Walter Reynolds, to stay up with him.

After one marathon session Howard's cook, Eddie, brought him the usual Hughes dinner on a silver platter—steak, peas, vanilla ice cream, and cookies. Walter eyed the meal, and he finally said, "Christ, Howard, I'm hungry, too!"

Howard seemed startled by Walter's comment. "Oh, sorry, Walter," he said. He turned to Eddie and added, "Tomorrow night bring some dinner for Walter, too."

As an afterthought Howard gave Walter a cookie. To avoid physical contact, he put the cookie on a spoon and handed it to Walter.

On another occasion, Howard called Walter to the studio to drive him home. Walter had a brand-new Buick, and he decided to take his wife and two young children for a ride in it while he drove the boss to his house. When Walter arrived, Howard said he wanted to run a reel of *The Outlaw*. He continued running the same reel over and over again until three hours had elapsed.

"Howard, I've got my family in the car," Walter remarked.

"Oh, really, Walt?" he said. "Then we'll go right now."

Walter came within three blocks of Howard's house when a tire blew out. "I'll fix it," Howard said. Despite Walter's protests, Howard jumped out of the Buick and unwrapped the tools, which had never been used before. He jacked up the car, changed the tire, and drove on to his house with the Reynolds family.

It was during the war period that he decided to sell the Muirfield house and auction all the furnishings, including the family silver. He moved to a rented house in Bel-Air, and from then on he never owned his own home. He conducted much of his business from the Bel-Air house. He also used an office at Goldwyn studio, smaller than the one with a private entrance I had fixed up for him during the early 1930s.

Howard's attitude toward the war was equivocal.

When it appeared certain in the early stages of World War II that gasoline would be in short supply on the home front, he sank large tanks on his property in the San Fernando Valley and filled them with gasoline. He also stored up a large supply of skeet shells, anticipating the shortage of ammunition.

I suppose that you might rationalize that Howard's attitude toward the government stemmed from his detestation of taxes. Even though he was receiving millions from the

United States for military contracts, he gave no favors in return.

For instance, the *Cassiana*. It was a huge yacht which Howard had picked up in Florida before the war at a bargain. The owner, a New York investment banker, claimed the boat was worth $100,000. Howard offered $30,000. The country was in a recession, and yachts were not selling.

When the owner objected to Howard's price, Howard told him: "I'll give you the thirty thousand, and we'll make a contract. If you can better the price within four months, I'll either meet the price or return the yacht and you give me back the thirty thousand."

The owner was desperate to sell, so he agreed to Howard's terms. Four months passed, and no better offer was forthcoming. So Howard got his bargain yacht—which he hardly ever used.

With the advent of war, the Coast Guard badly needed large vessels for patrolling the Caribbean. The *Cassiana* was ideal for such purposes, but Howard wouldn't part with it. Finally the Coast Guard threatened to requisition the yacht, and Howard agreed to sell it—for $75,000.

The government managed to get the five Stratoliners away from TWA, but Howard held onto his own. It spent most of the war in a hangar at Lockheed.

Howard also tried to keep his Sikorsky amphibian. The Army Engineering Corps pressured him for it, but he kept stalling, claiming that he was experimenting with the plane.

When he could stall no longer, he agreed to deliver the Sikorsky to the Engineers. But first he insisted on a final test flight before delivery. He said he wanted to test the modifications that he had made in the engines.

Howard flew the plane to Lake Mead for landings and takeoffs, taking along two Civil Aeronautics Administration pilots, a flight engineer, and a mechanic. As Howard was dropping down for the last landing, a wing dipped into the water. The plane was torn apart, and one of the CAA pilots died instantly. The mechanic later succumbed to injuries.

Howard himself was severely injured and almost drowned in the sinking plane. He and the others were rescued before the Sikorsky dropped to the bottom of Lake Mead.

As soon as Howard recovered, he announced his intention to raise the Sikorsky from the lake bottom.

"Good God, Howard, why don't you just let it stay there?" I suggested. "It will simply be a big expense—for a plane that has tragedy attached to it."

"I want to rebuild it," Howard said.

"For what?" I asked. "What would you use it for?"

"I want to rebuild it," Howard repeated.

There was no arguing with him when he set his mind to a course of action. The raising of the Sikorsky was an expensive task—and a grisly one, too. Fragments of human bone and flesh still clung to the wreckage.

The Sikorsky was rebuilt but never put back into service for the Hughes organization. Later Howard decided he wanted to unload it, and he told me to "jam it down Del Webb's throat." Webb was doing a lot of construction for the Culver City plant, and Howard figured Webb would be beholden enough to buy the plane, whether he needed it or not.

Webb wasn't so easily swayed. I had session after session with him, and I told him, "The old boy says if you don't buy the Sikorsky—and buy it at his price—you won't get any more business from him."

Even that argument failed to work. Howard eventually sent the plane down to Houston with the instructions "Don't do anything with it until you hear from me."

The years have passed and still it sits in Houston, 35 years old, waiting for word from Howard Hughes.

CHAPTER TWENTY-EIGHT

Putting the Hughes Affairs in Order

The end of World War II found the Hughes enterprises in a state of disarray.

Hughes Aircraft had been laboring over two projects to help the war effort—the F-11 and the Hercules—and at the time of the victories over Germany and Japan, no deliveries had been made. The army rescinded its order for the hundred F-11s and instead contracted for three of the planes. After pouring $20,000,000 in the Hercules, the government called a halt to further expense; Howard plunged stubbornly on, lavishing his own millions on the hopeless project.

The Hughes Tool Company had a better record of delivery to the government, having supplied cannon in large numbers and on time. But Toolco itself still suffered from its longtime ailments of absentee ownership and mismanagement. The company simply wasn't performing up to its potential.

TWA, like all airlines, encountered difficulties with the end of the war. But TWA's troubles were compounded by the poor management of Jack Frye. The airlines had been misled by the 96 percent load factor in the months following peace. As soon as the soldiers got home, the load factor plummeted to 58 percent; in most cases, that was below the breakeven point. Despite such hard facts Jack Frye continued forward with his expansionist dreams. At one point he sent a memo to department heads instructing them to make plans for the following year based on employment of 45,000 "because of expansion." TWA was employing 17,000 at the time. Such executive thinking was idiotic. Yet Howard continued to place his trust in Jack Frye.

To add to the clutter of his affairs, Howard had returned to moviemaking.

He had formed a partnership with Preston Sturges, the brilliant, erratic writer-director of such films as *The Miracle of Morgan's Creek* and *Hail the Conquering Hero*. Howard liked to take his dates to dinner at The Players, a café on the Sunset Strip which Sturges owned. Together they concocted a scheme to produce a series of films, some of which Sturges would write and direct, some he was to produce only. Howard's main motivation was to fulfill his promise to make a star of Faith Dorn, the teen-age starlet he had spirited away from Warner Brothers. Howard restored her real name, Faith Domergue, and she had undergone a long period of singing, dancing, and dramatic lessons. She had grown impatient with Howard's unkept promises, and so he hired Sturges to plan movies for her.

The area of greatest urgency in the Hughes empire during the immediate postwar period was Hughes Aircraft.

Progress on the Hercules and F-11 had been painfully slow. Partly this was due to Howard's own dilatory habits, partly because of plant supervision. I had become convinced that the appointment of Chuck Perelle as general manager was a mistake. I tried to convince Howard of this. But he was always reluctant to fire managers. Even though Hughes Aircraft had lost $5,000,000 during Perelle's first year of operation, Howard kept him on.

The change came on the first Christmas of peace, 1945.

I was home in Houston, preparing for a quiet family Christmas with my wife and our three young children. On Christmas Eve came the call from Howard. How typical of him. Christmas Eve meant nothing to him—not even the fact that it was his fortieth birthday.

"Noah," said the high, thin voice, "I want you to fly out here and fire this son of a bitch Perelle."

I was pleased that Howard had finally come to the decision, but appalled at his timing.

"Howard, nothing in this world would prompt me to leave my family on Christmas Eve, " I said.

"But this is important!" Howard insisted.

"I know it is, Howard. But even if you could convince me to fly to California and leave my family, I wouldn't do it."

"Why not?"

"Because it would be the worst possible public relations to fire an important executive on Christmas."

The thought had never occurred to Howard, and he agreed to allow me to spend Christmas with my family. On the day after Christmas, I arrived in California for the execution of Charles Perelle. I was curious about what had brought Howard to the point of firing him.

"Well, I remembered you told me about how we lost five million during Perelle's first year," Howard said.

"And that's what convinced you?"

"No."

"What was it then?"

"The son of a bitch sent me a letter ruling me out of my own goddam plant!"

"What?"

"That's right. I had been going down to Culver City at night, trying to figure out why the plant wasn't working right. The guards all know me, of course. Then the word got back to Perelle that I was visiting there. He had the effrontery to send me this letter warning me that if I persisted in making my nocturnal visits without notifying him in advance, he would have all the locks changed and inform the guards to keep me out! The nerve of the bastard!"

That was the end of Perelle. He sued, of course, but settled for a reasonable amount. I had hoped the firing of Perelle would bring a turnabout in the fortunes of Hughes Aircraft. But that was too much to hope for. Howard placed Frank McDonnell, the Toolco controller, in temporary command. Howard still wanted to run the Culver City plant as his own suzerainty, even though he was unwilling to devote the time and attention to the immense task of converting a war plant to peacetime production.

The strength of the Hughes operation—the tool company—still was not achieving its capabilities. As early as 1930 I had told Howard that he needed to modernize the Toolco methods. I continued my urgings after I moved to Houston in 1936. Howard insisted on operating the company in his own haphazard manner. He refused to hire efficient managers from other companies; his passion for secrecy would not allow outsiders moving into Toolco. As a result, the company had a succession of ineffective managers. One of them died while running the plant, another committed suicide.

When the war was over, Howard had a change of heart. Hughes Aircraft, TWA, and his movie operations were racking up big losses. Again, the golden goose had to accelerate its egg-laying.

In 1946 Howard said to me, "Noah, why don't you take full charge at Toolco?"

That was exactly what I had been waiting for. First, I needed a production mind. Through Jesse Jones, I had become acquainted with General William Knudsen, who had left the General Motors chairmanship to head the War Production Board. I went to Knudsen and explained my needs for a topflight production engineer.

"You're lucky," Knudsen said. "Fred Ayers is available. He laid out the Cadillac plant for us, and he's the best production man I know. He went to England during the war to advise on production matters, and also served as consultant to the Soviet Union. Now he's back."

I arranged a meeting with Fred Ayers and was impressed with him from the outset. He was a frail little man, no more than one hundred and thirty pounds, and he spoke with a touch of British accent from his wartime stay in England. He had the esthetic air of an artist, and indeed, what he could do with a production line was truly a work of art.

Fred liked the challenge of bringing order out of Toolco's chaotic ways, and I paid him a hefty salary as a convincer. Howard had given me carte blanche to revive the plant, and I began making outlays without consulting him.

I spent $5,000,000 out of company reserves in my campaign to bring the plant to peak efficiency.

Fred Ayers installed giant machines that performed dozens of operations; most of the procedures had been done by hand before. Finally Toolco had a production line that could turn out drilling bits in a smooth, efficient manner. I eliminated many of the bit sizes, discontinued unprofitable products and stepped up the advertising campaign.

As a result, the Hughes Tool Company once again dominated the market, accounting for 80 percent of the drilling-bit business. Profits mounted to a phenomenal 51 percent of the sales dollar.

Profits skyrocketed. The biggest annual profit of Toolco's previous history had been $6,000,000. After the reconversion, the return rose to $9,000,000, then $13,000,000, then $22,000,000, then $29,000,000, then $35,000,000.

Then the Toolco profits soared into the stratosphere: $60,000,000 for three straight years. And with no unusual advance in gross!

In the eight years following changes at the Hughes Tool Company, it poured out $285,000,000 in profits. Howard's cup runneth over.

He was scarcely aware of what was going on with Hughes Tool. I never even consulted him about establishing plants in Ireland and West Germany after World War II. A year or two after it had been accomplished, he said to me: "What's this I hear about our having factories in Europe?"

"That's correct, Howard," I said.

"But why?"

"Two reasons: Labor costs are cheaper over there; transportation costs are much less to our customers in Arabia and Russia."

He seemed pleased at the development and didn't question the fact that he hadn't been consulted. I had good reason for not consulting him: it would have taken months or years for him to give me a yes or no.

The upturn in Toolco profits proved a pivotal point in

Howard's fortune. If the tool company had continued making profits at a fixed rate of $6,000,000 or less, he could never have taken the giant financial strides that he made in the following decade. He would have run out of money to maintain Hughes Aircraft and TWA, just as he had been forced out of movie production in the early 1930s.

But with Toolco pouring forth gold, he could lavish millions on the aircraft and airline operations until they also began to prove winning enterprises.

Howard was now on his way to becoming a billionaire. Was he grateful?

He responded in typical fashion: "Noah, you're a genius. Now, here's what I want you to do next. . . ."

CHAPTER TWENTY-NINE

The F-11: Sequel

Howard was determined to vindicate the F-11. Although his contract had been cut from a hundred to three of the air reconnaissance planes, he continued to lavish money on the F-11's development. The plane almost killed him.

The Hughes Aircraft engineers had experimented with a new propeller technique—two sets of double counter-rotating propellers with four blades on each. It was believed that greater speed could be achieved with the eight blades on each side of the airplane.

On July 7, 1946, the new technique was ready to be tested. Howard had a rather romantic attitude about testing his own planes, and he insisted on taking the F-11 up for its first flight. After a few hours of taxiing the plane up and down the Culver City runway, he felt confident enough to attempt a flight.

The F-11 soared off beautifully, clocking more than four hundred miles per hour, an excellent speed for that era of aviation history. Then trouble developed.

Howard felt the plane pulling inexorably to the right. No amount of manipulation of the controls could stop the drift. The F-11 was losing speed and altitude rapidly, and he couldn't turn left because the starboard motor was powerless. The homes of Beverly Hills were drawing closer and closer. He saw the wide green fairways of the Los Angeles Country Club and tried to steer the plane in that direction.

He didn't make it. The landing gear sliced into the roof of one house and one wing sheared off a telephone pole.

Then the plane struck 808 Whittier Drive. Both the house and plane burst into flames with the impact. A Marine sergeant who was visiting nearby rushed to the scene and pulled Howard from under the wreckage. Howard told him there was no one else in the plane.

"Was anyone hurt in the crash?" Howard asked. Miraculously, no one was.

Howard was rushed to Good Samaritan Hospital, where his personal physician, Verne Mason, examined him. The injuries were severe: nine broken ribs, broken collarbone, possible broken nose, severe head cuts, bad burns on the left hand, chest, and buttock, bruises and cuts all over his body. His left lung collapsed and filled with blood.

When the crash occurred, I was en route from New York to Houston by automobile. I had stopped in Hot Springs, Arkansas, and that's where Dr. Mason reached me.

"What do you think his chances of survival are?" I asked.

"I would say about fifty-fifty," Dr. Mason told me.

"Would you ask Howard if he would like me to come out there?"

Dr. Mason called back later and said that Howard had said, "Tell Noah not to come here. Tell him just to keep on running things."

I drove on to Houston, then decided I should fly out to California. I made no attempt to see him, because the hospital had indicated no visitors would be allowed. Then Howard's favorite aunt, Mrs. Annette Lummis, arrived from Houston and came to see me in my office.

"I tried to see poor Howard, but I couldn't get inside," she told me. "Can you help me?"

I went to the Good Samaritan with her, and I sent a note to Howard saying that Mrs. Lummis was there and she would just like to put her head in the door and tell him, "Hello, Howard, I love you."

The answer came back: "No."

Now I found myself caught in the middle. Mrs. Lummis accused me of poisoning Howard's mind against his relatives—she hadn't forgotten her suspicions when Howard had made his disappearance in 1944.

I composed another note to Howard. This time I told him: "Howard, you are putting me in a very embarrassing position. Your aunt charges that I have come between you and your relatives to such an extent that you no longer are willing to see them. While this is not important to me, it apparently means a great deal to your family. I think it would be a fine gesture if you would allow your aunt to look in your room just long enough to say hello."

I showed the note to Mrs. Lummis, and she approved it. But the answer from Howard was the same: No.

Next, Dr. Fred Lummis came from Houston. He was the husband of Howard's aunt, a distinguished, European-trained physician. He requested permission to examine Howard. Same answer.

Before returning to Houston, Dr. Lummis visited my office and sympathized: "Now I can better understand your problems in dealing with Hughes. I don't understand him at all!"

Howard passed the critical stage and started on the way to recovery. He did it the hard way—no sleeping pills, no opiates of any kind. He was an amazing man in that respect. Even though the pain was excruciating from the burns, fractures, cuts, and bruises, he refused anything to kill the pain. If he was going to die, he was going out conscious, with full awareness of what was happening to him.

An amazing man—a hypochondriac, terrified by germs, yet unwilling to submit to a painkiller. Pain seemed to hold no terror for him. I remember once when he was married to Ella and he suffered a severe cold. His doctor gave him an injection every morning to combat the cold. One day the doctor's assistant arrived for the injection and readied the hypodermic needle. Howard grabbed it from him and said, "What good does it do just putting the needle under my skin? It'll never get in the bloodstream." So he jammed the needle an inch into the fleshy part of his arm. The next morning he had a swelling the size of an egg.

Characteristically, Howard sought a mechanical means to escape the pain of his plane injuries.

Every time he made the slightest move in bed, Howard suffered the pangs of hell. He figured there must have been a way to ease such painful movements, and he imparted his wish to Glen Odekirk: "Build me a bed that will permit me to move part of my body without disturbing the whole bed."

Glen rushed back to Hughes Aircraft and went to work with the engineers. Within twenty-four hours they came up with a special design, a mattress divided into thirty-two separate squares, each operating independently by means of a switchboard. The bed designers thought of everything—they even devised a special gap to accommodate a bed pan.

Despite one relapse Howard began to recover. His famous Hollywood friends came to visit him, and wellwishers sent messages from all over the world. One of them was President Truman, who sent a medal that Congress had voted for Howard because of his around-the-world flight. Howard had declined to go to the White House to collect the medal, and he might never have received it if he hadn't crashed.

Howard grew impatient with the hospital life and walked out, despite orders by the doctors to remain longer. He refused to submit to surgery that would have corrected the webbing caused by burns to his left hand. Because of his stubbornness, he would go through the rest of his life being unable to play golf or otherwise make normal use of his left hand.

After he recovered his health, Howard was intent on determining what had gone wrong in the F-11 test. He decided that the fault lay in the right propellers; despite a proper reading on the gauges their counter-rotating blades —an innovation at the time—had malfunctioned, with the resultant loss of power.

Howard filed a claim against the Hamilton-Standard Division of United Aircraft, threatening suit if a claim was not paid. The company settled for $175,000, and Howard was particularly proud that the payment came in the settlement of personal injury; thus it was his own tax-free money, not a settlement to Hughes Aircraft.

The payoff for the crash ended Howard's interest in the F-11. He had created three of the planes—one was a static test model that went to the air force, one burned in a hangar fire, and the other crashed and was destroyed in Beverly Hills. I never heard Howard mention the F-11 again.

Aftermath:

The man who rescued Howard from the flaming wreckage on Whittier Drive captured the admiration of the nation. He was Marine Sergeant Willian Lloyd Durkan. Howard's reaction to Durkan's heroism was interesting.

Durkan was awarded $200 a month, presumably for his lifetime. For some reason or other, Howard urged the Marine to remain in the service. I was present when Howard argued with him: "You must serve out your full enlistment with the Marines. It's your duty to your country. Then, when you come out of the service, I'll establish you in any line of business that you select."

The sergeant followed Howard's advice. Years later, Durkan emerged from his tour of duty with the Marines. He telephoned me to say: "Mr. Dietrich, you remember the agreement I had with Hughes?"

"Yes, I remember," I said.

"Well, it was just an oral agreement, but he promised to set me up in business. Well, now I'm out of the Marines; I put in my full thirty years. I'm ready to start in with my own business now. I'm still getting the two hundred a month, but I would need some more to start something going."

"Have you tried to reach Mr. Hughes?" I asked.

"That's just it," he said. "I *have* tried. But his secretary tells me that even she can't reach him. I was hoping that maybe you could help me."

I had to tell him that my own relationship with Howard Hughes had been severed. There was nothing I could do to help him.

CHAPTER THIRTY

Adventure in Washington

To millions of Americans, it seemed just like the Frank Capra movie *Mr. Smith Goes to Washington*—the lean, handsome young man tilting against the corrupt Establishment of the United States Senate. In this case, the protagonist was not Jimmy Stewart but the barefoot millionaire, Howard Hughes.

To understand the events, you must have a picture of the times. It was 1947, the era of the 80th Congress. The one that Harry Truman ran against in 1948, and won.

But things looked mighty good for the Republicans in 1947. They had captured control of Congress for the first time in two decades, and they were hellbent to win the White House. Having been out of power for so long, some of the Republican leaders were over-eager to discredit the Democrats in order to further their own cause.

One such Republican was Senator Owen Brewster of Maine. He had worked his way up the political ladder from state assemblyman and senator to governor of Maine, then member of the House of Representatives. In 1947 he was serving his second term in the United States Senate. He had his eyes set on becoming the Republican nominee for Vice-President in 1948. An ambitious man. But in the end, a foolish one.

Brewster had taken over as chairman of the Special Committee to Investigate the National Defense Program, presiding in the same position that had propelled Harry Truman to national prominence. It could do the same for him, Brewster believed. He needed big game to give the press something to write about. What better prospect than Howard Hughes?

Howard presented a most attractive target. He was world famous, a fabulous figure who evoked headlines whatever he did. He had entered into $90,000,000 worth of contracts for airplanes that had never been delivered. Furthermore, one of those contracts had been recommended by Elliott Roosevelt, son of the late President.

The first inkling we had of an investigation came when the Committee's Chief Assistant Counsel, Francis D. Flanagan, arrived in California. He was armed with subpoenas for the Hughes records. This, of course, infuriated Howard. He wanted no one, congressional investigator or otherwise, snooping around company records.

I was as upset as Howard over this intrusion on corporate policies. I told Flanagan: "Why do you investigate Hughes aircraft? He had only ninety million dollars' worth of war contract. Why don't you go after General Motors or General Electric or Chrysler? They had billions of dollars' worth of contracts."

Flanagan was tight-lipped about his mission: "I'm here to investigate Hughes."

"Yes, and I know why," I told him. "You Republicans are out to destroy the Roosevelt family, and you figure you can do it through Howard Hughes. This is a scattergun attempt, and I don't like it one goddam bit."

Of course my indignation made no impression on Flanagan, who was simply an errand boy for Owen Brewster. And Owen Brewster was simply an errand boy for Juan Trippe and Pan American Airways.

There wasn't much secret about that. Senator Brewster had been bald-faced in his advocacy of Pan American. He had been the airline's number-one spokesman in the Senate and had done Juan Trippe's bidding in introducing the one-carrier bill. That was a piece of legislation designed to give Pan American a monopoly for overseas travel, just as Air France, Lufthansa, and BOAC enjoyed exclusive contracts on air travel out of France, Germany, and England.

The Brewster Bill struck at the heart of TWA's plans to

extend its routes around the world. Howard Hughes wouldn't stand for that.

In some matters, Howard could teach a few lessons to the master of manipulation, Machiavelli himself.

Howard's first offensive was to open negotiations with Trippe, the head man of Pan American, for a merger with TWA. Trippe responded to the proposal. He flew in his private plane to Palm Springs for a rendezvous. Howard made the trip in his own plane, and I came from Houston in mine.

We met in a private house that Howard had rented in the desert specifically for the negotiation. Howard was extremely cordial to Trippe, even though he hated Trippe's guts for his efforts to monopolize overseas air travel for Pan American. The talks continued into the evening of the first day and were resumed on the morning of the next day.

As far as Trippe was concerned, it seemed like an honest negotiation for the merger of two great airlines. Howard had no such thought in mind. He was simply buying time to plot his strategy against the Brewster-sponsored legislation to freeze TWA out of the overseas market.

I continued the negotiations with Trippe in New York. The Pan American boss and I had more meetings at my hotel in Manhattan, and we went so far as to exchange balance sheets of our two airlines. But then it became apparent to Trippe that Hughes had no real intention of merging. Brewster scheduled his inquisition.

I went to Washington for a series of meetings with those who were conducting the investigation. The chief counsel was William P. Rogers, later to become Richard Nixon's Secretary of State. I was meeting in Rogers' office one day, going over Howard's bank statements, which had been subpoenaed for the Committee. As we were talking, Senator Brewster stuck his head in the door, and he inquired what we were doing.

When Rogers explained that we were examining Hughes' bank records, Brewster asked, "Do you call that compliance?"

Rogers spoke right up to him: "Senator, I call that compliance." Brewster quickly departed.

Senator Homer Ferguson, a Republican of Michigan, was designated subchairman of the hearings, and I had meetings with him before the proceedings. When we first met, he seemed impressed with my grasp of the legal aspects, and he said, "You're a lawyer, Mr. Dietrich?"

I guess I must have seemed like one; Howard was forever involved in litigation of one kind or another, so I had to educate myself. "No, I'm not a lawyer," I told the senator. "In fact, I don't want to be a lawyer—I don't even want to be a senator."

Senator Ferguson was amused by this, and we got along well. He asked me if I could assure the presence of Johnny Meyer. I had some misgivings about allowing Johnny to testify, but I realized that it would have been an admission of guilt to attempt to hide him.

"Mr. Meyer is in Cannes," I said, "but I'll try to get him back here."

I cabled Johnny to return, and I met him in New York before he went on to Washington. I wanted to be sure that Johnny did not trap himself—and the Hughes organization—on the stand. With my CPA mind, I had insisted that Johnny account for every expenditure in his pursuit of favor for Hughes Aircraft.

"Johnny, be sure to make one thing plain before you testify," I said. "Tell them that you often made up your expense accounts a month or six weeks later, so that you might be sketchy about what happened when. In that way, you can't be trapped on placing people in places where they might not have been."

Meyer followed my advice when he appeared before the Senate committee in that summer of 1947. That helped save his skin. But no amount of backtracking could prevent the damaging testimony that was exacted from Johnny Meyer.

Johnny was fair game for the Senate head-hunters. His testimony provided headlines galore about wild parties and wicked women and their contributions in securing war contracts for the Hughes interests.

Senator Ferguson reviewed Johnny's expense accounts before the watching nation. Here is some of the testimony:

Q. Now, what is your next item?

A. The next item is Saturday night. It says, "Some girls at hotel late." They obviously didn't have dinner.

Q. How much did you pay?

A. Fifty dollars.

Q. What do you mean, "They didn't have dinner" when you paid fifty dollars?

A. I mean they probably joined us late at the Statler.

Q. How do you account for the fifty dollars?

A. Probably some presents.

Q. What does this have to do with the production of aircraft?

A. I felt this was a Hughes Aircraft item, so I charged it that way.

Q. Now, was this entertainment for Colonel Roosevelt and the party you had? Is that why you charged it?

A. Yes.

Ferguson went on to question Johnny about some expenses involving Faye Emerson.

Q. Next item.

A. That afternoon, some nylon hose that I bought Miss Emerson as a present—one hundred and thirty-two dollars.

Q. And the next item?

A. Cash to travel home—twenty dollars.

Q. Now can you tell me why you were charging up to Hughes Aircraft Company one hundred and thirty-two dollars for nylon hose for Miss Emerson and twenty dollars to go home?

A. Because she had been very charming.

Q. Very charming?

A. Girls are very pleasant.

Q. What has that to do with aircraft production?

A. They just went along. Every company in the business did it. We were no different.

The tabloids spread the Meyer testimony over their front pages, and both Howard and I were appalled at the impression which it created in the minds of the American public.

Hughes Aircraft was made to seem like a tawdry operation which used free booze and other inducements to seek government contracts.

Howard's first inclination was to run for cover. He had become a master at the art of convenient disappearance, and he intended to duck out of sight until the headline-hunting expedition was over. I convinced him that such a course would be the worst possible public relations—an admission of guilt. It would be far better for him to present his own case to the public in a confrontation with the senators.

He took my advice and flew from California to Washington in a B-23 he piloted all night. He arrived exhausted, wearing his butler's coat, a size or two small for him, and carrying an extra shirt in a cardboard box. He had promised to appear before the Committee at ten that morning, but he told me, "Noah, I've got to get some rest; ask them to postpone the hearing until the afternoon."

That morning I made the request for postponement, and it was granted. Then I went to a department store and bought some fresh shirts and ties for Howard to wear, and I returned to rouse him at the Carlton Hotel.

I couldn't wake him up. I rang the doorbell to his suite, which consisted of a parlor with a bedroom on each side. No answer. I pounded on the door. Nothing happened. I went to the telephone and called him, but there was no reply.

Now I was getting worried. I summoned the hotel manager, and he brought along the house detective and the housekeeper. They unlocked the door, but Howard had attached the chain lock inside. I called inside, but Howard didn't respond.

As the hotel employees conferred on the next move, I said, "Get me a coat hanger." The housekeeper provided one, and I twisted it and pushed it inside the door to release the chain lock. I hurried to Howard's bedroom and found him lying still. For a moment I was fearful that he was dead. Finally I was able to rouse him. The combination of his deafness and being exhausted had prevented me from waking him before.

Howard arrived an hour late for his 1 o'clock appointment with the Committee. Then he performed in splendid style, taking over the proceedings with a sureness that astonished everyone, including me.

He refused to be trapped over the damaging testimony by Johnny Meyer concerning the buying of favors.

"All the aircraft companies were doing the same thing," Howard insisted. "I believe Meyer patterned his work after what he saw in the other companies. It certainly did not seem fair for all of my competitors to entertain while I sat back and ignored the government and its officials.

"If you can pass a law that no one can entertain army officers and you can enforce it, I'll be glad to abide by it. I never wanted to bother with it. If you can get the others to do business that way, I'll be glad to do so, too."

Next, Howard adopted the shrewdest of techniques: he turned his defense into an attack—on Senator Owen Brewster.

While he was buying time to combat the one-carrier overseas airline bill, he had not only bargained for the phony merger with Pan American; he also had courted the bill's promoter, Senator Brewster.

"I specifically charge," Howard declared in the floodlighted hearing, "that during luncheon at the Mayflower Hotel in Washington in the week beginning February 10, 1947, in the suite of Senator Brewster, that the senator told me in so many words that if I would agree to merge TWA with Pan Am and go along with this community airline bill, there would be no further hearing in this matter."

Brewster, expectably, responded with apoplectic indignation. He denied making any such proposal. That meant that either he or Howard Hughes was a liar. Reporters dispatched reams of copy about this confrontation.

After much debate Chairman Ferguson permitted Howard to submit a series of questions to Senator Brewster. At first Brewster parried the questions with the ease of an experienced parliamentarian. But then the going got rougher.

Brewster admitted that he had discussed the single-carrier bill with Hughes, that he had accepted air transportation from Pan American and from TWA, that he had vacationed at the Florida home of a Pan American vice-president. Brewster's answers became less cool. I watched him become flustered and frantic, as if he could see his dream of the vice-presidency vanish before his eyes.

After Brewster stepped down from the witness stand, Howard had his turn to testify. He summed up his opinion of his opponent: "I understand that Senator Brewster has a reputation for being a clever, resourceful, and a terrific public speaker, a man who can hold an audience in the palm of his hand, and that he has a reputation of being one of the greatest trick-shot artists in Washington, one of the most high powers behind the scenes."

Then Howard turned the spotlight on himself: "Now let us examine my reputation. I am supposed to be many things which are not complimentary. I am supposed to be capricious. I am called a playboy. I have been called eccentric, but I do not believe I have the reputation of being a liar. As far as I know in twenty-three years, up to yesterday, no one has ever questioned my word. In fact, I believe I have the reputation in that respect which most Texans consider important. That is to say, if I may use a corny phrase, I believe most people consider my word to be my bond."

I was sitting beside Howard when he made this speech, and I had to wince. I suddenly realized why the movies that Howard personally supervised always failed: he had a fondness for corn.

As the proceedings continued, it seemed apparent that Howard had the upper hand. He had succeeded in calling Brewster a liar and making it stick. Senator Ferguson struggled valiantly to rescue his colleague, but it wouldn't work. Like a senatorial Captain Queeg, Brewster had convicted himself with his own testimony. Howard brushed off attempts to return to the real purpose of the hearing: to investigate his performance on war contracts. It was a masterful performance.

The climax of Howard's defiance of his inquisitors came when Senator Ferguson struggled to get Johnny Meyer back for testimony. Johnny's subpoena had expired, and we hustled him off to Europe to get him away from the clutches of the senators.

"Where *is* Johnny Meyer?" Senator Ferguson demanded.

"I don't know where he is," Howard replied.

The senator persisted, and Howard told him, "I have twenty-eight thousand employees, and I can't know where all of them are all of the time."

"Do you know where Meyer is?" Ferguson continued. "No."

"Will you see that he is here by two P.M.?"

"I don't know that I will. Just to put him up here on the stand beside me and make a publicity show. My company has been inconvenienced just about enough. I brought Meyer here twice. You had time for unlimited questioning."

"The chair feels that as president of the company you should know where Meyer is. I must warn you of possible contempt. Give me your answer to the preceding question." Ferguson was becoming red-faced and petulant.

"I don't remember," Howard answered blithely.

"I just asked you what your answer was."

"I don't remember. Get it off the record."

"Will you bring Mr. Meyer in here at two P.M.?" the Senator was furious.

"No," Howard said quietly. "No, I don't think I will."

The audience loved that moment. So did newspaper readers from coast to coast. Even though Howard Hughes was a rich and powerful man, he symbolized the little man defying entrenched, corrupt authority. He had fought City Hall—and won.

I had also been summoned to appear before the Senate committee to answer questions concerning financial matters. On the evening before I was to testify, Howard and I had a conference in his suite at the Carlton Hotel. We started talking in his parlor, but then he shook his head and said, "Let's go in here."

He led me into the bathroom and began again. Then he put his finger to his lips.

"They probably have the bathroom bugged, Noah," he said. "They could easily put a microphone in that ventilator shaft. We'd better go out and drive around in a car while we talk."

And so we drove through the darkened streets of Washington as we discussed the strategy for the rest of the hearings. Howard knew that I was scheduled to testify about certain expenses for the company, and he urged me to bend the facts so the company would look better.

I refused. "Howard, I might have a convenient memory, so that I can fail to remember certain things," I said, "but I won't lie for anybody."

At the time, I was amused by Howard's insistence on secrecy in our conversations. As it turned out, he was correct. Both his room at the Carlton and mine at the Mayflower Hotel had been bugged by a police detective, who had been paid a thousand dollars for the job. Paid by whom? There could be little doubt that various interested parties were behind this bugging.

The hearings of the Special Committee to Investigate the National Defense Program continued through the summer of 1947, but the rest was anti-climax. Senator Brewster had aimed at the reputation of Howard Hughes, but in the end it was Brewster's own reputation that had been damaged. Yet he had little to fear. He had been elected in November of 1946, hence he had five more years before facing the voters of Maine once again.

The only person who really got hurt in the investigation was General Bennett Meyers.

He was a pitiable figure, a man who had been pushed into a position far beyond his capabilities and one who allowed his own avarice to upset his judgment. It was no secret that Howard Hughes had used him, buying him with favors and holding out promises of hiring him to command Hughes Aircraft. The promises proved to be hollow, and Meyers suffered disillusionment.

Before the Senate hearings, I met with Benny in New York. He was in an agitated state, seeking fulfillment of Howard's pledges of employment.

"He promised me a contract, and I want it!" the general insisted.

"Benny, we're going into an investigation of the Hughes

Aircraft contracts with the government," I reasoned. "The worst thing in the world would be for you to be on our payroll during all the questioning."

I convinced him to hold off on his demand, knowing all the while that Howard had no intention of hiring Benny Meyers in any capacity. That was a problem we never had to face. Out of the Senate hearings came a charge that General Meyers had accepted a payoff from a subcontractor. Benny was tried and convicted. He was sentenced to seven years in the federal penitentiary.

Another Hughes sequel.

Howard never forgets an enemy. For five years he waited for the chance to get back at his opponent, Owen Brewster. Then in 1952 Brewster came up for reelection as senator from Maine. His principal opponent was Frederick Payne, a newspaper publisher.

"Give Payne whatever he needs," Howard instructed, "and the hell with what it costs."

Howard had hired the Carl Byoir publicity agency, largely to suppress newspaper and magazine articles that were planned about him. The Byoir agency also performed other functions. Such as twice transporting $30,000 to the state of Maine, to be used for the candidacy of Frederick Payne. Payne was also supplied copious information about the nefarious activities of Owen Brewster.

Maine is not a large state, and $60,000 supplied a lot of clout in a political campaign. Billboards for Payne appeared all over, and the radio blared forth commercials for the candidate.

Owen Brewster, who had once believed that he had a fine chance to capture the nomination for Vice-President, was. defeated at the polls. His long political career had ended, because of the long memory and unlimited funds of Howard Hughes.

CHAPTER THIRTY-ONE

The Flying Boat: Sequel

I can only tell you that I designed every nut and bolt that went into this airplane. I designed this ship to a greater degree than any one man has ever designed any of the recent large airplanes, down to one-half the size. . . . If the flying boat fails to fly, I will probably exile myself from this country. I have put the sweat of my life into this thing, and seven million, two hundred thousand dollars of my own money. My reputation is wrapped up in it. I have stated that if it fails to fly, I will leave the country. And I mean it.

This was Howard's valedictory at the end of the Congressional hearings. It was an expensive piece of theatrics.

When Howard returned from Washington, he applied himself to the Hercules like a man possessed. Expense meant nothing; he assigned around-the-clock crews to the task of getting the flying boat ready for tests.

Finally, on November 1, 1947, he felt the time had come.

Howard conducted the Hercules test as he did a premiere of one of his movies. Dozens of newspaper writers were flown to Los Angeles at his expense and entertained like visiting dignitaries. The wine flowed freely, and starlets mingled with the visitors.

There could be no doubt that Howard himself would be at the helm for the test. The water at Long Beach was choppy that day, and he announced the first run would probably not go over forty miles per hour. He gave the visitors a three-mile voyage across the harbor, then returned to the dock for the visitors to get off.

Howard took the huge plane back to the harbor. When he began his final taxiing run, observers noticed that he was picking up speed. The Hercules hurtled through the water at one hundred miles per hour, then Howard opened the throttles and the plane rose majestically into the air.

The Hercules climbed to seventy feet, then Howard eased it downward and onto the water. He had flown the plane for slightly over a mile, just long enough for photographs to be taken for the front pages of the world's newspapers.

It might have been the greatest moment in Howard's life. He had vindicated his honor, his technical know-how. He had smitten his enemies, the venal politicians of Washington, the hostile generals of the Hate Howard Hughes Club. He had proved himself to be not an eccentric playboy, but a lonely dreamer who had made the world's largest plane fly.

If only he had let it go at that!

But no. He had to press on with the Hercules, pouring his money into a plane that was already obsolescent when it made its brief flight—nobody wanted a plywood airplane, of any size.

Howard wouldn't be dissuaded. He built a permanent hangar at Long Beach and kept a crew of 300 on the project. The government owned the plane—and still does—but no further funds were forthcoming. He leased the Hercules for $800 a month on the excuse that he was using it for research.

My only connection with the Hercules was to pay the bills. Before long, the bills came to more than $3,000,000 a year. The expense seemed senseless to me. Three million dollars per year with no possible way to recover the investment. It was a big drain on the Hughes treasury; only the immense profits of the tool company could accommodate such an expense.

Howard wouldn't talk about the plane. His other associates realized how touchy he was about it, and they prudently overlooked the subject. But it was my duty to face Howard with harsh facts.

One day I asked him, "When do you plan to make the final test flight of the plane?"

"I don't know," he replied. "I hesitate to try to fly it in a real test flight."

"Howard, this plane is costing you three million dollars a year. How on earth do you expect to recover that money?"

"I don't know," he shrugged. "I haven't thought about that."

It was useless to point out that other plane manufacturers were already pushing into the jet era, designing swept-wing planes that would fly several hundred miles per hour. Compared to them, the Hercules was a leviathan Model T Ford—a plywood propeller-driven plane that could fly only 180 miles per hour at top speed.

Even though the Hercules contained no secrets that a competitor would want to steal, Howard insisted on keeping the project as guarded as an atom-bomb plant. Over the years he went to fantastic lengths to keep the flying boat under wraps.

He paid a Long Beach lawyer $35,000 to negotiate an unprecedented lease with the city for the hangar site. It was a watertight contract that forbade anyone, even the members of the City Council who approved the lease, from entering the hangar.

The lease was tested when a fire inspector arrived at the hangar for a routine inspection of the property. He was given the bum's rush by the Hughes guards. The Long Beach Fire Chief was enraged; no one had ever challenged his jurisdiction before. A new city attorney ventured the opinion that the lease was invalid, because it deprived the fire department of its rights under the city charter. A controversy raged in Long Beach, but in the end Howard Hughes prevailed. He kept his lease, and the fire inspectors didn't set foot in the hangar.

The Hughes dictum against visitors ran headlong into an insurance problem that could have cost Howard $200,000.

A fire broke out in the hangar. Fortunately the hangar crew was able to extinguish the blaze, but not before a considerable amount of damage had been done to the Hercules. When Howard assessed the damage, he insisted that the insurance company pay. But he would not permit the company's inspector to review the damage.

It was an impasse, which I resolved by a curious coincidence of names. The name of the inspector happened to be George Strake. A longtime and valued customer of the Hughes Tool Company was a Houston oil man who also bore the name of George Strake. He was coming to California on vacation.

I called Howard and told him, "George Strake is coming to town, Howard, and he wants to see the flying boat."

"He does, huh?" Howard said. "Well, I guess it's all right, as long as he doesn't make a detailed inspection of the boat."

So he arranged a pass for George Strake to enter the sacred precincts of the Hercules hangar. The insurance man made his inspection, and we were able to collect the $200,000 due for fire damage.

Howard went to great lengths and considerable expense to keep the Hercules out of the nation's press. Every so often a writer would arrive from the East with an assignment to write an article on "Whatever Happened to Howard Hughes' Spruce Goose?" That's when the Carl Byoir anti-publicity agents would swing into action.

The writer was wined and dined and dazzled with passes on TWA. When he was in a particularly pliant mood, he was told: "Nobody wants to read about that flying boat—it's old stuff." Many a writer fell for that line.

Others did not. For the recalcitrant ones, another approach was employed. The editor or publisher of the magazine or newspaper was approached with the argument that Mr. Hughes would be greatly displeased to read an article about his pet project. There were many avenues of persuasion. I recall one publisher who had assigned a flying boat article; he also owned a movie magazine which had been sued for libel by a famous actress who had once been a Hughes sweetheart. The libel action was dropped, and the flying boat article was quietly shelved.

Through the efforts of the Hughes "*sup*press" agents, the flying boat was largely forgotten by the public until September 17, 1953. On that day I received a telephone call from the Long Beach hangar. The supervisor was near-hysterical, and he was shouting something about a disaster. I calmed him down, and he told me what had happened.

"A barge was being pulled past the hangar, and it broke loose," he told me. "It swung out of control, hitting the cofferdam outside the hangar. Water poured in, and the plane is a shambles. It's terrible, Mr. Dietrich. The hull, the stabilizers, the ailerons, the wings, and the tail are all crushed. The whole hangar is filled with water and mud five feet deep."

I listened to his sad tale, and my heart danced. At last, a way to escape the crushing expense of the flying whale!

I telephoned Howard at the Beverly Hills Hotel and told him I was coming over. On my way, I picked up an afternoon paper with the blaring headline: "GIANT HUGHES PLANE TOTAL LOSS."

Presenting the headline to Howard, I made my pitch: "This is the best possible thing that could happen, Howard. You can junk the plane now, and nobody could possibly criticize you or raise any questions as to why it doesn't fly."

"Junk it, hell!" Howard responded. "I'm going to repair it. I'm going to sue the hell out of Long Beach and get enough money to repair the plane the way it was."

My hopes were dashed. Howard was prepared to begin another ruinous round of monumental expense.

He filed suit for $12,000,000 against the city of Long Beach, even though the errant barge had been privately owned. The enormous suit angered the city fathers of Long Beach, who were already perturbed by Howard's high-handed ways. Howard wouldn't even allow city inspectors into the hangar to inspect the damage he claimed.

Since Howard was inaccessible, I bore the brunt of the

civic wrath. Nothing I could say would placate the enraged politicians. They now were plotting to retaliate by pulling Howard's lease out from under him. It was soon due for renewal.

A member of the Harbor Commission telephoned me to report in an icy manner: "I would appreciate it if you would notify Mr. Hughes that he will have a hell of a time getting his lease renewed. The moment it expires, out go his hangar and his big wooden plane."

"I'll give him the message," I said.

"And you can tell him that I hope he has to come down here personally and carry it out on his back."

I told Howard what the man had said. He was more resolved than ever. If he could take on the United States Senate—and win, he certainly wasn't going to fear the city of Long Beach.

His counterattack showed Howard Hughes at his most devious. He knew that Long Beach had been embroiled for years in a controversy with the State of California over the tideland oil pools that lay beneath the harbor. Hundreds of millions of dollars in royalties were involved in the lengthy dispute. At last a formula was devised to make a division of the funds between Long Beach and the state. The solution seemed to please everyone, and the legislation was about to go through the Senate and Assembly in Sacramento.

Howard summoned his two high-paid lobbyists.

"Get up to Sacramento and kick Long Beach in the ass on that tideland oil settlement," he ordered.

The lobbyists started working their wiles. They had used Hughes' money to pay the campaign bills for many of the assemblymen and senators. The underpaid legislators were beholden to Hughes, and overnight the tidelands bill began to grind to a halt.

The Long Beach interests panicked. After years of trying, they had finally arrived within reaching distance of those oil millions. Now a petulant millionaire was throwing a wrench in the legislative process.

Truce was called. Long Beach granted a ten-year lease

to Howard Hughes for his Hercules. In return, Howard dropped his $12,000,000 suit against the city and settled for a half-million. And the tidelands bill sailed through the Legislature. Thus Long Beach was granted millions to play with. Out of the windfall came another enormous white elephant, which ended up as next-door neighbor to the Spruce Goose. I refer to the *Queen Mary*.

A nice irony, that. The *Queen Mary* cost the City of Long Beach $50,000,000 and its berthmate has taken 50 of Howard Hughes' millions. But at least Long Beach has a chance of recovering some of its investment through tourist and convention trade. How can Howard recoup any of his money?

Over the years I have been asked many, many times what Howard had in mind for the flying boat. Why did he continue pouring money into it?

The Hercules has been the source of innumerable rumors. Howard was going to use the plane in a movie. He was going to equip it with an atomic reactor. He was going to convert it into a swept-wing jet.

As far as I know, he never had any of those plans in mind. Or any other plan.

Howard never explained why he kept on pouring a fortune into the useless enterprise. He rarely explained any of the things he did. His attitude was always the same: "It's my money, and what I do with it is my business, nobody else's."

I believe that in the early years he found himself in a dilemma. He had sworn before God and everybody that he would leave the country if the Hercules didn't fly. Yet he was frightened that the plane was so unsafe that it would prove to be his own coffin. So he kept the whole thing in limbo, neither terminating the project—which would have been an admission of defeat and denial of his vow to leave the country—nor trying to complete it—which might mean his own demise.

Another element comes into play here.

As a longtime observer of the Hughes phenomenon, I have developed a theory which might be called Dietrich's

Law. It is simply this: *Any order by Howard Hughes must continue to be carried out until it is countermanded by Howard Hughes—and it won't be.*

Sounds ridiculous, doesn't it? Yet I have seen it happen over and over again in the years since I left Howard. For instance, he gave orders that the Sikorsky amphibian, the one he crashed into Lake Mead and rebuilt, remain at Houston until he gave orders for its disposal. The orders never came, and the Sikorsky sits in Texas year after year.

There have been two B-25s, a Convair, and an A-20 at Santa Monica Airport under the same ukase. They remain under guard, rusting away in the California weather. There are other planes at an airport across from San Francisco. Howard has forgotten them, along with automobiles under the same orders. No one in the Hughes organization has the nerve to dispose of the unused planes and cars, and so millions of dollars of equipment go to waste.

The same with the Hercules.

I am dead certain that no one with access to Hughes has mentioned the Sikorsky plane to him in years and years. Dietrich's Law prevails. Work will continue on the Hercules until Howard Hughes countermands the order.

CHAPTER THIRTY-TWO

Howard in His Forties

The Washington adventure had a profound affect on Howard's behavior. The confirmation that our hotel rooms had been bugged made him even more secretive than he had been before.

"I don't want anyone spying on me," he said, and he took extreme precautions to assure his complete privacy. One of his devices was to purchase twenty Chevrolets.

"Why on earth would you want twenty Chevies?" I asked him.

"Simple," he replied. "I'm going to use them as my personal cars. But I'll use a different one every day. Nobody would be able to bug twenty different cars—it's impractical. And they'll never know which car I'm going to choose."

Howard also figured that the modest Chevrolets would permit him to travel incognito.

One Christmas he gave me a magnificent Mercedes Benz 300 SL as a present. When I first drove him in it, he seemed as delighted as he had been with his old Duesenberg, the one that I saved from Multicolor creditors.

"This is one hell of a car, Noah," he enthused. "Get me one just like it tomorrow."

He telephoned me that evening with a change of plans.

"Don't buy me a Mercedes, Noah," he said. "I've been thinking it over, and it's not such a hot idea. If I drove one around town, everybody would say, 'There goes Howard Hughes!' "

Following the Washington hearings, Howard set up the

famous message center at 7000 Romaine. He never visited there, but he insisted on around-the-clock staffing of the Romaine headquarters. The purpose: to satisfy his desires at any hour of the day or night.

If Howard wanted a steak at 4 A.M., the message center would get it for him. If he desired to speak to a movie actress at the Cannes Film Festival, the call was put through. Any whim could be satisfied.

The message center required trained, loyal personnel. For his secretary he had chosen Nadine Henley, a calm, quiet, efficient woman who had worked for one of the Hughes Aircraft engineers with whom Howard had worked closely. Howard admired her easy, effective manner, and he transferred her from the engineer's office to his own. Nadine performed ably until the rigors of employment with an eccentric boss got to her. She quit and retired to Arizona. Howard insisted that I pursue her and use all my persuasion to convince her to return: I managed to do so.

The early years of the 7000 Romaine message center brought the Advent of the Mormons.

"I think Mormons as a whole have the most integrity of any group of people in the country," Howard told me. "They take care of their own people, and they won't accept help from charity or the government. And I like the idea that they don't drink liquor. You can trust them."

Howard began staffing the message center and the fleet of Chevrolets exclusively with Mormons. One of them was Bill Gay, who was later to become a power in the Hughes organization.

The passion for secrecy was carried into Howard's own residence. He allowed no one in his bedroom, not even the maid to change the bedsheets. The linens were left outside the bedroom, and Howard changed the bed himself. He did a great deal of business over the telephone in his bedroom, and he was afraid that the servants, inadvertently or on purpose, might remove the notes that he made on the bedside table.

For a couple of years after the war, Howard occupied the Beverly Hills mansion of Cary Grant, who was spending much of his time in Europe making movies. Grant was one of the few close friends that Howard had.

Later Howard decided to reside in one of the luxurious bungalows at the rear of the Beverly Hills Hotel. There are two suites to each bungalow, and Howard wanted no one to reside next to him—too much danger of spying.

Howard wanted to rent one-half of the bungalow, but he insisted that the hotel keep the other half unoccupied, at no cost to him. I tried to argue that this was not a very equitable arrangement for the hotel management.

"Why should I pay for a suite that I'm not using?" he argued.

"Then why not let them rent the other suite?" I suggested.

"Absolutely not! Somebody could use the place to listen in on my conversations."

There was no arguing with him. I was faced with the chore of negotiating with the hotel. I tactfully pointed out to the manager that the bungalows were not always rented; in fact, they could be vacant for weeks at a time during the slow season. If Howard Hughes were to rent a suite for five years on a year-around basis, the hotel would certainly not suffer by keeping the other half of the bungalow unoccupied.

The manager saw the wisdom of my argument. Not to mention the publicity value of having Howard Hughes as a regular resident.

At the same time as he was chiseling the Beverly Hills Hotel out of the rental of half a bungalow, Howard was paying rent on five expensive houses which he kept available for his protégées.

Indeed, Howard continued his search for the "perfect female face and figure." He had help in his pursuit—a series of "talent scouts" who kept a lookout for advertising models, little-theater actresses, college coeds, and movie starlets who might capture Howard's fancy. Among those who served in an unofficial capacity for this purpose were Pat DiCicco, Cubby Broccoli, Johnny Meyer, Greg Bautzer, and Walter Kane.

When a girl met the Hughes standards, she was installed

in one of the rented mansions and sent to classes for acting, voice, dance, and other graces. Some never met Howard himself. They continued their lessons for months,
sometimes years, and finally were let go, to vanish once
again into anonymity. Others did meet Howard, and a few
were promoted to stardom.

Whether he was having an alliance with a protégée or
not, Howard did not like to have the girl tampered with.
Therefore he employed a half-dozen "safe" gigolos whose
duty was to take the girls out to dinner and a show and get
them home safely, without any hanky-panky.

Howard had a peculiar predilection about glamour
girls. He liked to court them just after they had left their
husbands. That was true just after Susan Hayward had a
violent parting with Jess Barker. It also happened when
Ava Gardner left Mickey Rooney. Ava and Howard
began a torrid romance, but he was unable to devote
enough time to her—he was too busy with the flying boat
and other distractions. Ava felt neglected, and she took up
with a Mexican bullfighter. Howard heard about it, and he
stormed into her house and confronted her with the information.

Ava's temper is well-known, and she told off Howard in
no uncertain terms. He slapped her so hard that she fell
down on the davenport, then he turned on his heel and
started to stalk out of the house. She grabbed a piece of
bronze statuary and rushed after him, clouting him over
the head. He was knocked unconscious, and I think she
would have done more damage if the maid hadn't heard
the commotion and pulled Ava off.

Such encounters were rare in the life of Howard
Hughes, who preferred his romances to follow a well-or-
dered course. Most of the actresses—they were always actresses—were willing to await Howard's pleasure. To a favored few, he held out the prospect of matrimony. He
stalled them off by saying he *wanted* to get married, but
the press of business made it impossible at the moment.
The promises continued until the ladies became worn
down with waiting and moved on to other fields. Their loss
never seemed to bother Howard.

The germ phobia was getting worse.

He began establishing strict procedures for all those who came in personal contact with him. The typists who typed documents that were to be presented to him and the couriers who delivered them were required to wear white cotton gloves. These gloves were bought by the gross from an undertaker's supply house. No papers intended for him could be touched by naked hands.

I found it hard to understand his logic. If he was aiming at an antiseptic atmosphere, he wasn't going about it in a scientific manner. The white cotton gloves were clean, but they weren't sterile. There was no assurance they didn't carry as many germs as ungloved hands.

I rarely saw Howard shake hands anymore. He always stood back at an introduction and made no move to extend his hand. If the other person offered his hand, Howard would manufacture some excuse—he had cut his finger or spilled something on his hand.

He had an aversion to touching doorknobs. He generally maneuvered himself so that someone else would open the door for him. If that failed, he would surreptitiously take out a handkerchief and apply it to the doorknob.

Once I questioned him about his fear of germs.

"Everybody carries germs around with them," he said. "I want to live longer than my parents. So I avoid germs."

CHAPTER THIRTY-THREE

Taking Care of TWA's Troubles

One of the most pressing problems that faced Howard after the war was TWA. The airline had always been a problem child under Jack Frye's management, and now it was growing into a delinquent adult.

All of the airlines had trouble adjusting to the peacetime economy, but TWA had more than most. Frye's inept handling of costs, his inefficient operations, his extravagance with new purchases of equipment—all these factors combined to nosedive the TWA stock from 71 at the war's end to 9 in 1947.

Howard still resisted my entreaties to dump Frye. The pair of them combined to go on a shopping spree for new airliners. I had urged them to pick up some surplus DC-4s and convert them for TWA use during the difficult time of transition to peace. But no, they wanted new equipment to dazzle the customers with. The trouble was, there weren't enough customers.

While other airlines were largely buying Douglas DC-4s and Boeing Stratocruisers, Howard favored Constellations by Lockheed. He had an affinity for Lockheed ever since he used the Lodestar to fly around the world. He sometimes bragged that he designed the Constellation wing. The basis of that story was this: an inventor came to me with a design for an airplane wing. I checked with experts who told me that the design might have merit. So I paid him $2,500 for it. I showed the plans to Howard, and he took them to Bob Gross at Lockheed. Howard may have added his own ideas. I don't know about that.

At any rate, he ordered forty Constellations for TWA before the war. The price was a reasonable $425,000 apiece, but the planes were never delivered. The war intervened.

When the war was over and airplanes were again available for civilian use, Howard again placed his order for Constellations. But by now the price tag had inflated from $425,000 to a whopping $2,700,000.

The only bargain Connies that Howard acquired were four army surplus planes. He had them flown to Hughes Aircraft, and we entered into negotiations with Lockheed for converting them to airline use. Howard himself conducted most of the negotiations directly with Bob Gross, Lockheed's president. They arrived at an over-all price of $400,000 per plane, then Howard got down to the nitty-gritty details of specifications.

One night I was dining with my brother in Hollywood when I received a telephone call from Howard.

"You won't believe this, Noah," he said, "but I was thrown out of Bob Gross's office today."

"You're right, Howard," I replied. "I don't believe it."

"But I was!"

"Howard, Bob may have become annoyed with you and ended the conference, but I can't conceive—"

"Noah, I'm telling you it happened! I was thrown out. Bodily. He called for two plant security men and ordered them to escort me off the premises. They took me by the arms and deposited me at my car. And they didn't leave until I had driven off the lot."

"Howard, what on earth did you do to warrant such treatment?"

"Nothing. I was just telling Bob what I expected in the way of specifications."

"It must have been something more than that."

"Now I'm stuck. He won't allow me inside the gate, and I want to finish up this contract with him. What'll I do?"

"Howard I'll see you in the morning, and we'll talk about it."

I met with him the following morning, and he presented a list of thirty-four specifications that he was seeking from

Lockheed. He had checked eleven of them as "must" items.

"You go talk to Gross," Howard said. "If you can get those eleven items, I'll be satisfied. I don't care so much about the rest of them."

"All right, I'll see what I can do," I said. "Write out a little note saying that I'm authorized to sign the contract for you."

The next evening, Howard called me and asked, "How did you get along with Gross?"

"The contract is all signed," I said. "I got your eleven items."

"Great!"

"And nineteen others, too."

"Thirty out of the thirty-four items! How the hell did you manage that?"

"Simple. Every time we came to a sticky point, I said, 'Bob, do you want to settle this thing with me, or do you want another dose of Howard Hughes?' And every time he said, 'All right, you can have it!' "

I never heard Howard laugh so hard. He thought it was a delightful story, especially since it had redounded to his advantage.

The four reconverted Constellations were a minor help to TWA's economy, but the cost of the new Connies was crushing the company. The deficit was mounting.

TWA was not a primary concern of mine, since I had dropped most happily from the board of directors. My major purpose was to keep Hughes Tool Company pouring forth profits to support TWA and Howard's other ventures. I was pursuing such a course in Houston when Howard called me with concern over the airline's future.

"TWA needs money, Noah," he said. He told me about the plans for financing that had been devised by Jack Frye and his treasurer, Lee Tallman. They had lined up a $17,000,000 loan from bank and insurance company sources.

"But that won't even begin to straighten things out," Howard admitted.

"How much do you think they need?" I asked.

"Thirty million as a minimum," he said. "Forty million would be better."

"If Frye can only come up with seventeen million, thirty million won't be easy."

"See what you can do."

Frye had also applied to the Export-Import Bank for a $150,000,000 loan, on the basis that TWA was now an overseas carrier. He was confident that the loan would come through. I wasn't.

After I spoke to Howard, I started telephoning. Within two hours, I had a commitment for $40,000,000. I can't really claim all the credit for my financial acumen; lady luck played a big role in my achievement.

I telephoned a friend, Maury Bent, at Merrill Lynch, Pierce, Fenner and Beane. I told him of TWA's needs.

"This is a real coincidence," he said. "Just yesterday I was having lunch with Parkinson, the headman of Equitable Life Insurance. He told me that Equitable wants to get into airline financing. He thinks that is the coming business. He asked me to find something substantial to invest in."

I assured Maury that Prudential could find no more substantial investment in the airline business than TWA.

Within an hour, Maury called me back with the information: "Hell, Parkinson said you could have thirty million on a straight debenture, with another ten million behind it if you need it. How's that for action?"

I agreed that it was somewhat more than all right. I telephoned Howard and told him: "You know that forty million you asked me to raise for TWA? I made a phone call and arranged it. Tell Frye to go to Equitable and make the arrangements."

I presumed that Howard was pleased. He didn't say so, but then, he rarely did.

One of the stipulations of the Equitable loan was that no part of it was to go for deficit financing. Howard had assigned me to watchdog the TWA operation, and I had established an office with TWA in Washington, D.C., where I could keep a closer view on the situation. It was not long before I detected a violation of the Prudential agreement. The loan funds were being used to cover the growing TWA deficit.

I blew the whistle.

When I reported to Howard that the airline was losing $20,000,000 for the year and much of it was being covered up by misuse of the Equitable loan funds, he finally lost his patience, blaming a key man for the trouble.

"Okay, Noah, I'm fed up," he said. "Fire him. I don't care how you do it. Throw him out on his big fat ass."

Those were the words I had been waiting to hear. But they weren't easy to execute.

I had exacted from Howard a promise to pour $10,000,000 of Hughes Tool Company money into TWA to tide it over in an emergency. Then I went to Parkinson and told him how the Equitable loan had gone down the drain to pay for TWA's losses.

"The airline is out of money and can't even meet its payroll," I told Parkinson. "Hughes is willing to pump ten million dollars into TWA, but not with the present board of directors. Either they go, or Hughes will put in no money. He wants the whole lot of them out."

When I had agreed to drop off the TWA board Howard had been told that signed letters of resignation from all board members would be kept in a safe, to be delivered whenever Howard gave the word. When Howard finally asked for them, they were not forthcoming.

Parkinson was reluctant to take precipitate action. He sympathized with my argument but pointed out that the loan contract called for semiannual financial reports from TWA. Until the next report, Equitable would not be officially notified of TWA's default. He argued that he couldn't act until the default became official.

"The situation isn't going to wait," I said urgently. "The till is almost empty, and Howard isn't going to put in another dime until the board is fired."

Parkinson finally agreed to take up the matter with the board and see if they would not remove themselves gracefully. He didn't know them.

The next day Parkinson called me and said, "I suggested

that Howard's proposal be accepted. Then all hell broke loose."

Parkinson hadn't figured with the board's strong ties in Washington. For years some members of the board had been spending immense amounts of TWA money to win friends and influence legislation in the nation's capital. Their efforts paid off in their time of need.

The first call came from Robert E. Hannegan, Postmaster General of the United States. He made a vigorous protest over the proposed ouster of the board of TWA. The Postmaster General carried a great deal of weight, since all airlines were dependent on air mail contracts.

Next came a call from Tom Clark, the Attorney General. He also wielded a great deal of power over airlines, being the number-one prosecutor of the nation. Clark urged Parkinson not to depose the board.

They were not the only ones with political connections. I telephoned my good friend Jesse Jones. He was still fuming over being ousted as Secretary of Commerce to make a place for Henry Wallace, and he was itching to get back at his fellow Democrats.

"Hannegan and Clark have no business intervening in this case," Jones said. "If they persist, I think there ought to be a Congressional inquiry into the activities. I'm sure one could be arranged."

That was possible. This was in 1947, when the Republicans had regained control of the Congress. One of my good friends was Charlie Halleck, the Republican House leader who had gone turkey-shooting with me in Texas. I apprised him of the TWA difficulties, and he was indignant.

"I'm with you and Jesse Jones," he declared. "Whether or not the board of TWA remains as it is is of no concern to the Postmaster General and the Attorney General. If they persist, I can tell you there *will* be a Congressional investigation."

That was all I needed. I went back to Parkinson and told him that the opposition was ready to combat any threats by the Democrats in the administration.

"Hannegan and Clark must be bluffing," I argued. "They couldn't possibly defend their positions if it came to a public showdown."

I told Parkinson that he could call Jones and Halleck and confirm their opinions. He did so, and he was ready to act.

He sent the same letter to every member of the TWA board, informing them they would be held financially responsible for losses if they rejected Hughes' offer to provide $10,000,000 worth of financing and if Equitable lost money on its investment.

During my negotiation with Parkinson, a fortuitous event happened. TWA's labor relations officer told me: "We're really in trouble now, Mr. Dietrich. The pilots' union has just served notice of a strike."

"Great! I'm all for it!" I replied. The poor man thought I had lost my marbles. He didn't know what I knew: that TWA was deeply in debt to the oil companies and was in danger of running out of fuel for its planes. The company was having trouble meeting any of its bills. A strike would be ideal.

As soon as the pilots struck, I placed the entire personnel on furlough. Through that lucky happenstance the financial drain on the company was stemmed—for the moment.

Now I returned to the problem of the board of directors. I personally delivered the Parkinson letter to the board members. They saw the light. Frye was removed, Howard's offer of $10,000,000 was accepted, and eleven members were added to the board, giving Howard full control.

Howard's strong new position at TWA resulted in an enormous windfall, thanks to my maneuvering.

Howard at first would not take stock for his $10,000,000 addition to the TWA treasury. At my suggestion the board voted to give him the right to convert the loan into TWA stock at any time during the following three years. The price of the stock would be the average closing market price during the ten days prior to the purchase.

If he had converted the loan right after Frye was ousted, he could have garnered a million shares, since the price was hovering at 10. But he held off.

With the management reforms that I helped push through, TWA began to recover its financial health. The price rose to 15. Howard fretted and fumed that he hadn't converted his $10,000,000 earlier. Now he could only buy two-thirds of a million shares.

"Howard, why don't you protect yourself by converting half of the loan to stock?" I suggested. "The price will very likely go higher as business gets better."

But Howard went through another one of those agonizing periods when he couldn't make up his mind. The opportunity passed.

Soon the stock reached 20. Now he was getting frantic. The success of his airline mitigated against his chance to make a killing by adding new shares. When TWA hit 21, he was beside himself.

"We've got to do something, Noah," he said.

"Let me look into it," I replied.

What I did was not exactly according to the Marquis of Queensberry rules, or even those of the Securities and Exchange Commission. But it was child's play, compared to some of the machinations of the market.

First of all, we opened two brokerage accounts, one in Washington, another in New York, and started trading TWA stock in 100-share lots under the market. With shares being sold two points below the market price, no one was likely to sell at 21.

Next, TWA began issuing reports that indicated an unfavorable atmosphere in the company. For instance, we implied that TWA would have to pass the next interest payment installment on the $40,000,000 loan from Equitable.

Suddenly TWA dropped to 18.

At that time, National Gypsum announced it was offering a public stock issue with preemptive rights to stockholders at $3 less than the offering price. The SEC didn't object. So I reasoned with Howard that he might be able to convert his loan to TWA stock at the price of $15.

"I can't vote on the matter as a TWA director," I told him, "but I can see that the offer goes before the board."

Meanwhile, I discussed the matter with an important brokerage executive.

"With Howard's conversion right hanging over TWA," he remarked, "you'd have trouble with a public stock issue. It would be to TWA's future advantage for Howard to convert now. Maybe you can get approval for less than fifteen dollars."

I didn't mention to him that Howard detested any dilution of his ownership and would do everything in his power to prevent a public offering.

His opinion was presented to the board, and I excused myself from the room during the voting. To my astonishment, the board voted to convert his loan at *$10 per share.*

Howard had given me authorization to act, and I converted the $10,000,000 immediately. He received 1,039,000 shares of TWA stock—the extra 39,000 shares representing accrued interest on the loan.

I couldn't suppress my delight over the coup. Instead of the market price of 18 or the discounted price of 15, I had managed to win him 1,039,000 shares at 10—a saving of at least $5,000,000. When Howard ultimately sold the shares in the 1960s, those million shares were worth $83,000,000.

I made a hurried trip to California so I could present my gift to Howard in person. When I showed him the stock certificates, he glanced at them and said, "Okay, Noah, put 'em in the safe."

That was all. My God, what a man!

The following day Howard had another matter to take up with me, and he took me out for a drive in one of his secretive Chevrolets. He talked about his problem for a while, and then he noticed that I was staring out the window.

"You're not paying attention to me, Noah," he said. "What the hell's bothering you?"

"You!" I replied.

"Me? What the hell have I done?"

"It's what you didn't do. That stock deal was a brilliant operation. Any other man in your position would have done something—or at least said something—to show his appreciation. My God, I broke my neck to put that one over for you. And all you can say is, "Okay, Noah, put 'em in the safe.' "

"Well, for crissake, Noah," he said, "if you feel that way about it, why don't you take the thirty-nine thousand shares?"

My stubborn pride took over, and I snapped, "I don't want your goddam thirty-nine thousand shares if I have to get them this way!"

As far as Howard was concerned, that ended the matter. "Now, about this other deal—"

It was a rare moment in the life of Howard Hughes, and I blew it. I'm not speaking only of the money, though that was certainly a consideration; TWA stock later rose to 100, and I could have pocketed $3,900,000.

The important thing was that I had denied Howard the one chance that I could recall for him to say thank-you. Of course he would have done it in the only manner he knew how—with money. But at least he would have done it, and it might have made a difference to Howard, if only for a moment.

The opportunity never arose again.

There was a sequel, as always.

Six months later I was in Houston on one of my rare visits home; I was spending most of my time in Kansas City, trying to straighten out TWA. Howard called me from Los Angeles.

"I've been talking to Jack Frye," he said.

I was dumbfounded. "Jesus, the last thing you told me about Frye was that you'd never give that guy a chance to rat on you again," I said.

"Yeah, I know I said that," Howard continued. "But dammit, he spent an awful lot of my money building up influence in Washington. Why should I let all that go to waste? Now I'm not thinking about putting him back in the airline management. I just thought it would be a good idea to hire him as our political representative."

"What kind of money are you thinking of?"

"Well, he wants a hundred thousand a year, the Lockheed Lodestar with a pilot, and an unlimited expense account."

"Howard, you're looking at a quarter-million dollars a year."

"That's just about the way I figured it."

"Well, I would never vote for it, Howard. But you're the boss."

"Don't give me your answer tonight, Noah. I want you to think it over and let me know tomorrow."

The following morning brought the outbreak of a national telephone strike, so I was unable to speak to Howard. I sent him a telegram which read, "As far as I'm concerned, Howard, you have to choose between Dietrich and Frye. You can't have both. Period."

I never heard another word from him about it.

CHAPTER THIRTY-FOUR

A New Toy for Howard: RKO

Howard's movie partnership with Preston Sturges had gone sour. Sturges was an erratic genius who had made some brilliant social comedies for Paramount. Lacking the discipline of a big-studio operation, Sturges went wild as an independent filmmaker. He had the idea of bringing back Harold Lloyd, who had been off the screen for ten years.

Sturges concocted the notion of starting the picture with Lloyd's old silent, *The Freshman,* then bringing it up to date with Lloyd today. The modern part of the movie was a frenetic comedy which Sturges filmed at a leisurely pace, figuring Howard Hughes would pay the bills. Among the bills was a $150,000 payment to Lloyd for his services and the use of *The Freshman.*

The film was first called *The Sin of Harold Diddlebock.* United Artists released the film to widespread apathy. It was brought back and retitled *Mad Wednesday,* with a whole new advertising campaign. Same result.

The principal reason for Howard's return to films was his youthful protégée, Faith Domergue. Sturges produced a costume adventure, *Vendetta,* which was designed to fit her slim talents. The distinguished German director, Max Ophuls, directed the film at the start. Howard drove Sturges and Ophuls to distraction with his constant interference, and they eventually left the project.

Vendetta went through a number of changes in the next three years as Howard hired new cooks to brew his Sicilian stew. Meanwhile, Faith Domergue was blossoming into womanhood, and her appearance in the early scenes didn't match those taken in the later versions.

Howard sank $5,500,000 into *Mad Wednesday* and *Vendetta*, and they were almost total losses.

In 1948 Howard telephoned me in Houston.

"Noah, I have something of great importance to discuss with you," he said. "It's so important that I don't even want to discuss it on the phone."

"All right, Howard," I replied. "I'll come to California immediately."

As I flew westward in my private plane, I pondered on what might be Howard's latest brainstorm. A design for a new plane? An atom-bomb contract? It was useless to contemplate, because Howard had a knack for coming up with the most illogical proposals.

When I arrived in Los Angeles, I telephoned Howard's attorney, Loyd Wright. "What's Howard up to now?" I asked.

"He wants to buy control of RKO studios," Loyd replied. "But for God's sake, don't tell him I told you. He swore me to absolute secrecy."

So that was it! Howard wanted to buy a major studio. He couldn't have picked a worse prospect than RKO, which was traditionally the sickest of the big companies. But at least RKO did have some important assets, including its backlog of old movies and a theater chain.

Howard picked me up in one of his Chevrolets the next day, and he drove around town without saying a word. I said nothing, either. Finally he arrived at a deserted spot by the beach. he seemed ill at ease, as though he was trying to find the words to present the proposal in the best possible light.

"Noah, I'd like to get your reaction to an idea I have," he began.

"I know. You want to buy RKO."

It was one of the few times that I saw Howard surprised. "You and that goddam gestapo of yours!" he exclaimed. "You know everything that's going on. Well, what do you think?"

"I think it's a great idea."

Now he was even more surprised. "You do?"

"Sure."

"But why? I thought you'd give me hell for even thinking about it."

"Howard, if you're going to make pictures again, it's much better that you do it with O-P-M—other people's money. You've lost millions on movies; at least you'll be able to stop your own losses. And RKO's not such a bad buy. It has some assets that will enable you to get your bait back when you sell out later on."

Even though Howard wasn't pleased with my reasoning, he was delighted that I gave my acquiescence.

Now the question arose: how to finance the purchase?

Howard had been negotiating in his usual cloak-and-dagger manner with his friend Floyd Odlum, head of the Atlas Corporation. In 1935 Atlas had bought out Radio Corporation of America for control of RKO. Atlas owned 929,000 of the almost 4,000,000 shares, and Odlum was concerned that RKO in particular and the movie industry in general were going downhill.

Howard asked me to go down to Odlum's estate at Indio and negotiate the purchase price. Odlum wanted to sell for 10½ and Howard wanted to buy for 9½. I had a few rounds with Odlum, then I had to return to Houston on urgent Toolco business. Howard completed the negotiation at slightly less than 10. The total came to $8,825,000.

He didn't want to use Hughes Tool Company money for the deal. "I want to do this on my own," he said. So I borrowed $10,000,000 for him from the Mellon Bank in Pittsburgh. Actually it was a kind of ring-around-the-rosie transaction. Hughes Tool had a heavy deposit in the Mellon Bank, so in effect it was lending Howard his own money at a respectable rate of interest.

The deal between the two friends, Howard Hughes and Floyd Odlum, was completed. Each was seeking to profit from RKO's divestment of its theaters. The government had forced all the film companies to get rid of their theaters because of the anti-trust laws. Howard had signed the consent decree with the Justice Department, indicating he would retain either the production company or the theater chain. Odlum knew that Howard was interested in the studio, not theaters, and so he put a special clause in the purchase agreement. If Howard received an offer for the theaters, Odlum would be given a chance to meet it.

Along came Stanley Meyer, a theater man and son-in-law of Universal board chairman Nate Blumberg, and Matty Fox, a veteran wheeler-dealer in the film world. Meyer and Fox wanted to buy the 124 RKO theaters, and Howard told me to negotiate with them.

I had several meetings with Meyer and Fox, and they put $1,500,000 in escrow as initial payment for purchase of the theaters.

Then Howard reneged. I didn't learn until afterward that he had no intention of selling to Meyer and Fox. He was simply establishing a purchase price so he could get rid of friend Odlum's option to match it. Then the RKO parent company sold its theater subsidiary to Albert A. List.

Hollywood was waiting to see what would happen to RKO with Howard Hughes in charge. Peter Rathvon, who had been Odlum's handpicked president, announced bravely that Howard had promised to keep his hands off the operation of RKO.

I knew differently. It was like turning a boy loose in a candystore and expecting him not to touch the merchandise.

The first casualty was Dore Schary. He had been production head at RKO, and he had been doing a pretty fair job. But he and Howard were destined for incompatability. Schary was a liberal thinker who believed movies could be meaningful as well as entertaining; he injected his films with pleas for tolerance. Howard was a devotee of what the trade called "tits and sand" pictures.

The blowup came over *Battleground*.

Schary had planned a saga about the Battle of the Bulge in the recently ended war. Howard said the moviegoing public didn't want war pictures. He told Schary to cancel *Battleground*. Schary quit and went over to head production at MGM. He induced Howard to sell him *Battle-ground*, which turned into MGM's biggest hit of 1950.

Peter Rathvon was the next to go. When Howard summarily fired seven hundred employees, Rathvon resigned.

Howard wanted someone as chairman of the RKO board who could give financial stability to the company. I was distressed by his choice of nominee: Noah Dietrich.

I had no knowledge of the inner workings of a movie corporation, and I had no real ambition or time to learn. But Howard insisted that I take the title, and I agreed to do the best I could. I placed Sid Rogell in charge of production, figuring that he was a levelheaded film veteran who could keep studio operations on a sensible basis.

He might have—if it hadn't been for a fellow named Howard Hughes.

Howard insisted on overseeing every operation. He read all the scripts, did all the castings, approved the costumes and sets, and ran a small army of would-be starlets through the casting office. Getting decisions out of Howard was no easier than before. As a result, RKO, which had been averaging thirty pictures a year, made only nine during the first year of the Hughes regime.

Adding to the chaotic operation of RKO was the fact that Howard never visited the studio. New places filled with people would subject him to contamination by germs; hence he ran RKO from his familiar surroundings at Goldwyn Studio, two miles away.

This long-distance management provided some odd situations. At one time he had romantic ambitions with Janet Leigh. He borrowed her from MGM for a musical, *Two Tickets to Broadway*. Janet was no dancer, so he hired the noted couple, Marge and Gower Champion, to coach her. Not at RKO, where the picture was to be made. Howard had sets built at Goldwyn, and he watched her rehearse nightly for hours at a time.

While he seemed to have no real interest in having RKO turn a profit for its stockholders, Howard wasn't adverse to making some money with the company for Howard Hughes.

He devised a scheme of selling his independently made

movies, including *Hell's Angels* and *Scarface,* to RKO. Naturally the sale would have meant a nice capital gains for Howard. I agreed to present the proposal to the board, which approved of it. To ascertain the value of the films, three appraisers were appointed; all were leading figures of the movie industry. Howard contacted them and insisted on an inflated price for his films. The appraisers flatly refused to continue, and Howard's scheme died a-borning.

Howard could go to extremes in his deviousness.

One of his pet projects was *Jet Pilot*, which he announced would be the *Hell's Angels* of the jet age. But again he defeated himself. He tinkered with the picture for more than two years; meanwhile jet airplanes had become commonplace and the impact of the film was dissipated.

Still, Howard was jealous of his picture. John Wayne had starred in it with Janet Leigh, and Howard feared that Wayne would make another movie that would reach the screens before *Jet Pilot*.

So Howard devised an intricate scheme which would keep Wayne away from alien cameras. He proposed a goodwill trip of South America, to be paid for by RKO. Glen Odekirk flew Wayne in a PBY and they visited major capitals and stopped to fish and hunt along the way. Wayne had a great vacation, but he didn't realize that it was simply designed to keep him from working for other producers.

I figured in another example of Howard's protection of his properties.

Howard planned to use his valuable film property, Jane Russell, in big-budget RKO pictures; she was to be loaned by Hughes Productions at a reasonable fee, considering her worth as a star. But prior to the RKO acquisition, Howard had loaned her to an independent producer, Hunt Stromberg, who had made a medium-budget western, *Montana Belle.* Howard was worried that Stromberg would get his film into release early and lower Jane's value as an attraction.

I was chosen as the instrument of Howard's deception. As chairman of the RKO board, I was to enter into negotiations with Stromberg for merging his interests—particularly *Montana Belle*—into RKO. The talks were to take place in New York.

Realizing how Howard operated, I bade farewell to my wife and children and flew off for a lengthy stay in New York.

The Stromberg experience was useless except for one thing: I received a closeup education in the mating habits of pigeons.

When I checked into my suite at the Mayfair Hotel, I noticed a couple of pigeons on the window ledge. They were engaging in ardent love-making.

Following Howard's plan, I opened negotiations with Hunt Stromberg. He made a proposal. I made a counter-proposal. He made a counter-counter-proposal. I made. ... Well, this went on for days, weeks.

Meanwhile, the pigeons were busy. They brought twigs and pieces of string to the window ledge and constructed a neat little nest. One day after a long session with Stromberg, I returned to find the mother pigeon sitting on the nest. Underneath her were two eggs.

More proposals, objections, counter-objections.

The eggs hatched. Mother and father brought offerings of worms to the hungry little beaks.

Back to Stromberg and offers for the release of *Montana Belle*. He makes a proposition. I plead for time to study it. I leave with the excuse of an urgent appointment.

I return to the Mayfair. The fledglings are being pushed out of the nest to try their wings.

Finally Stromberg is overcome by frustration and flies back to Hollywood. I follow, having completed the life cycle of the pigeon, as well as my mission for Howard Hughes.

In the end, Howard bought *Montana Belle* from Stromberg for $600,000, so he himself could hold it out of release until after his more substantial RKO films with Russell could appear.

Here's a postscript. The Hollywood lawyer who concluded the purchase claimed a $60,000 commission for his services. Later I learned that the same lawyer also collected $60,000 from Hunt Stromberg.

"Howard, that's double-dealing!" I protested. "That man has no right to collect ten percent from both parties."

Howard refused to share my indignation.

"What the hell do I care?" he said. "I got what *I* wanted."

CHAPTER THIRTY-FIVE

Politics

I have often been asked: what were Howard Hughes' politics? And my answer has been: he had none.

I never met a more apolitical man in my life. He cared nothing about candidates or issues—unless they had some effect on Howard Hughes.

And if they did, he figured he could buy his way to favor. "Everybody has a price," he always said. And he was willing to offer that price—to a city councilman or the President of the United States.

Democrat or Republican, it didn't matter. I don't recall Howard ever contributing money to a Communist or a Prohibitionist. But I'm sure he would have, provided those fellows could have done him some good.

An example of Howard's ambivalence can be seen in his attitude toward Harry Truman.

When Truman was running for Vice-President in 1944, he bore much of the campaigning burden for the ailing President Franklin D. Roosevelt. On a visit to Los Angeles, he was visited at the Biltmore Hotel by Howard Hughes and his attorney, Neil McCarthy. Howard waited in the outer room while McCarthy conferred with Truman, wished him luck in the campaign, and handed him a cash contribution of $12,500 in an envelope.

During their chat Howard burst into the room and said bluntly, "I want you to know, Mr. Truman, that is *my* money Mr. McCarthy is giving you."

Truman managed to laugh off Howard's lack of diplomacy, but McCarthy had an uneasy moment or two.

The Democratic ticket won in 1944, and in 1945 Truman succeeded to the presidency when Roosevelt died. By the time Truman ran on his own in 1948, his popularity had dipped, and all the polls were predicting that the Republican candidate, Thomas E. Dewey would be the winner.

Howard read the polls and figured he should climb aboard the Republican bandwagon. He called me and said, "We'd better put some money into the Dewey campaign."

I took $25,000 back to New York to offer it to Harold Talbott, the New York investment banker. I had some trepidation about facing Talbott. His brother Nelson had been on the TWA board when he died of a heart attack. Harold called me and said, "Noah, there's nothing I'd like better than to succeed my brother on the TWA board." I said I thought it was an excellent idea and recommended it to Howard. He approved, and I told the president of TWA, Ralph Damon, to bring it up at the next board meeting. I couldn't attend the meeting to follow up. Damon was angry with Howard at the time and nominated a friend of his own, the president of a distilling company. Naturally Talbott didn't accept my excuses.

As I expected, my reception with Harold Talbott was chilly. The election was in its final weeks, and the entire Dewey camp was enjoying the euphoria of certain success. When I offered the $25,000 to Talbott, he turned it down.

"Take that money back to Hughes," he said haughtily, "and tell him we don't need his help."

I returned to California with Howard's $25,000 undonated. I guess I could have been excused a chuckle of satisfaction on that November morning when Harry Truman fooled all the experts by being elected President of the United States.

During the late 1940s and throughout the 1950s, Howard's political contributions ran between $100,000 and $400,000 per year. He financed Los Angeles councilmen and county supervisors, tax assessors, sheriffs, state senators and assemblymen, district attorneys, governors, congressmen and senators, judges—yes, and Vice-Presidents and Presidents, too. Besides cash, Howard was liberal in providing airplanes for candidates.

Contributions were usually made in person through one of Howard's political lawyers or by an official of the Hughes organization. Some office holders received a regular check of $5,000 each year, whether they were running for reelection or not. It could be treated as donation for a past deficit or future campaign.

Federal law prohibited corporations from making political contributions. I made sure that Hughes Tool Company was not involved in the donations. Then one day I found an easy way to circumvent the contributions law.

Remember those talks with Juan Trippe about a merger of Pan American and TWA? They were phony and fruitless, but one important piece of information came out of them.

After a lengthy session I asked Trippe how he managed to wield so much influence in Washington—the Pan American lobby was enormously effective, and not only with Senator Brewster.

"Well, you know," he confided, "the law says nothing at all about contributions from *foreign* corporations. We have a subsidiary in South America that takes an intense interest in our U.S. elections."

I mentioned this to Howard on our next meeting. "Great idea!" he said. "Set it up."

Our lawyers agreed that a plan like Trippe's was feasible. I arranged for the sales in Canada to be handled by a subsidiary of the Hughes Tool Company. The income regulated to what Howard was spending politically—between $350,000 and $400,000 per year.

It was a curious operation: Money from the use of Hughes drills in Canada flowed to the Bank of America branch in West Hollywood and thence to politicians' coffers from Sacramento to Washington.

When a politician was tendered a testimonial dinner, the Hughes organization took a table, whether it was for $100 or $1,000 a plate. The Hughes lobbyists had learned a lesson from glad-handing Johnny Meyer and avoided the free booze and broads. But hotel bills and steak dinners were picked up for those who occupied policy-making positions.

These lobbyists were not so foolish as to twist arms or make payments in dark alleys. They were entirely businesslike and said: "All we ask is what Mr. Hughes is rightfully entitled to—no more, no less."

Well, sometimes it was a little more.

For instance, the Marina Del Rey. The County of Los Angeles wanted to develop the Playa Del Rey area into a marina for boat lovers. To do so, the county had to acquire one-tenth of the 1,200 acres Howard had bought for Hughes Aircraft.

He didn't want to part with one foot of his land. For two years he stymied the county officials who sought his land. Finally, after long and tedious negotiations, the politicos decided that Hughes was stalling. The county filed a condemnation suit.

Now Howard realized he wasn't going to be able to forestall the building of the marina by political contributions. He had done so for two years, with cash contributions to the right parties.

"I won't give up that land for less than thirty thousand an acre," Howard insisted. He had paid an average of $2,000 an acre for it.

Howard stalled. Now the officials were getting desperate; they needed to begin dredging at the mouth of the channel. They asked if they couldn't get one and a half acres at the ocean, and they offered $54,000 per acre. In Howard's absence, I took the bull by the horns and signed a contract at $84,000 for the acre and a half.

When Howard returned, I told him I had sold the land to begin the marina.

"Jesus Christ, Noah!" he said. "I didn't want them to have any of that land."

"Howard, it was either making a deal or letting them condemn the land on their terms. You told me you wanted thirty thousand an acre, and I did better than that."

"How much?"

"Fifty-four thousand."

There was a long silence on the other end of the telephone.

"Well," he finally said, "don't let them have any more."

In the end, the county got the land it needed for the marina, and Howard earned an enormous profit.

On another occasion, Howard was able to prevent the violation of his Culver City property. The State of California wanted to route Highway 1 down the coast through the acreage of Hughes Aircraft. Even though the property the state wanted was not being put to any use, Howard would not part with it. He used the argument that his was the longest runway on the West Coast and hence of use in case of enemy attack. But the runway wasn't threatened.

He put his Sacramento lobbyist to work. A bit of persuasion in the right places caused Highway 1 to be rerouted so that it did not impinge on Hughes property.

Howard failed, however, to stop the Loyola campanile.

On a bluff overlooking the Hughes Aircraft plant, Loyola University had been founded by the Jesuit Fathers. Howard tolerated the incursion of the Catholic educators —as long as they continued their quiet studies up on the hill. But then the Jesuits decided that they wanted to construct a bell tower atop the bluff. Howard blew his top.

He was convinced that the campanile would be a menace to landings at Hughes Aircraft. It became a fixation with Howard, and he insisted that I do everything possible to forestall the construction of the tower.

I did what I could. I became acquainted with the Catholic fathers and donated an oil painting to the University. Still, the Jesuits were intent upon raising the campanile.

"It'll be an aircraft hazard," Howard insisted. "Notify the CAB, the FAA."

I notified the CAB and the FAA. Both government agencies investigated the matter and concluded that the campanile was no hazard to airplanes. And so, much to Howard's distaste, Loyola University raised its bell tower to the celebration of man's devotion to God.

Whether it was God or the President of the United States, Howard never gave up trying. TWA found itself bettered by Pan American in the matter of overseas routes. Howard was greatly distressed, and he figured he could exert some pressure on the Civil Aeronautics Board, which issued the route permits.

The best place to start was at the top, Howard figured. He instructed Jack Frye, who was still TWA president at the time, to make representations to Truman, reminding him of the $12,500 contribution by Howard Hughes. Frye was very reluctant, but Howard insisted.

Frye maneuvered an invitation on the Presidential yacht. During a cruise down the Potomac, Frye mentioned his quest and reminded Truman of Hughes' $12,500 donation.

Frye told me later that Truman blew his top, and Frye himself was lucky not to be forced to swim ashore.

A notable example of Howard's political clout came following an unfortunate episode concerning Hughes Tool Company employees in 1948.

On April 23, 1948, the United States Grand Jury in Honolulu indicted the Hughes Tool Company, two Hughes employees and two others for obtaining six Douglas C-47s from the War Assets Administration by fraudulent means. The Grand Jury charged that the Hughes company had used veterans as a front for acquiring surplus planes on priority.

Specifically, Hughes was accused of paying $105,000 for planes that were worth $600,000.

One of the veterans in the case had turned state's evidence. So it seemed like an open-and-shut case, one which could bring serious damage to the Hughes reputation. Howard claimed no knowledge whatsoever of the underhanded transaction. I certainly had none; I had specifically warned our employees not to attempt to use veteran status to aid the company.

"Get Hughes Tool Company out of the indictment," Howard told me. "I don't give a damn what it costs or how you do it."

I called on Tom Clark, the U.S. Attorney General, whom I had known slightly in Houston. He took me to the office of the chief criminal prosecutor. I made a strong plea, but the prosecutor was unconvinced that Hughes Tool Company should be eliminated from the indictment.

I met with him on other occasions, and still he remained adamant. Then I learned that he had announced his intention of running for the Senate from his home state. I called on a high official at Democratic National Headquarters and offered him a donation of $100,000, to be applied at the rate of $5,000 to any twenty campaigns he designated.

"That's very generous of Mr. Hughes," he replied. "Tell me, is there anything we can do for him?"

That was my opening. I made my plea that the tool company bore no guilt in the Honolulu case and should be dropped as a defendant. The man lifted the telephone and called the criminal prosecutor. He explained my case. I could tell that he was drawing opposition on the other end.

The official's voice adopted a tougher tone. "Look— you want to be senator, don't you? . . . Okay, then let's get Hughes out of this case." The argument was over.

I returned to California. Soon I received a list of twenty Democratic nominees, including the Justice Department prosecutor. I turned the list over to Hughes' political lawyer and transferred $100,000 to his account.

A week later, our attorneys in Honolulu suggested that the charges against the Hughes Tool Company be dropped. The United States Attorney agreed, and the judge granted the motion. The two Hughes employees pleaded *nolo contendere* to the charge of defrauding the government and were fined $10,000 apiece. Their fines were paid by Howard Hughes.

CHAPTER THIRTY-SIX

TWA after Frye

Following Jack Frye's summary departure from TWA, Howard chose LaMotte Cohu as his successor. He seemed like a good choice, having been a veteran in the aircraft industry and a TWA director since 1933. Cohu served a year, then was nominated for reelection. When the board members reelected him, he merely said, "Thank you, gentlemen."

A month later I learned the reason for his reticence. I saw him in Washington and he said, "Tell Hughes I'm resigning. Odlum has offered me a top job at Consolidated-Vultee."

And so he went off to head up Odlum's aircraft company. It burned Howard that his friend Odlum would proselyte the president of TWA.

The airline continued without a president for a while. Then one day Ralph Damon called me. He was president of American Airlines, but I knew he was discontented with the policies of C. R. Smith, chairman of the board.

"Smith is selling our overseas operation to Pan American," Damon told me. "I don't approve. I plan to be leaving American."

I welcomed the news and said I would talk to Howard. "Sign him," Howard said. I drew up a five-year contract and Ralph Damon became president of TWA.

He should have known better.

Damon had two previous encounters with the eccentric Howard Hughes. Both occasions were disastrous.

The first was in 1942. I was in my office at 7000 Romaine during one of my summer visits; I made a policy of spending three summer months in Los Angeles to escape the Houston heat. A telephone call came from Ralph Damon, whom I had met and liked.

"It's nice to hear from you, Ralph," I said. "Where are you?"

"At the Beverly Hills Hotel."

"Oh, you're in town? What are you doing here?"

"That's what I called *you* to find out, Noah," he said.

He angrily spilled out the whole story: Howard had asked him to come to California for secret talks. Howard was planning to dump Jack Frye and install Ralph as president of TWA. Acting on Howard's suggestion, Ralph had executed an elaborate ruse to avoid letting anyone at American Airlines know that he was going to see Howard Hughes.

"I've been sitting here for four days, waiting for Howard," Damon complained. *"Four days* in a hotel room, and no Hughes! No message from Hughes, either. He hasn't even called, and I can't get him to answer my messages. Who the hell does he think he is, keeping me waiting four days in a hotel room?"

His indignation was understandable. After all, he was president of a huge airline; now he had been summoned across the country to sit in a hotel room and wait for the bidding of Howard Hughes.

"Ralph, I don't know where Howard is," I admitted. "But I certainly will try to locate him."

"Don't bother," Ralph snapped. "I'm checking out and going back to New York. Tell Hughes I never want to hear from him." He slammed down the phone.

I made several attempts at reconciliation, but to no avail. I figured the chances of getting Damon over to TWA were nil. But Howard didn't let a little thing like standing up the President of American Airlines stop him.

Less than a year later, Howard came to Houston for talks with federal officials about production of the F-11. He checked into the Rice Hotel under the name of "Mr. Harrison," and we had our conference there. I took the officials out to dinner and Howard stayed in his room.

When I returned home that evening, I found a message to call Ralph Damon at the Texas State Hotel. It surprised me that Ralph would be in Houston, and I quickly called the hotel. I was told that Mr. Damon had checked out.

I knew the manager of the Texas State, and I asked him to try to find out where Ralph had gone. The manager did some investigating and found a bellboy who said that Ralph had ordered the taxi to take him to the railroad station. I paged him there, and he responded.

"Ralph, what are you doing in Houston?" I asked.

He was so apoplectic he could scarcely speak.

"He did it again!" Ralph ranted. "He did it to me again!"

I tried to calm him down and get the story out of him. I learned that Howard had invited Ralph to Houston to talk about the presidency of TWA. But when Ralph telephoned the Rice Hotel, he was told there was no Howard Hughes registered.

"But that's because Howard registered as Harrison," I said. "It's an old trick of Howard's. He didn't mean to stand you up. Please stay over. I'm sure Howard wants to see you."

"He certainly doesn't act like it. I'm leaving."

"On the train?"

"Yes, the train. There are no more flights out of Houston tonight, so I am leaving on the first train!"

Once again he slammed down the phone. I figured that Ralph was lost to TWA forever. But with the passage of five years, the hurt was finally forgotten, and he took over as president in 1948.

Ralph Damon was a sensitive man, too sensitive, perhaps, to work for Howard Hughes. TWA was Howard's private domain, and he ran it according to his own whim. Damon was a keen businessman and an executive of vision. He couldn't cope with the eccentricities of Hughes.

Under Damon, TWA began making strides toward financial stability. The deficit was eliminated, and the stock rose into the 60s. Damon introduced policies that became standard in the industry.

The most important of these was multi-class service.

"On a train you can get four or five different kinds of accommodation," he explained to me. "The steamships do the same. Why shouldn't airlines? We could offer first-class service which would give the traveler special treatment. Then we could have the economy section, where people would figure they were getting a bargain in travel."

Howard liked the idea, and Damon applied for two-class service with the Civil Aeronautics Board. Approval was given, and TWA inaugurated economy service in the front of the planes, first-class in the rear (because of propeller noise, the front was less desirable). The policy was so successful that all of the other airlines followed suit.

Ralph Damon lasted seven years as president of TWA. Those years of working for Howard Hughes took a toll, and he ended up a sick and embittered man. Once I saw him become so furious about the interference of Hughes that he broke down and cried. Finally a heart attack killed him.

After Damon's death, the presidency of TWA remained unfilled for a year. Howard seemed to think he could run the airline himself. He couldn't, and the independent members of the board of directors—men like Nelson Talbott of National Cash Register, Powell Crosley, and Arthur Eisenhower—became angry with his inaction on the TWA presidency. Finally, at one of the monthly meetings, they appointed me as a committee of one to nominate a new president at the next meeting.

I had submitted a number of names to Howard, and he rejected them all. Then I brought up the name of Carter Burgess. He had a strong business background and then was serving as Assistant Secretary of Defense, in charge of manpower, for the Eisenhower administration.

Howard was intrigued with the suggestion. "Can you get in touch with the President and find out what he thinks of Burgess?" he asked me.

"I'll try," I replied.

I was staying at the Waldorf-Astoria in New York. So was my fellow board member, Arthur Eisenhower. I paid him a call.

"How well do you know your brother Ike?" I asked facetiously.

"What do you mean?" he asked.

"Do you know him well enough to get him on the telephone?"

"Sure."

Within three minutes, he had reached the President in the White House.

"Mr. President, we are considering Carter Burgess as president of TWA," I began. "Before we go ahead, I'd like to know what you think of him."

"Why, Carter Burgess is one of the most intelligent, personable, and capable men I've ever known," Mr. Eisenhower replied, and he continued at length on Burgess's qualities.

I couldn't find a better recommendation than that. I immediately called Howard and reported our conversation. "Hire him," he said.

Next I called Burgess and told him of Howard's decision. I asked him to come to New York immediately, and we worked out a five-year contract at $75,000 a year. It was approved at the next board meeting.

Burgess took over as president of TWA in January of 1957. He lasted eleven months. Never did he lay eyes on Howard Hughes. Burgess was thwarted at every turn by orders Howard had given without consulting him.

One day after I had left Hughes, I received a telephone call from Carter Burgess. His voice sounded desperate. "Jesus Christ, how did you stand that man Hughes all those years?" he asked.

I suggested that if he would come out to California, I would try to instruct him in the ways of dealing with Howard Hughes. Burgess accepted my invitation. But a few days later he called back.

"I'm not even coming out there," he said. "I'm quitting."

CHAPTER THIRTY-SEVEN

Trying to Make a Change

By 1948 my duties for Howard had become immensely onerous, and I yearned to be relieved of some of my burdens. I was nearing sixty, an age when a lot of businessmen start slowing down. But my life was accelerating as Howard embroiled himself in increasingly complicated enterprises. He was relying on me more and more.

If an executive had to be fired, "Noah can do it." If millions had to be raised overnight, "Noah can do it." If a politico or a starlet had to be paid off, "Noah can do it."

Noah was getting tired of doing it.

Furthermore, I was getting to the point where I didn't have to do it in order to prosper financially. Through my connections with oil men in Houston, I had invested in a number of drilling ventures that had paid off handsomely. so much so that Howard himself wanted to get into the act.

"I'm only working for you because I like you," I once kidded Howard. "My oil leases are bringing me in fifteen thousand a month."

Howard's eyes lighted up. "Get me in on it, too," he insisted. So we formed an oil partnership, thus ending a longtime Hughes tradition; his father had established the policy of no oil investments, lest Toolco come in competitition with its customers.

It was the oil money that was stiffening my independence. Not my income from Hughes.

I was in a financial position that would have been ludicrous if it hadn't been so sad. Howard Hughes, my boss, was well on his way to becoming a billionaire, yet he paid less than $20,000 in income taxes. My own net worth was less than a million, and I was paying fifteen to twenty times Howard's income tax.

Nobody can really sympathize with the financial problems of those who are paid a large amount of money. I don't ask the reader to shed any tears over my plight. Simply consider the inequity.

Howard paid himself only $50,000 in salary. Nearly all of his living expenses were paid by the Hughes Tool Company. The millions that his companies earned were sheltered by plant expansion and in real estate. His millions kept piling up and up.

I was being paid a half-million dollars per year—a princely sum. Out of the first $100,000, federal and state tax collectors exacted $70,000. The balance was subject to federal and state taxes of 93 percent, leaving me with seven cents out of every dollar.

I figured that on an eight-hour-a-day basis, I was working seven and a half hours for the government and a half-hour for myself.

Most major corporations in the United States realized the tax hardship on their executives and instituted stock option deals. In that way the executives' rewards were subjected to a capital gains tax, which took only 25 percent.

I mentioned my problem to Howard.

"I want to do something about that, Noah," Howard said earnestly. "Draw up a capital gains arrangement and let me look it over. We'll come up with something."

I formulated a capital gains plan and submitted it to Howard. He fell into dead silence. Finally he said, "Well, that wasn't exactly what I had in mind. Let's try something different."

So I tried something different. Again the silence. This time it was longer. He needed time to study it. Months, years, went by and he made no comment. I reminded him of the plan, and he said, "I'm sorry, Noah; that just isn't the right formula."

That's the way it went. In 1948, encouraged by my oil income, I made a proposal to Howard.

"Look, Howard," I said, "I want to cut down. As an alternative to complete retirement, let me suggest something different. I'll continue to make my headquarters in Houston, and I'll look after the tool company, the brewery, and TWA. You get someone else to handle the West Coast operations—RKO and Hughes Aircraft."

Howard thought it over for months and finally said, "All right, Noah. You find someone to take over your duties with RKO and Aircraft. If I think he is qualified, I'll consent to the arrangement."

So I started my search. My first candidate was Ed Thomas, president of Goodyear Tire and Rubber Company. I had known Ed for years and felt a kinship with him—he, too, had come into his company as a certified public accountant and had worked his way up to the top. I induced him to come out to California for a talk with Howard. The offer was to be $200,000 a year with stock options. I was surprised when Howard agreed to the stock options; he had never done so before. In spite of the attractive offer, Thomas declined the job.

I made some other suggestions for my successor on the West Coast, but none satisfied Howard. Finally he came up with the suggestion: "Why don't you go back to the Harvard School of Business and ask the dean for a list of the ten outstanding graduates?"

This amused me. It harked back to my own hiring in 1925, when Howard wanted to know how I had finished in the CPA exams. He still had the notion that he could choose an executive on the basis of how he had scored competitively with his contemporaries.

"Howard," I said, "if these men are the ten outstanding graduates, the chances are that they have jobs so good that they wouldn't want to leave."

"Try it anyway."

I got such a list from Harvard. As I expected, most of those on it were in such prestigious positions that they wouldn't have contemplated a change. But then I came to the name of an investment banker who had worked for one of the big financial families of New York. I knew the headman and I called him for information about the prospect.

"The guy has a lot of ability," I was told, "but you've got to watch him or he'll get your job."

I laughed. "That's exactly what I want him to do," I said.

I met my prospective successor and he was about what I expected: gray-suited, well-groomed, precise in his manner. He came out to the coast, and Howard approved of him. He was put on the RKO board and I began breaking him in to take over my duties.

As my friend in New York had predicted, the new man didn't need any breaking in—he started taking over my job immediately. That was all right with me, up to a certain point. That point came when I decided he wasn't taking good care of the company's interests.

When he started attending RKO board meetings, I didn't go. But I kept an eye on the proceedings. One item caught my eye: the sale of a theater chain in Wisconsin and Michigan. The price seemed low. I checked with some friends in the theater business, and they agreed that the sale was a fantastic bargain for the purchaser.

I mentioned this to Howard. Nothing made him more concerned than the possibility that his assets were being squandered. He summoned the new man to Goldwyn Studio for an explanation.

"Why wasn't I consulted about this sale?" Howard asked.

"Mr. Hughes, RKO is a corporation," the man answered stiffly. "I am a member of the board. The board has power to determine corporation policy."

Goodbye, Mr. Gray Flannel Suit.

As soon as he left the office, Howard told me: "Take him off the payroll." Then he added: "But keep him on a retainer at twenty thousand a year. He's privy to too many of our secrets. I don't want him talking."

So I had failed to find a successor for myself. It seemed too burdensome to search for and train another, so I decided to stay on. I still had hope that Howard would fulfill his promise and set up a capital gains setup that would allow me to keep more of my money.

I told Howard of my decision to stay on, and he was delighted. I had come to the conclusion that I could better perform my duties with a base in California. Howard said I could have any place to live I wanted. I suggested trading my Houston house for the Bel-Air mansion on Sarbonne Road, which had been used as a stopping place for visiting executives. Howard readily agreed.

Now I was right back where I had started. I was running the whole show for Howard—Toolco, TWA, Aircraft, RKO, the works. After fifteen years in Houston, I was back in California and therefore even closer to Howard's reach. Such was his dependency on me that he wouldn't allow marital difficulties to interfere with the performance of my duties.

My marriage had gone sour. I honestly believe that I did everything in my power to keep the marriage going, though I'll admit that being Howard Hughes' right-hand man could strain any husband-and-wife relationship.

I made concessions and agreed to reconciliations, always with the hope that I could preserve our home. It didn't work. Each new crisis brought more emotional strain, and Howard couldn't help notice what was happening to me.

He made up his mind that I had to get a divorce.

One night he picked me up at the Bel-Air house. With him were Loyd Wright, his attorney, and doctor. Howard took the car up to Mulholland Drive and for hours we drove around the hills.

"Noah, you must divorce that woman," Howard insisted. He offered one argument after another, pleading my own wellbeing depended on a clean break from my wife. What he really meant was that the unhappiness was showing on me and he feared loss of efficiency in my management of his affairs.

"Supposing you're a kid in Podunk, Noah," Howard reasoned. "You grow up with a girl, go to school with her, and you call it love. You get married. But then you have to go out to Hollywood to live. You must leave your wife behind. When you're out here, you meet another girl. You discover your wife isn't the only woman in the world. You can be just as happy with a new one."

The argument was supposed to persuade me that a change would be good for me. I remained unconvinced.

At one point Howard exclaimed in typical Hughes logic: "For crissake, Noah, I can get you a dozen girls who are better looking, have better figures, and are better lays than the one you've got."

The drive continued. Loyd Wright made comments on the legal aspects of my problem. The doctor discussed the state of my wife's rationality. At Howard's suggestion, the doctor had been invited to my house for dinner so he could observe my wife. He indicated that she was not totally rational, at least in regard to me. But he wanted another interview with her before he decided that continuance of the marriage would be undesirable.

Finally at 5 A.M. I was worn down and seeking rest. I agreed to have the doctor observe my wife once more.

"If the doctor thinks that I should call it quits," I said wearily, "then I will."

The following morning, the doctor called me and said, "You know, after you left last night, Howard turned to me and said, 'You know what your answer's got to be.' So I wanted you to be prepared for my answer when it comes, Noah."

My wife and I separated in February of 1951. I'm sure that the marriage would have ended sooner or later. Howard made sure that it happened sooner.

CHAPTER THIRTY-EIGHT

Problems and Promises
with Hughes Aircraft

Like most war plants, Hughes Aircraft had shrunk after the coming of peace. But the effects of the peacetime economy were felt more at Hughes Aircraft, which had no record of success in supplying material to the military. Far from it. The plant had produced only the now-defunct F-11 and the ever-building Hercules. From a wartime high of 6,000 employees, Aircraft had dipped to 800 a couple of years after the war had ended.

"What are you going to do with Aircraft?" I asked Howard.

"I haven't any plans at the moment," he said.

"Howard, I really believe you should think about shutting it down. We simply aren't getting any contracts, and it is becoming a financial burden."

"No, I won't shut it down." Howard vowed. "Something will turn up."

Something did. The Hughes luck came through once more. But it took more than luck to turn Hughes Aircraft into a winner. It also took money—and guts. Howard had plenty of both.

The idea came from a brilliant engineer named David Evans. He perceived the forthcoming boom in electronics. Why shouldn't Hughes Aircraft corner all available electronics engineers and be ready to move into that field when it develops? Howard liked the idea, and he ordered it put into motion.

Obviously he needed a strong new management to supervise the conversion to electronics. His devious mind reasoned that since he would be seeking contracts with the government, he should hire someone who had an "in" with the military. Why not an air force general?

Howard had become acquainted with General Ira Eaker during the war. Eaker, deputy commander to General Carl Spaats, had recently retired from the air force and he seemed like a strong choice to head Hughes Aircraft. But Eaker was a West Point man with no business experience. Howard chose another general to pair with Eaker: Harold L. George, who had commanded the Air Transport Command. At least George had a modicum of administrative experience since retiring from the service; he had been running Peruvian Airlines.

Generals George and Eaker were accustomed to command, and they wanted autonomy in running Hughes Aircraft. Surprisingly, Howard gave it to them. The first test of their ability to act independently of Howard came with the selection of an administrative head. They chose Charles (Tex) Thornton, who had been one of the "whiz kids" of Ford Motor Company, along with Robert McNamara.

Howard and I interviewed Thornton, and both of us had a negative reaction. We argued with the generals about appointing Thornton, but in the end Howard acquiesced.

"Look, Noah," he told me, "I promised the generals autonomy, and I'm going to stick by it."

"That's fine, Howard," I said, "but don't hold me responsible."

"Well, you hold onto the purse strings."

My position as holder of the purse strings was not calculated to win me any popularity contests. I became an irritant to George, Eaker, and Thornton, but that was what I was paid to do. They fought me every inch of the way. At one time they barred my private auditors from the plant, but that didn't stop me from finding out what I needed to know.

The plan for Hughes Aircraft was to make it an unofficial laboratory for the air force. That required experts in the electronic field, and the plant went on a hiring spree that corraled the greatest collection of scientific talent since the Los Alamos project. At one time Hughes Aircraft employed 3,300 Ph.D.'s.

Heading the electronics research department were two brilliant young scientists, Dean Wooldridge and Simon Ramo, both graduates of Caltech. Wooldridge had been with Bell Telephone and Ramo with General Electric, and their talents combined for an excellent partnership.

Hughes Aircraft grew fast. Howard poured the Toolco profits into plant expansion, gambling that the government contracts would be forthcoming. And they were. Hughes Aircraft became the sole supplier of a fire-power control system for all new fighter planes and an electronically controlled air-to-air missile, the Falcon. Howard authorized an entire Falcon plant that was built in Tucson even before the funds were authorized by the government.

By 1953, Hughes Aircraft was employing 17,000 and had almost a monopoly on air force electronics systems, with a backlog of $600,000,000 in federal contracts.

This tremendous growth produced problems to match. This electronics team was a new breed, not the kind you would have encountered in other industrial plants. The scientists were bright, super-intelligent and sophisticated. They viewed Howard Hughes as a necessary evil, an eccentric, distant moneyman who was more of a hindrance than a help. He was someone to be out-maneuvered, deceived, outsmarted.

As Howard Hughes' surrogate, I ranked only slightly lower on their list of unfavorite people. Some days I placed even higher, because Howard at least was invisible. My presence was felt at all times. No expenditure of more than $10,000 could be made without my approval. And I studied every outlay that came along.

It was in 1950 that I first had an inkling that the geniuses were getting restless. Ramo and Wooldridge had been urging further expansion of their laboratory staff; they wanted to double the capacity, at a cost of many millions of dollars. I had negotiated a loan of $35,000,000 from the Mellon Bank in Pittsburgh for such an expansion, but I controlled its use.

The generals thought that I had been high-handed in this regard. But I wasn't. They had excluded me from first-hand knowledge of the plant's operation. Without that knowledge, I couldn't possibly authorize such a huge outlay to expand.

Howard was becoming increasingly unavailable. He had moved his residence to Las Vegas and had made his announcement that he was considering the shift of Hughes Aircraft operations to Nevada.

That shot more holes in the plant's morale. The electronics staff members were horrified at the prospect of moving their families to the honky-tonk gambling capital, far from the research facilities of Caltech, UCLA, and the University of Southern California.

The top echelon at Hughes Aircraft was also upset by Howard's unkept promise about arranging a capital gains plan. The plant executives figured that they had built Aircraft into a booming enterprise, and they deserved to share in the rewards.

Howard vowed that he would take care of them, but of course he never did. He simply could not bring himself to let anyone share in his ownership.

The irony of this situation was that the Aircraft officials blamed me!

They thought I was the villain who was holding up their plan to enjoy the benefits of making Hughes Aircraft an industrial giant. They didn't know that Howard had also failed in his promise to me for a capital gains setup.

As if the spirit at Hughes Aircraft were not bad enough —the news then came that Howard was negotiating to sell the plant.

Howard let the word out that he might unload Hughes Aircraft if the right price were offered. Other corporations had eyed the Aircraft operation with envy, and they came a-running. Was Howard serious about selling? I don't know. I'm not sure that *he* knew himself. Perhaps if the right price had been offered, he might have sold out. But I doubt it. Howard's pride of ownership seldom allowed him to part with any of his holdings.

For instance, the beer company. The Toolco subsidiary, Gulf Brewing Company, had done well before and during the war, earning $2,300,000 in its peak year. But then the national breweries were attracted to Texas with the prospect of a year-around market. Offers were made for Gulf Brewing, and Howard could have sold out for a nice profit. But the brewery was on Toolco property, and Howard wouldn't allow any invasion by outsiders. The national beers took over in Texas, and Gulf Brewing went steadily downhill. With losses mounting, I shut the operation down. Later I negotiated an offer of $7,000,000 from Schlitz. Howard refused to sell, and the plant has remained idle.

Westinghouse, General Electric, and other big corporations made attempts to negotiate a purchase of Hughes Aircraft, and Howard held long, secret talks. The trouble was that he enjoyed negotiating. He loved to hold clandestine meetings and discuss deals in the hundreds of millions of dollars. He enjoyed the negotiating so much that he didn't like it to end. And so the talks would go on and on until the exhausted negotiations finally had to conclude that he wasn't really serious about selling. He was simply "counting his chips"—determining how much Hughes Aircraft was worth.

His most bizarre negotiation was with Robert Gross of Lockheed, who was very serious about buying Hughes Aircraft.

Howard expressed his eagerness to discuss the sale with Gross. I flew Bob up to Las Vegas in my plane, and we checked into a hotel to wait for a call from Howard. At that time Howard had a hotel suite, but he was living in a bungalow out in the desert.

After a wait of several hours the call finally came. We were picked up by a member of the Mormon guard and driven to the bungalow. Howard greeted us there and instructed us to get into one of the Chevrolets. He slipped behind the wheel and started driving further into the desert on dirt roads.

All of the car windows were closed, and Howard wanted them kept that way, even though the desert heat was stifling. Howard also told Bob and me to stuff our handkerchiefs in the heater vents; he didn't want any conversation to flow out through the vents.

Howard had a sniffling cold.

"Jesus, Howard, I've got to have some ventilation!" Bob finally said.

"Oh, sure, Bob," Howard said.

He pulled the Chevy off the road for two hundred yards. "No conversation while we're sitting here," Howard ordered. He got out of the car and walked through the sage brush in widening circles, trying to determine if there were any listeners.

He returned to the car and said, "Now we can talk."

While Howard was carrying on his fruitless negotiation with Bob Gross, I uncovered some deeply disturbing developments at Hughes Aircraft. The internal audit staff told me there had been an overcrediting of the inventory accounts. The result was a corresponding increase in the recorded costs of a $200,000,000 government contract.

Since our profits were limited by law to 11 percent of our costs, this amounted to defrauding the government.

My CPA mind went to work. I consulted with the plant auditors and with our auditing firm of Haskins and Sells. The conclusion was inescapable: the government had been overcharged by many millions of dollars.

I immediately told Howard about the matter, emphasizing its seriousness. My recommendation was an immediate initial refund of $5,000,000 to the government. Then I suggested that we ask the air force to join with us in determining the actual amount of the overcharge.

Howard met with Generals George and Eaker at their request. The generals, neither of them experienced in industrial production, took a defensive attitude. They claimed that I was mounting a personal attack and hinting at malfeasance. I wasn't accusing anybody of willful wrongdoing; I merely pointed out that Hughes Aircraft was in deep trouble unless the situation could be righted.

Howard procrastinated. He used the opposition of the generals as an excuse to bide his time, despite my warnings of a ruinous scandal. To bolster my arguments, I ordered a complete audit by Haskins and Sells.

In January of 1952, Haskins and Sells refused to give Hughes Aircraft a clean certification of its 1951 financial statements. This constituted a default of our Mellon Bank loan agreement.

At last Howard realized something *had* gone wrong. Hughes Aircraft ended up refunding $43,000,000 to the government.

The Aircraft scientists were not aware of the potential scandal. They accused me of interfering and attempting a power grab. I became the convenient son of a bitch who was poisoning Howard's mind against them and interfering with their dreams of a capital gains settlement.

Howard's absentee ownership, his moves to sell Aircraft, his lack of decision and unwillingness to share his ownership with anyone—these factors sent plant morale to new lows. In July of 1953, Ramo and Wooldridge confronted Howard with his unkept promises. He promised to reform, but of course he didn't.

The exodus began.

Ramo and Wooldridge were the first to go. They joined with Thompson Products Company and eventually formed the successful electronics firm of Thompson, Ramo, and Wooldridge.

Tex Thornton followed. He secured backing and bought a small firm that grew into the giant conglomerate Litton Industries.

General George tried to gain some assurances from Howard, but George despaired and submitted his resignation.

Howard's reaction to the departures was in character.

"Lock up his office!" he ordered as each key man left. Again, the memory of how Reed had walked out of the Hughes Tool Company with Big Howard's blueprints.

The executive suites of Hughes Aircraft had been emptied. With most corporations, it would have been a fiscal upset, nothing more. But with Hughes Aircraft, the national security was involved.

The Pentagon had become increasingly concerned with reports of troubles at Hughes Aircraft. Now, with the mass exit of the top management, that concern became alarm.

The new Republican administration had taken office in 1953, and guess who turned up as Secretary of the Air Force. Harold Talbott. The same Harold Talbott who had been affronted by the snub to his request to replace his dead brother on the TWA board. The same who turned up his nose when I offered Howard's $25,000 contribution to the Dewey campaign in 1948.

Talbott came flying out to California with fire in his eye. He demanded an immediate meeting with Howard Hughes, and Howard was in no position to refuse. I think that for once in his life, Howard was worried. He wanted me to be present at the meeting, for moral support and guidance.

The meeting at the summit took place in Howard's rented bungalow at the Beverly Hills Hotel. Present were Howard, Talbott, myself, and Roger Lewis, Assistant Secretary of the Air Force.

Howard had good reason to be concerned. Talbott gave him a dressing-down such as Howard had never heard before.

"You personally have wrecked a great industrial establishment with gross mismanagement!" Talbott exclaimed. "I don't give a damn what happens to you, but I am concerned for this country. The United States is wholly dependent on Hughes Aircraft for vital defense systems. It would take at least a year to set up alternative sources of supply. That could be a national tragedy. It was a terrible mistake entrusting the nation's security to an eccentric like you!"

There was little that Howard could say to reply. Talbott delivered his ultimatum: "Either sell Hughes Aircraft to Lockheed or accept a new management that I myself will designate.

"Take your choice, Mr. Hughes. I give you seventy-two hours to decide. If you don't do one or the other, I'll see to it that all of your contracts are cancelled and you'll get no more business from the government."

Howard seemed stunned. Perhaps the enormity of the situation had not struck him before that moment. He offered no excuses, no explanations. Yet he didn't capitulate, either. He simply seemed immobile.

I moved into the impasse.

"Harold, may I talk to you alone for a moment?" I asked.

Talbott stalked into the adjoining bedroom. I closed the door behind us and started to reason with him.

"I wonder if you realize the position you're in, Harold," I said. "You yourself have said that Hughes Aircraft is your sole supplier and that it will take a year to start getting electronics systems from a new manufacturer. Then in the next breath you threaten to cancel all the Hughes contracts within three days. We can't move that fast. We need time to straighten things out. Give us ninety days."

"All right," Talbott replied tersely. "Ninety days. And I mean *ninety* days."

We returned to Howard and told him of our agreement. As soon as Talbott had left, Howard became his old self.

"Who the hell does he think he is?" Howard ranted. "Nobody—not even the Secretary of the Air Force—is going to dictate how I manage my plant. It's *my* plant!"

"Yes, Howard," I said. "But without air force contracts there would be no Hughes Aircraft."

Howard was perverse enough to take the entire ninety days to make his decision. In the end he accepted Talbott's nominee for a man to run Hughes Aircraft: William Jordan, retired president of Curtiss-Wright Aircraft and a capable executive. Jordan took over on a temporary basis and began to get things back in order. Howard instructed me to hunt for another manager to take over when Jordan completed his stay.

While this was going on, Howard came across a scheme which he believed was the panacea to his problems with the air force. It had been suggested by his Houston lawyer,

Tom Slack. For years Howard had been toying with the idea of creating the Hughes Medical Foundation as the ultimate heir of his fortune. After all, Howard had no heirs, no wife, no immediate family to assume the burdens of his empire.

Slack proposed the idea of putting Hughes Aircraft under the control of the Hughes Medical Foundation. That would place the entire aircraft enterprise under control of a public trust and hence remove the personal element that had come under the criticism of the Pentagon establishment.

I was against the idea. I pointed out to Howard that while the air force might have been more receptive to dealing with a public trust, his power would be greatly dissipated. He would be deprived of access to Hughes Aircraft's assets for collateral or preceeds of sale. This would mean a severe setback in his financial condition.

Howard would not listen to my arguments. In December of 1953, he established the foundation and he transferred Hughes Aircraft to the new organization on January 1, 1954. The foundation gave Hughes Tool Company a note for $18,000,000 in payment for the next current assets. Hughes Tool retained title to the land, buildings, and equipment. The foundation leased the real property from Toolco and subleased it to its 100 percent-owned subsidiary, Hughes Aircraft Corporation. Howard was the sole trustee of the Foundation. The foundation's working capital consisted of the difference between the rental it paid Toolco and the rent it collected from its subsidiary—approximately $2,000,000 per year.

I could not prevent the transfer of Hughes Aircraft to the foundation. But I was fortunate in locating a new chief officer for Aircraft—L. A. (Pat) Hyland, who had been vice-president in charge of engineering research for Bendix. I had several conversations with him, and I decided that he had the forthright qualities that were needed to direct the destinies of Hughes Aircraft—and to deal with the egocentric ways of Howard Hughes.

Hyland drew a hard bargain: a ten-year contract at $100,000 a year, a home in the Holmby Hills section of Los Angeles in exchange for his house in Detroit, a percentage of the profits of Hughes Aircraft, and a capital gains arrangement that would provide him with a minimum of $250,000 after taxes.

Howard was in a delicate spot, still being subjected to the scrutiny of the air force. He agreed to all of the conditions—except the capital gains setup.

"But you agreed to it orally," I said to Howard.

"I know I did, Noah," he answered. "But that puts me in an embarrassing position. I've made the same promise to you and other executives, and I haven't come through on it yet."

"I know," I said knowingly.

"But I will," he added. "I'll take care of it. I just don't want it in writing."

I explained the situation to Pat Hyland. My argument was that if Pat could not accept the oral commitment of Hughes, then he shouldn't go to work for him at all. Pat agreed to go through with the arrangement—without the capital gains stipulation in the contract.

Pat Hyland took over Hughes Aircraft and did a splendid job. That job continues to the time of this writing. The odd part is that Pat has seen Howard only once in his lifetime—at the initial job interview. They have talked twice on the phone, so his total interviews with Howard amount to three since his employment in 1954.

What about the promise of a capital gains settlement? Pat Hyland is still waiting for it.

After I left Hughes, Pat sent word about the default of the agreement. The blame was conveniently laid on me. "I thought Noah had taken care of it," said Howard. "I'll see that it is implemented right away."

Two years passed. No action. Finally Pat Hyland came to my home and sought my advice. He offered this idea that he would put an annuity plan on the agenda for the next meeting of the board of directors of Hughes Aircraft —and give Howard notice of the fact. The board would then approve, and the plan would become binding in two years, barring Howard's objection. The board consisted of Hughes, Hyland, and Howard Hall, chief counsel.

"What do you think?" Pat asked.

"In the first place," I said, "Howard won't appear at the board of directors' meeting. In thirty-two years, I never knew him to appear at a board meeting anywhere. Secondly, if you are ever going to get anything out of him, this is the only way to do it."

Pat Hyland went ahead with the plan and achieved it, since Howard was nowhere about to countermand the order. And so, many years and many promises later, Howard finally fulfilled one of his promises to share his wealth with the executives who helped provide it.

The fulfillment, I might add, was by default.

CHAPTER THIRTY-NINE

Buying RKO; Also, Some Personal Matters

While all the turmoil with Hughes Aircraft and TWA was going on in the early 1950s, Howard somehow found time to run RKO by remote control. Remote, indeed. He never set foot on the studio property, yet he dictated policy, right down to the matter of Jane Russell's brassiere.

Under Howard's erratic management, RKO had gone steadily downhill. When he took control in 1948, the studio had 2,000 employees. By 1952, only 500 remained. The stock had plummeted from 9½ to 2⅞ in 1954.

In most of Howard's other enterprises, he could have mismanaged affairs and suffered no consequences; he had nobody to answer to but himself. But RKO had hundreds of stockholders besides Howard. And they began to squawk.

They had good reason to complain. The number of films released by RKO had fallen precipitously, because of Howard's insistence on passing judgment on everything. When he did make a decision, it was often a king-size boo-boo, such as casting John Wayne as Genghis Khan in *The Conqueror*. In his exploitation of Jane Russell's bosom, he managed to incur the wrath of the censoring Catholics. As with *Scarface* and *The Outlaw* in times past, Howard once again fought the battle against censorship over *The French Line*. He won in the end, but it was a hollow victory.

Howard had replaced Sid Rogell with Sam Bischoff as head of production. But neither Sam nor Sid could really function, as long as Howard was hovering in the background, calling the shots. The next team to take over was

Jerry Wald and Norman Krasna, who announced a brave program of $50,000,000 worth of movies. But Wald and Krasna became frustrated by the continual interference of Howard.

The other stockholders became restless. I don't blame them. RKO was losing money steadily, and Howard Hughes' conduct of the company's fortunes was obviously to blame. A derivative stockholder suit for $35,000,000 was filed.

Howard discussed the problem with me, and I pointed out the value of the corporation, especially in the old film library, which was carried on the books at one dollar. Television stations were then desperate for entertainment, and they would have paid millions for the old RKO movies.

"But I can't sell those old pictures to television," Howard countered. "The theater owners would get up in arms and refuse to buy the new RKO pictures."

"Somebody's got to break the ice," I said.

"But we'd ruin our theater business."

"All right, so you don't sell now. But at least you have that value in the library. The stockholders don't know that. They just want to come out without too much loss. You've got a new group of stockholders; the ones who bought the stock at twenty-five sold out a long time ago. This new crowd sees the stock at two and five eighths. If you were to offer them five dollars a share, they'd grab at it."

Howard liked the idea. But he went even further.

"Hell, I'll offer them six dollars," he said.

The RKO board in 1954 passed a resolution accepting his offer of $24,000,000 for the four million shares, including the ones that he himself owned. He included $6,000,000 for his shares as evidence of good faith.

Innocent stockholders, even after Howard's public offer, continued to sell stupidly at prices below six dollars. Floyd Odlum was smart enough to realize this, and he began buying up RKO stock in large quantities. He became a larger stockholder in RKO than Howard.

When all the other stockholders had picked up their

marbles, Hughes and Odlum were left with $17,000,000 in the till.

Odlum had a plan. The uranium fever was on, and he wanted to buy the Hidden Splendor Mine for $15,000,000. He convinced Howard to merge RKO with the Atlas Corporation, in which Howard then became the principal stockholder. This presented a problem, because Atlas controlled Northeast Airlines, and Howard was already the controlling stockholder of TWA. He was forced to place his Atlas stock in escrow to avoid a conflict of interest charge. The merger was effected, and Odlum bought the mine with the help of RKO's ready cash. The mine proved to be a loser, and Atlas stock took a tumble, but later recovered.

Howard had tired of the complications of trying to run a movie studio, and he began negotiations to sell RKO to Thomas Francis O'Neil, president of General Teleradio, a subsidiary of the General Tire and Rubber Company. In the summer of 1955, O'Neil paid Howard $25,000,000 for RKO studio and its backlog. Howard had already profited $10,000,000 on the sale of the theater interests. Howard paid $10,000,000 for the RKO stock and put $24,000,000 in escrow. He got $10,000,000 in Atlas stock and $25,000,000 from General Tire.

So he netted a profit of one million dollars for his seven-year ownership of RKO. That wasn't much of a return—less than simple interest—considering the money and time that he had put into the movie company. But, as I pointed out to him at the outset, it could have been worse. He could have lost millions, as he had before, in putting his own money into the making of movies.

Howard's involvement with RKO had other motivations than the pursuit of profits and furtherance of the art of the cinema. It also aided the exercise of his libido. I was never certain throughout Howard's long association with the motion picture industry whether his amours were an offshoot of that activity or film production was a screen for his romantic ventures.

In other words, which came first, movies or sex? I never knew for sure.

RKO had offered a logical excuse for Howard's massive search for appealing females. The five mansions, which were rented and charged to the Hughes Tool Company, entertained a succession of famous and never-to-be-famous beauties.

I couldn't keep track of all of Howard's romances (neither could he). His personal life was his own affair, I had enough trouble trying to keep his business matters straightened out.

But along the line I did pick up a few notes about some of Howard's affairs. At one time he moved into one of his rented homes a lovely and brainy young actress who was becoming a star in light comedies. Her parents apparently were liberal-minded, because she invited them to the house when they were visiting Hollywood.

"I'm living with Howard, and I'm going to marry him," she announced to her father and mother. "I want you to meet him."

She led them into the hallway and called upstairs.

"Howard!" she said. "My parents are here. They'd like to meet you."

The meeting was not exactly what she had in mind. Apparently wakened from a nap, Howard appeared at the top of the stairs, stark naked.

"Tell them to get the hell out of here," he growled.

That marked the end of that romance. The actress soon afterward married one of Hollywood's biggest and richest stars.

Another protégée of Howard's was remarkably beautiful and alarmingly young. She was only sixteen when Howard moved her into his house. This was one occasion when I interceded in his romantic career.

"Howard, you are playing with dynamite," I told him. "This girl is under-age, and you can get into serious difficulties by living with her."

This was after some famous Hollywood stars had gone to trial because of their sexual didos with teen-age girls. The same could have happened to Howard, but he was deaf to my arguments. He continued living with her and fostering her acting career. She was totally untalented, at least on the screen.

Howard was indeed threatened with trouble when the girl's father started telling people, "I've got Howard Hughes by the nuts." News of the father's mutterings reached Howard, and he told me, "Take care of him." I arranged a well-paying job at Hughes Aircraft, and that silenced the father.

The affair with the young actress was an expensive one for Howard. He lost a fortune in trying to promote her career. Finally he gave up the task and went on to other projects—and girls. She married a young man and was going to live with him in a foreign country. Before she left, she paid a final call to Howard.

"Is there anything I can do for you?" Howard asked.

"Well, yes," she said. "The baby is coming, and I could use some money for that. And my mother's teeth need fixing."

His final payment to her was a few thousand dollars. Even with the money he lost on her movies, he came off well. The romance could have cost him a lot more.

Another candidate for Howard's long list of beauties was Elizabeth Taylor.

After she had divorced Nicky Hilton, Howard attempted his move. As usual, he sent one of his emissaries to make the contact—reliable Pat DiCicco.

"Howard is very anxious to talk to you about your career," Pat said. "But you know how he is—he doesn't want anybody to know about it. He has a house in Palm Springs which you can use. He'll meet you there."

Elizabeth had other things on her mind, but the call from the fabulous Howard Hughes was too enticing to resist. She went to the Palm Springs house and waited—and waited. She was about at the end of her patience when Howard finally arrived. He gave her the pitch that he would make her a greater star than MGM had. She was unimpressed. She told him that she was going to London to see Michael Wilding, whom she intended to marry.

Howard was distraught. Elizabeth was adamant. No

amount of sweet-talk could dissuade her. As a last desperate measure, he sent Pat DiCicco on the plane with her to London. Pat argued all the way, but the young lady had her mind set on marrying Michael Wilding. And she did.

Elizabeth Taylor was one that got away.

Two other young ladies did not.

The first story concerns Terry Moore.

She had been a child actress in films like *Gaslight* and *Son of Lassie*, then developed into a buxom and beauteous young lady. Inevitably, she came to the attention of Howard Hughes. A romance developed—or at least she thought it was a romance. Indeed, Howard was most attentive, and he gave her career a big push. But no girl could retain his interest for long, and he wandered off to other pursuits.

Along came Glenn Davis, the famed football star of West Point. He fell in love with Terry and gave her the big rush. She concluded that Howard Hughes had forgotten his promises to her, and she married Glenn in 1951. They went to live in Lubbock, Texas, where he was engaged in business.

About three months after their marriage I received a curious telephone call.

"Mr. Dietrich, this is Terry Moore."

"Yes?"

"What was the result of your trip to Texas?"

The question set me aback. I had just returned from one of my periodic visits to Houston, but I couldn't possibly imagine why a movie actress would be inquiring about my trip.

"Well, Miss Moore," I said, "I *have* just returned from Texas, and I have reported on my visit to Mr. Hughes. You must understand that my relationship to Mr. Hughes is one of extreme confidence. You'll have to get your information from him—unless he releases me to talk."

After I finished talking with her, I quickly called Howard and told him about the call. "Why on earth does Terry Moore want to know about my trip to Texas?" I asked.

"Oh, Noah, I forgot to tell you!" Howard said. "I told her I wanted you to explore the divorce laws in Texas."

That was the first I knew that Terry Moore was separated from Glenn Davis. Later I found out what had happened. After the newlyweds had settled in Lubbock, Terry received a telephone call from Howard Hughes. He wanted her to come to Los Angeles for "some screen tests." Terry discussed the matter with her husband, and Glenn agreed to let her go.

She had said the tests would only take four or five days. But her stay in California extended five weeks. Then she telephoned Glenn and said, "I want a divorce so I can marry Howard."

Glenn was thunderstruck. He took the next plane to California and arranged to meet Terry at her parents' house in Glendale after she finished work at the studio. Howard was going to join them later.

Terry's parents were present at the Glendale house, and it was an uncomfortable situation. "I'll wait in the yard," Glenn said. "You call me when Hughes arrives."

A short while later, Terry appeared at the back door to say that Howard had made his appearance. As soon as Glenn walked into the living room and saw Howard, his temper flared. Without a word he stalked up to Howard and leveled a haymaker at Howard's face.

Glenn told me later that he didn't remember hitting Howard again, but he was told that he leaped on Howard and landed some more blows. Then he picked up Howard and pushed him onto a couch.

"You sit there, you son of a bitch," Glenn muttered, "and don't open your mouth or I'll kill you." Howard knew enough to avoid antagonizing an outraged husband; he sat and listened.

"You've just broken up my marriage," Glenn said, "and I know you haven't the slightest intention of marrying Terry. Well, in a way you did me a favor. At least I found out how things stood. This is the best thing that could have happened to me—to find out about her before we had any children."

Glenn turned on his heel and walked out of the house.

That night Howard called Glenn at his hotel. Howard carried on at length about how *he* was the aggrieved party, that Terry had been his girl and Glenn had taken her away. The entire conversation made no sense to Glenn.

The following day I had a conference with Howard at the apartment of Walter Kane, an agent who had become the latest of Howard's talent scouts. Howard often used Walter's place for conferences and rendezvous.

I was startled to see Howard's face. He had a shiner on one eye and scratches and bruises on his cheeks.

"What the hell happened to you?" I asked.

"Oh, I was coming out of Walter's apartment last night," Howard said, "and I walked right into a parked car and fell on my face."

The divorce went through, and Terry Moore went on to minor triumphs in RKO movies. But her plans to get Howard Hughes to the altar fell short of victory. Like all the other girls, she got tired of waiting.

One girl waited—and won: Jean Peters.

She was an Ohio State coed who came to Hollywood in the classic manner—by winning a beauty contest and a screen test. But unlike the thousands of other girls who had that experience, Jean succeeded. Twentieth Century-Fox gave her a contract and soon she was starring opposite Tyrone Power.

It was in 1946 that Howard first saw her on the screen. He wanted to meet the lovely brunette, and she was willing. I never heard of any girl who turned down a date with Howard Hughes.

A romance ensued, along with the usual promises of marriage by Howard. And the usual procrastination.

I met Jean Peters only once, and our meeting had a wry aftermath. Howard invited me out with him and Jean, and I had a delightful evening. I found her to be a charming, intelligent young lady, and she and I talked animatedly throughout the evening. Howard, of course, was devoid of talent as a conversationalist, and he remained silent most of the time. And, as I look back on the evening, a bit sullen.

The next morning, Lee Murrin, the handyman who paid the bills for Howard's romantic attachments, telephoned me to say: "What happened last night?"

"What happened? Why, I spent a charming evening with Miss Peters and Howard. Why do you ask?"

"I was just wondering. Because today Mr. Hughes told me, 'Don't ever let Dietrich get near Miss Peters again.' "

I had to laugh. I don't really think that Howard had any concern about the romantic competition of a man who was seventeen years his senior. My conclusion was that he didn't enjoy being shown up in the coversation department.

Like all of the others, Jean Peters grew weary of Howard's unfulfilled promises. Another man entered her life: Stuart W. Cramer III, a handsome young man from North Carolina, son of a textile industrialist whose father had been a close friend and former West Point classmate of Dwight D. Eisenhower.

Jean went off to Rome for the filming of *Three Coins in the Fountain,* and she met Stu there. After a quick courtship, he asked her to marry him, and she accepted. They were wed May 29, 1954, in Washington, D.C.

The newlyweds settled down in Washington and began taking part in the capital's social scene. To everyone, including Stu, theirs seemed to be an idyllic marriage.

Jean's studio, Twentieth Century-Fox, wanted her to return to Hollywood to appear in *A Man Called Peter.* Stu agreed to let her go. After she had been gone four or five weeks, Stu was puzzled when he could not reach his wife on the telephone. She simply didn't return his calls. Stu called Jean's mother in Ohio, and she reported her suspicions that Howard Hughes was interfering in Jean's marriage.

Stu became alarmed and he flew to California. At first Jean would not see him, and Stu got in touch with Howard on the telephone. Howard seemed solicitous and offered his services in attempting a reconciliation. But when Stu met with Jean he recognized that she was in a highly emotional state. She seemed to feel guilt for having run out on their marriage, yet she also seemed concerned about Howard's intentions toward her.

There seemed to be no chance of repairing the marriage. Jean went off to Florida for the purpose of filing for divorce. Stu followed her and tried to talk her out of it. But she remained in an emotional state and was unresponsive to his pleas. She filed for divorce in Florida, but didn't process the case. Finally she returned to California and began divorce proceedings there.

Curiously she failed to pick up her final decree at the end of the one-year waiting period. What happened? Did Jean have a showdown with Howard, threatening to return to Cramer if Howard didn't make good his promise of marriage? At any rate, she claimed the final decree on January 17, 1957, and she and Howard were married in Tonopah, Nevada, on March 13, 1957.

It was a strange kind of marriage. After he moved to Las Vegas, she visited him only every three or four weeks and then for only a half hour at a time. Eventually she tired of the arrangement. She divorced him in 1970.

CHAPTER FORTY

The Nixon Loan

The telephone rang in my office at 7000 Romaine. Howard's political lawyer was on the other end.

"I've been talking to Nixon," he said. "His brother Donald is having financial difficulties with his restaurant in Whittier. The Vice-President would like us to help him."

"Help him in what way?" I asked.

"With a loan."

"How much?"

"Two hundred and five thousand dollars."

I couldn't refrain from a whistle of astonishment. "Jesus, I've never transferred that much money to the political account," I protested. "I can't do it on my own responsibility. You'd better talk to Howard."

When I hung up the telephone, I had a very uneasy feeling. I had never gone along with Howard's penchant for dabbling in political favors. This time I felt he was going too far. It was one thing to support the campaigns of councilmen or even senators. It was something quite different when you started making personal loans to relatives of the Vice-President. Richard Nixon had been re-elected only a few weeks before in the Eisenhower landslide of 1956. The whole thing had a bad smell to it.

Donald Nixon was a personable chap, but apparently not much of a businessman. He had opened a restaurant in the Nixon home town of Whittier and featured a sandwich called the Nixonburger. The place had been operating in the red for a year.

Howard himself called me on the day after I had talked to the political lawyer.

"I want the Nixons to have the money," he said briskly.

"Do you know how much is involved?" I asked.

The amount seemed unimportant to him. "It's all right. Let 'em have it."

So I had the $205,000 transferred from the Hughes Tool Company Canadian subsidiary and turned the money over to the lawyer. The more I heard about the transaction, the less I liked it. I liked Richard Nixon; I had voted for him as United States Senator and twice as Vice-President. I supported President Eisenhower and served with his brother Arthur on the TWA Board of Directors (in 1949, I had loaned my Waldorf-Astoria suite to the Eisenhower family for the celebration of Ike's birthday). I didn't want to see anything happen to bring disrepute to Eisenhower or Nixon.

But the machinery for the loan was already in motion.

The $205,000 was to be provided as a loan. The only security was a vacant lot owned by Nixon's mother, Mrs. Hannah Nixon. A gasoline station was to be built on the lot with $40,000, with a lease to Union Oil at $800 a month. The rest of the money was to be used to pay past debts for the restaurant. No one was to be held liable for the repayment of the loan if it went into default. The Nixons would simply surrender the lot to Hughes Tool Company.

What was the collateral? Donald Nixon had applied for a loan from a commercial lending firm and had been offered $93,000 for the entire package.

This raised some serious questions:

Why would Hughes lend $205,000 for an enterprise on which only $93,000 could be borrowed?

Why would Hughes Tool Company, which was not a lending agency, make the loan?

How would the transaction look for a company that was deeply involved in defense contracting and in a government-regulated airline?

Even though the loan was for Richard Nixon's brother,

not himself, the whole thing seemed fishy. An ordinary citizen with a failing restaurant wouldn't have a prayer of achieving such a loan. Obviously the reason was in the fact that Richard Nixon occupied the number-two position in the nation. And his chances of becoming number-one had been increased since Dwight Eisenhower's heart attack and other ailments.

I was thoroughly convinced that the loan was wrong— for Nixon, for Hughes, for the state of political ethics. After fretting over the matter for several days, I made a bold move. Without consulting Howard, I flew to Washington in an attempt to halt the loan.

I had no difficulty in obtaining an appointment with the Vice-President. He was extremely cordial and showed me around his office, pointing out mementos of his visits to foreign lands. Then we sat down for a serious talk.

"About the loan to Donald," I began, "Hughes has authorized it, and Donald can have it. I realize that it involves a loan to your brother and not to you. But I feel compelled to tell you what's on my mind. If this loan becomes public information, it could mean the end of your political career. And I don't believe that it can be kept quiet."

He responded immediately, perhaps having anticipated what I had said.

"Mr. Dietrich," he said, "I have to put my relatives ahead of my career."

Nothing further was said about the subject. We had lunch in his office, and I departed more troubled than when I had arrived. I could not believe that he was so naïve as to think that the affair could be kept secret.

Having failed to scuttle the transaction, I did everything I could to put it on a businesslike basis. The high-paid executives of the Hughes empire were challenged with the problem of rescuing a modest Whittier restaurant from insolvency.

Pat DiCicco, who had the industrial feeding contract at Hughes Aircraft, headed a management committee to survey the enterprise. When Pat first visited the place, he kiddingly suggested dropping the name of "Nixon's"—"After all, Democrats eat, too," he reasoned.

The committee made a number of proposals for improving the operation of the restaurant, but Donald Nixon resented the intrusion. His displeasure was relayed by Richard Nixon to me.

"But I believe the restaurant will fail within ninety days if changes aren't made," I said.

"My brother wants to run it his way," the Vice-President said.

So the Hughes task force abandoned its effort. Not much later the restaurant closed its doors.

That was the end of my connection with the Nixon loan. In 1957 I broke with Hughes and was happily divested of such concerns. But I was amused—or appalled—by the ensuing events.

The rest of the story had all the aspects of a farce—except for the far-reaching effects on the national destiny. If anything, the affair proved that highly complicated attempts at secrecy can be self-defeating.

It seems that the $205,000 went from Hughes Tool Company to the political lawyer to Mrs. Hannah Nixon to her son Donald. Mrs. Nixon executed a trust deed with the gas station lot as collateral. To conceal Hughes' connection with the loan, the trust deed was transferred to a tax lawyer and then to a free-lance accountant.

After the restaurant failed, the accountant started getting $800 monthly checks from the oil company leasing the property. He tried to send them to the Hughes office but they were returned; obviously the Hughes people didn't want the risk of being connected with the loan. So the accountant cashed the checks, figuring they were in payment for his services.

A year and a half later a Houston accountant came across the mysterious $205,000 transaction. Where was the money? A squabble ensued among those involved in the whole affair. The matter came to the attention of a Washington lawyer who had close ties with the Kennedy family. This was in the closing days of the 1960 presidential race in which Richard Nixon and John Kennedy were running neck-and-neck.

The story was leaked to a few members of the press, but all declined to print it because of an aversion to printing scandal at the end of a campaign. The Nixon forces learned of the leaks, and they released a cleaned-up version of the loan to Donald Nixon. Drew Pearson, who had been holding back on the story until after election, came out with the full story—that the loan had come directly from the Hughes Tool Company.

After Kennedy had been elected, his brother Robert opined that the Hughes Loan was one of the three events that swung the narrow victory. I took no pleasure in witnessing confirmation of my initial fears over the consequences of the loan.

In his book *Six Crises,* Richard Nixon dismissed the whole affair in a short paragraph stating that his political opponents "had tried to connect him" with his brother's financial troubles. I noted his wording. He did not say that he had *not* been connected with the loan.

Something curious happened one month after the loan was made. The Internal Revenue Service made a reversal and ruled that the Howard Hughes Medical Foundation was entitled to tax-exempt status. The request for tax exemption had twice been refused by the IRS and the Treasury Department. But early in 1957, Howard was able to win that status for his foundation, which owned all the stock in Hughes Aircraft.

Was the timing coincidental? Or did Howard win a bargain for his $205,000?

Howard, of course, made no public comment on the whole affair. And I never learned if he found out that I had made a special trip to Washington in an effort to dissuade Nixon from becoming involved in a loan from Howard Hughes.

A curious postscript: A few years ago, Hughes Tool Company finally took title to the Nixon lot in Whittier. So, in addition to six Las Vegas casinos, 25,000 acres in Nevada, Air West, great real estate holdings in Los Angeles,

Tucson, and Houston, huge industrial plants, and God knows what else, Howard Hughes now owns a little filling station in Richard Nixon's home town.

CHAPTER FORTY-ONE

"Noah, I Can't Exist Without You"

The end of my life with Howard Hughes was approaching in late 1956. His eccentricities were becoming more ingrained, and he spent nearly all of his time in seclusion, surrounded by his Mormon guard, headed by Bill Fay. I remained in close contact with Howard by telephone, but I saw him less and less. On the occasions when I did see him, I was shocked by his appearance and behavior.

One of the last times I saw him was on a hot day in Las Vegas. He had sent for me, and I flew up and registered at the Sands Hotel. In time, one of the Mormon drivers arrived to take me to Howard's bungalow out in the desert.

As I was approaching the front door, I was signaled to halt. The guard knocked on the front door. Howard's voice came from inside: "What do you want?"

"Mr. Dietrich is here to see you," the guard reported.

"Is he in position?"

The guard came over to me and pointed at a chalked square, eighteen inches across, drawn on the cement sidewalk. "Stand in the center of the square, please," the guard said.

I stood inside the square, feeling as if I were playing some childish game.

"All right, Mr. Hughes," the guard announced. "Mr. Dietrich is in position."

The door opened a few inches, and I could see Howard behind it. "Come in quickly, Noah," he said.

I hurried inside, and he quickly closed the door. I was amazed at his appearance. He was as thin as I had ever seen him, and the damage to his face from the plane and car crashes could readily be seen. He was only fifty-one years old, but he seemed to have the appearance of an old man.

"How are you, Howard?" I asked earnestly, tossing my briefcase on the nearest chair.

His face suddenly stiffened, and he walked to a window to gain his composure. Then he turned and said, "Noah, do me a favor and never drop your briefcase in my presence again."

I couldn't imagine that he could be so concerned about being contaminated by the germs raised into the air when I dropped my briefcase. But that was the extent to which his germ phobia had been carried. The chalked square was another aspect of his fear. If his visitors stood further away from the door, then he would not be able to open and close the door as quickly.

The eccentricities of Howard Hughes were becoming more and more exasperating. Also, I was having guilt pangs about some of the missions I had undertaken for Hughes—missions that might not have seemed strictly legitimate to certain moralists. I wrestled with my conscience, and then I decided to seek expert advice.

One of my non-business functions was to serve on the Advisory Council of Notre Dame University. This put me in contact with many of the high-minded administrators of that fine institution. I laid my cards on the table to one of the priest-administrators.

"Father," I said, "in the performance of my duties for Howard Hughes, I have to do things that bother my conscience. There's no way that I can convert him to straight-thinking; he's beyond that. Do you think I ought to quit him?"

The good father thought for a while and said to me: "Noah, you're not going to accomplish anything by quitting. Stay where you are, and use as much good influence as you can. You'll do more good by trying to help him."

So I stayed. I thought perhaps I could help bring some order to the muddled affairs that Howard had gotten himself into. But as time went on, I realized how impossible a task that was becoming.

I went through the incredible events of January 1956, when I discovered that Howard had ordered almost a half billion dollars' worth of jet airplanes for TWA. It was staggering enough to realize that he had issued the orders without even remembering the amounts involved. Even more unbelievable was the fact that he had taken the action with no official capacity in the affairs of TWA.

True, he was the major stockholder, owning 78 percent of the TWA stock. But he held no office in the corporation; he was not an officer, not a director, not even a consultant.

"Howard, you can't make decisions like this!" I told him. "You're ignoring all standard practices of business You can't get away with it."

He was unhearing. He figured I would find some way out of his difficulty. I tried. I devised the plan to use $100,000,000 of Hughes Tool Company cash, plus a $300,000,000 convertible bond issue to be floated by New York bankers. And then Howard stopped the bond issue without consulting me. He had a monomania about not diluting his ownership.

Then came my safari, which Howard tried desperately to forestall. He did succeed in bringing me home prematurely, to attend to a trivial matter about an attorney's fee.

The jet financing crisis remained unsolved after my return; we were shoving out available funds to meet the periodic payments, but those funds were becoming exhausted. In March of 1957, I noted that in slightly over a month a bill for $80,000,000 would be coming due. I sent an urgent memo to Howard. My conclusion:

"It is unfortunate that we did not proceed with our refinancing program last summer prior to the change in the Federal Reserve Board rediscount rate and the general tightening of credit. It is for this reason that I am suggesting an interim loan of $100,000,000 to cover our needs for the next two years, which will give us that amount of time in which to work out a complete financing program to cover the jet program. Please bear in mind the April 15 maturities. This gives us approximately one month to negotiate such an interim loan."

A month passed without a decision from Howard. I learned that he was on the telephone importuning plane manufacturers for early deliveries.

Still unwilling to float a loan that might possibly jeopardize his ownership, he contemplated drastic solutions. The most drastic of all was selling Hughes Tool. The parable of the golden goose held no meaning for Howard; he was willing to sacrifice Toolco in order to hold onto TWA. Of all his possessions, TWA held a certain mystique for him. He didn't give a damn about the tool company, except as a source of wealth. Hughes Aircraft was an avocation for him, an outlet for his tendency to tinker. RKO was a heady diversion, an opportunity to pursue his sensual enjoyments.

But TWA was the nearest thing to a passion that this inordinately passionless man possessed.

A year before, he had toyed with the notion of selling Toolco, and he strung along a potential buyer for months until a price was established. The price was $400,000,000, based on a times-earnings formula. As soon as he learned the figure, Howard dropped the selling plan. Once again I suspected he was merely "counting his chips."

But this time he seemed in earnest. He told me: "Go on down to Houston and see if you can jack up the profits for 1957."

I knew what he was after. For every extra million I could muster, he could be paid an extra $13,500,000 by a purchaser. But I tried to argue the folly of his plan. I pointed out that Toolco had been a steady moneymaker over the years, while TWA had rarely turned a profit.

"Besides, business is falling off at Toolco, Howard," I warned. "We made sixty million in 1956, but I don't think we can do it this year. Money has tightened up, and the oil companies simply aren't drilling as much."

"I don't care," Howard said blindly. "I want you to raise the Toolco profits."

So I journeyed to Houston to see if I could possibly induce more eggs out of the tired old goose. I uncovered a gimmick. Hughes Tool had a practice of consigning drill bits to an oil company for each drilling site, but the consignment was not recorded as a sale until the firms actually put the bits in operation and so notified Toolco. The average time lag was ninety days.

I consulted with Haskins and Sells, our auditors. They agreed that I could shorten the time lag. This picked up an added $1,500,000 in the current month.

Returning to Los Angeles, I informed Howard of what I had accomplished. He seemed heartened and he said, "I want you to move down to Houston, Noah. I want you to watch the operation full-time and keep pumping up the profits."

"But, Howard," I said, "that won't do any good. That profit of a million and a half was on a non-recurring basis. The investment bankers will be fully aware of it before an offering can be made."

Howard offered no response. Nor did he respond to my pleas to formulate an orderly, longterm financing plan to tide TWA over during the difficult period of conversion to the jet age.

Instead, he vanished further into his isolation. Nearly all of my conversations with him were now by telephone. He had dictated instructions to his staff not to call him for any reason whatsoever.

"If I want anything, I'll call in," he said. "When I do, I'll tell you what I want. Do not introduce any new subject unless I ask for it."

His instructions to me were not as curt, but just as limiting.

"Noah, let's discuss only the problem I raise," he said. "I just can't concentrate on more than one subject at a time."

During this upheaval in early 1957, I learned some shocking news from one of Howard's Houston lawyers. He came to my office and paced up and down, in a state of obvious agitation. Finally he summoned up the nerve to tell his story.

"Noah, I think that Howard is out of his mind," he said.

"You know the problem we have—possibly defaulting on the payments for the new jets and no financing in sight to handle future deliveries. Well, I had a call from Howard. He wants me to go to Montreal and start negotiations for fifty Viscount prop jets!"

"What?"

"That's right. Capital Airlines can't pay for them, and Howard wants to pick them up for TWA. Can you imagine? Why, those planes will cost two and a half million apiece. That's another hundred and twenty-five million that Howard wants to commit. We've got our backs to the wall financially, and Howard wants to buy more planes!"

I shook my head unbelievingly.

"Noah," he continued gravely, "I think the time has come for drastic measures. I think you ought to start a legal proceeding to have a guardian or a conservator appointed for Howard. Otherwise I don't know what's going to happen."

I wouldn't even entertain the notion.

"Whoever initiates that move will be a dead duck with Howard—immediately," I said.

"Well," he said, "you want to retire, don't you? It seems to me—"

I laughed ruefully. "That's a sure way to retire, all right. But that's not the way I intend to go out."

Two weeks later I had a visit from Howard's personal physician and head of the Hughes Medical Foundation. I was startled to hear him make the same suggestion: "Noah, I think the time has come for you to have Howard declared incompetent."

"You've got the whole thing backwards," I said. "*You're* his doctor. If you think this thing should be done, why don't *you* do it?"

He shuddered at the thought. "I've got my position to protect," he said. "I'm getting fifty thousand a year with an unlimited expense account, and I don't have to account to anybody. *You're* the one who wants to quit. *You* should do it."

"I am not about to play doctor," I replied.

With no one to put the brakes on him, Howard continued driving his suicidal course. He had convinced himself that his salvation lay in jacking up the Toolco profits and selling the division off for a huge profit that could be poured into TWA jets. I was the one to pull off this caper for him. Always he had said, "Noah can do it." Once more he sent for Noah. I agreed to meet him at the Beverly Hills Hotel.

March 12, 1957.

I arrived at the hotel in the evening and called him from the lobby.

"Go to drawing room A; I'll talk to you there," he instructed.

I went to the drawing room and placed the call to Howard's bungalow. He moved me to another room. He wanted to be certain that our conversation was not being recorded. After the third move I tired of this CIA nonsense, and I said, "Howard, why can't we just sit down over a coffee table and talk this thing out?"

"No, I want to do it this way," he insisted. Once again he made his pitch for me to go to Houston and inflate the Toolco profits.

Finally out of weariness I said, "All right, Howard, I'll go to Houston, but—"

"That's great, Noah," he said. "I'm glad you came around."

"I haven't finished, Howard. I'll go under one condition."

He was silent for a moment. "What's that?" he asked in his chilliest tone.

"For fifteen years you have been promising me to put a capital gains agreement in writing. I want it before I go. It doesn't have to be a long, complicated contract. We can just write a one-page agreement. We can do it in longhand. We'll both sign it, and I'm off to Houston."

"I don't like this, Noah," he said. "You're pushing me."

My heart was pounding, but I was fully aware of what I was doing.

"Put yourself in my place, Howard," I suggested. "For fifteen years I've been living on your promises. That's a long time to wait for a simple agreement that would take only twenty minutes to draw up."

"Noah, we can talk about this later."

"Now, Howard. No more promises. We sign the agreement now, or I'm through."

Howard's voice became tight. "You're holding a gun to my head. Nobody holds a gun to my head."

"All right, Howard, forget it. I'm through as of this moment. We'll forget the whole damn thing. Don't telephone me. Don't try to reach me, except through your lawyers."

There was a silence on the other end of the phone.

"Jesus, you can't mean that. Noah, I can't exist without you."

It was the first time in thirty-two years that he had said that. They were the last words I was to hear from Howard Hughes.

"That's nonsense, Howard," I said. "Your operations are well organized. Just keep your fingers out of them and they'll do all right. Goodnight, Howard."

And I hung up.

CHAPTER FORTY-TWO

Again, My Life without Howard Hughes

"Lock up his office!"

That familiar cry, which I heard for departing executives, was now applied to me.

Within an hour after my last conversation with Howard Hughes, the locksmith we used at 7000 Romaine called me at home.

"Mr. Dietrich, I don't know how to tell you this, and maybe I oughtn't," he said hesitantly. "But I just had an order from Mr. Hughes to change all the locks at Romaine —and above all to make sure I changed the one on your office."

I had worked with the locksmith for years, and I didn't want him to feel bad. "Just relax," I said. "Everything is all right—go ahead and change the locks. I just quit, and he's afraid I'm going to run off with the records."

The next call was from Chuck Price, the company's financial vice-president.

"Jesus, Noah, what's going on?" he asked. "I just had a call from Hughes, and he exacted a loyalty oath from me. He said, 'Dietrich's quitting, and I want to know where your loyalty lies.' I had to tell him that he was my employer, and that's where my loyalty was. 'Okay,' he said, 'I want all payments to Dietrich stopped—compensation, expense accounts, everything. Incidentally, how much are you paying him?' I told him about five hundred thousand a year for the past three or four years, including a percentage of the profits. He made no comment about that."

The next call I had was from Loyd Wright in Washington.

"Noah, I'm chairman of the President's security council, and we're in session here in Washington," said Wright. "Howard wants me to drop everything and come out there to handle the situation that has developed between you and Howard. I told him I couldn't leave for twenty-four hours, but I would come out there and try to mediate."

"Loyd, there isn't anything to mediate," I said. "I'm through. Period."

"Will you talk to me if I do come out?"

"Certainly."

"Howard has given me his word that he'll be available as soon as I arrive."

Wright arrived the next evening, and he called me the following morning at 7.

"Noah, neither one of us can understand Howard," he said resignedly. "He promised that I would be taken directly to him when I arrived and that I could reach him at any time during my stay. Well, there was a Cadillac limousine waiting for me. The driver said his instructions were simply to pick me up and take me to my home. That's where I am now. I kept phoning Howard until I finally reached him at three this morning, and he promised to meet with me."

Wright stayed in Los Angeles four days, and he never did see Howard. But he did talk to him on the phone. Loyd asked me to come to his home, and I did.

"Howard wants you to change your mind and come back," Loyd said.

"Loyd, I have crossed my last bridge and burned it behind me," I replied.

"All right," the attorney sighed. "Now here's what Howard said he's going to do if you won't come back. He's going to take your house away from you. He's going to take away your interest in the oil properties you two are involved in. And he's going to sue you for all the compensation you have received in the last three years."

I could see how Howard's mind was working.

Number one, the house. I had bought it from RKO, which had used it as an executive house. My price was $25,000 above the nearest bid, from Cary Grant, and the board of directors had approved the sale.

Number two, the oil partnership. Howard had insisted that I take him in on my oil ventures, and he had put up $1,250,000 in eighteen months—but had promised to contribute $2,000,000 a year for five years. He had no legal claim on my oil money.

Number three, my compensation. In 1954, I had resigned my offices with Toolco and Aircraft to avoid a conflict of interest. At Howard's urging, I stayed on in the same capacities, with the same compensation but without a contract. Now he thought he could get my pay back on the grounds that I had been compensated illegally. He overlooked my accomplishments after 1954 and his efforts to prevent my safari vacation in 1956.

"If he won't mediate, I'll take everything he's got away from him," Howard had vowed.

He didn't get the house or the back pay. I finally relinquished the oil partnership, just to get rid of him. I believed we had no prospects of a big strike, anyway. Time proved me wrong; Howard made a killing later.

Loyd Wright went back to Washington without ever having seen Howard. In the next six months, investigators combed the corporation records in an effort to nail me with something. The key people in the Hughes empire told me about the search, and they were shamefaced about it.

"Don't worry," I told them. "Howard can hunt from now until doomsday and he won't find anything. I've got nothing to hide."

Still, Howard pursued his small-boy vindictiveness. My office at 7000 Romaine continued to be padlocked. Many of my personal effects were in there: my bank statements, personal checks, brokers' statements, jewel box, savings bonds, marriage licenses, birth certificates, car licenses, trip files, snapshots, brief case, personal correspondence,

$2,000 in cash in the safe, even my framed CPA certificate. I finally had to go to court and get a mandatory order for the return of my possessions.

The three airplanes that had been at my disposal were left to rot their hangars and so they remain today.

After I had first left Howard, I felt so relieved that I wanted nothing more to do with him. But as the months of freedom continued, I began to get sore. He was having gumshoes snoop around my records in an attempt to catch me in wrongdoing. Meanwhile, I did nothing about all the unkept promises he had made to me.

I decided to call him on one of them.

When I had tried to quit after my safari in 1956, Howard had pleaded with me to remain. "Just stay another six months," he urged. "I've got too many problems weighing down on me right now. I need you. If you'll stay just six more months, I'll give you an extra million dollars—and I'll try to put it on a capital gains basis."

I stayed eight months. And of course the million dollars never appeared. So I sued him for it.

Howard had to appear for a deposition prior to the suit, and his attorneys kept pleading his ill health. My attorney, Arthur Crowley, insisted that they produce Hughes or allow us to have doctors examine him. The Hughes lawyers kept stalling. When Howard failed to arrive on the deadline, Crowley arranged an extension until the following Monday at 11 A.M.

"But if he's not in my office at that hour, I insist on a penalty of one hundred thousand dollars," said Crowley. The desperate Hughes lawyers agreed.

"Arthur, you're out of your mind," I told my attorney afterward. "If you had asked twenty-five thousand, Howard might not show up."

It turned out that Crowley made a good gamble. Howard did not appear the following Monday, and the $100,000 was forfeited.

The case never came to trial. Howard settled for $800,000—and I lost. Why? Well, my lawyer took one-quarter, my former wife took another quarter. By the time

I finished paying high-bracket taxes, the suit had earned me peanuts.

More importantly, it severed me from Howard Hughes forever. I suspect that in time he would have wanted me back, and it's possible I would have returned. But my suit had attacked him in his area of greatest vulnerability: the alter ego theory—that Howard Hughes is the Hughes Tool Company, and the Hughes Tool Company is Howard Hughes. If that could ever be established in court, then the Hughes empire would be radically changed. He would have to face income taxes like ordinary citizens, instead of hiding his wealth behind a corporate curtain.

What has happened in the years since the Hughes-Dietrich divorce?

Like all Americans, I have followed the bizarre movements of Howard's life with fascination. After thirty-two years of closeup scrutiny of the Hughes psyche, I think I can offer some perspective on the peculiar goings-on.

The TWA fiasco, which I had tried to save him from, turned into one of the greatest bonanzas in the history of American finance. And Howard did everything within his power to prevent it.

Briefly, here is the sequence of events:

In 1960, Howard had exhausted every alternative and had to seek $165,000,000 financing from a consortium of eastern banks and insurance companies. The lenders laid down strict terms. Included was a proviso that if TWA's fortunes took a turn for the worse, Howard's stock would be placed in a three-man voting trust. The lenders would name two trustees, Howard one.

When TWA President Charles Thomas resigned, the lenders invoked the voting trust. The lenders appointed their own president, Charles Tillinghast. Hughes Tool Company sued, charging mismanagement. TWA countersued.

The case was fought through the courts for years. Hughes Tool lost its case and TWA won, finally, by default, because Howard refused to appear before the court.

Howard was ordered to pay TWA $137,000,000 in damages. The Civil Aeronautics Board ordered a show cause hearing and when Howard failed to appear it refused to dissolve the voting trust.

Howard had to admit defeat. He decided to sell his TWA shares which he couldn't vote—and that provided the bonanza. When he lost control of the airline in 1960, the TWA stock was selling at $13. By 1966 when he was forced to sell, the market price was $86.

His stock brought him a check for $546,549,771. Even after Toolco had paid the brokerage fee and the capital gains tax, it had about $450,000,000 left over.

Despite his unbelievable windfall, I do believe that Howard would have been willing to sacrifice it to have the airline back. He loved TWA and did everything in his power to hold onto it.

He lost TWA only because of his personal frailties. He would not adopt a reasonable method of financing the jets, because he feared dilution of his ownership. When the showdown occurred in court, he declined to appear. Why? Because he feared his powers of concentration were not sufficient to undergo cross-examination. If he appeared in public and raised severe doubts about his competence, he might lose control of everything.

So instead of fighting for his beloved TWA, he disappeared into limbo. His new address: Limbo, Nevada.

Las Vegas had always held fascination for Howard. He liked the gaudy atmosphere, the easy access to beautiful girls, the excitement of the gambling town. He also was obsessed by political power. Nevada was an easy state to buy. After he had become the biggest employer, the biggest taxpayer in Nevada, he figured he could make his influence felt. And he could.

He had to do something with the $450,000,000 from the TWA sale. He had learned my early lesson to keep pouring his excess money into expansion and real estate, where it would be overlooked by the income tax collector. So Howard went on a spending spree in Las Vegas, picking up casinos and hotels by the handful.

This time the investment went sour. Hughes Aircraft, Hughes Tool, TWA, even RKO if it had been properly managed—those industries had been solidly based on economic need. But Las Vegas had a slimmer base: human greed and the desire for entertainment. When expenses got out of hand and a recession kept customers away, the casino-hotels began losing at a perilous rate.

Howard needed a scapegoat. He found one in Robert Maheu, head of his Las Vegas operations.

This time Howard didn't have Noah to do the firing for him. Instead, he assigned the Mormon high command. Before the sentence was carried out, Howard vanished and turned up at the Britannia Beach Hotel in Nassau. Obviously he wanted to be far out of reach when Maheu filed the inevitable law suit.

I have watched all the developments with amusement. Also a feeling of great relief, since I do not have to be involved. Once in 1968 I visited Las Vegas and Bob Maheu asked me to have lunch with him. He pumped me for information about how to deal with his difficult employer.

"Don't count on any of Howard's verbal promises or expect any stock options or capital gains that aren't nailed down in a written contract," I warned him. "Take whatever he offers you while he needs you, because that's all you're going to get."

When I heard of Maheu's execution in December of 1970, I couldn't resist sending him a wire:

"Welcome to the club."

And what has happened to me in the years since 1957?

I have led a contented, productive, active, though slightly less exciting life. I married again, this time happily. My wife Mary and I live in a big house atop Beverly Hills, and the place is generally alive with the sounds of our children and grandchildren.

As of this writing, I am 83 years old, and I still go to my office in Century City every day. I maintain a lively interest in the business community and act as a corporate consultant on a wide variety of projects. In 1971 I retired as director of the Metropolitan Water District of Southern California after serving for sixteen years. But I have no intention of lapsing into complete retirement. I still feel like a young man, and my friends say I think and act like one.

Not long ago I took a drive down to Long Beach, primarily to take a look at the *Queen Mary*. But I was drawn irresistibly toward the *Queen's* monstrous neighbor, the *Hercules*. I counted thirteen cars in the parking lot, so I presumed that work was still continuing on the aging flying boat.

As I was staring at the hangar, a shipyard worker came strolling along at the end of his shift.

"Better not get too close, mister," he warned me. "Those guards get suspicious if they see anyone too close."

"They do, huh?" I said.

"Yeah. That's the *Spruce Goose,* you know. Howard Hughes' big flying boat. Nobody can get anywhere near it. You see that tower alongside the hangar?"

"Yes."

"They tell me he's got a telescopic camera up there. Anybody hangs around here a lot or gets too close, the camera takes a picture."

"Really? Then what happens to the pictures?"

"I dunno. Maybe they go alla way down to the Caribbean and Howard Hughes looks 'em over to see if it's anyone suspicious."

The shipyard worker went on his way, leaving me with my memories. I studied the hangar and thought of the $50,000,000 that had been squandered on the world's greatest toy. And all the drilling bits that had to be sold to pay for it.

I stayed for a while, hoping that I was suspicious-looking enough to be snapped by the telescopic camera, if one existed. And just for good measure I gave a friendly wave, as if to say, "Hi, Howard."

Sometimes at night the phone rings, and I answer quickly, as I always did. I half expect to hear that high-pitched voice at the other end say, "Noah, I got something I want you to take care of for me."

And you know what I'd say?

"Okay, Howard, tell me what it is now. . . ."